Access your Online Resources

Understanding Anxiety at School is accompanied by a number of print-able online materials, designed to ensure this resource best supports your professional needs

Go to https://resourcecentre.routledge.com/speechmark and click on the cover of this book

Answer the question prompt using your copy of the book to gain access to the online content.

T0384820

Understanding Anxiety at School

An increasing number of children face feelings of anxiety and isolation, negatively impacting their mental health and wellbeing, as well as their attainment in school. Having battled social anxiety herself, Rachel Thynne knows first-hand how hard it can be to be misunderstood and receive little help. By understanding the communicative function of behaviours and seeing the person behind their actions, staff can learn to support and nurture pupils with consistency, empathy and positivity.

This book explores anxiety in children and young people, unpicking social anxiety, situational mutism, school anxiety and separation anxiety within a school context, and shining a light on the importance of relationships, effective communication and self-regulation skills. A wealth of strength-based strategies are provided that can be implemented quickly and easily by busy school staff to alleviate anxiety, build self-esteem and increase feelings of safety and belonging. The book also supports sensitive and collaborative work with caregivers to achieve the biggest impact and includes real-life examples, case-studies and reflective opportunities to bring theory to life.

Little adjustments can make a huge difference and have a positive, lifelong effect on the individual but also on the other pupils. Advocating for whole school approaches to create a culture where all pupils can thrive, *Understanding Anxiety at School* will enable school staff, including teachers and special educational needs coordinators (SENCOs), to recognise signs of anxiety and to provide support empathically and compassionately.

Rachel Thynne is an experienced teacher and is currently an Outreach Lead Teacher and Specialist Leader in Education, providing training, advice and support for the effective inclusion of pupils with social, emotional and mental health (SEMH) within mainstream schools. She is author of the book *Behaviour Barriers and Beyond*.

Understanding Anxiety at School

From Personal Experience to Practical Pupil Support

Rachel Thynne

Routledge
Taylor & Francis Group

LONDON AND NEW YORK

Designed cover image: Getty Images

First published 2025
by Routledge
4 Park Square, Milton Park, Abingdon, Oxon OX14 4RN

and by Routledge
605 Third Avenue, New York, NY 10158

Routledge is an imprint of the Taylor & Francis Group, an informa business

© 2025 Rachel Thynne

British Library Cataloguing-in-Publication Data
A catalogue record for this book is available from the British Library

Library of Congress Cataloging-in-Publication Data
Names: Thynne, Rachel, author.
Title: Understanding anxiety at school : from personal experience to
    practical pupil support / Rachel Thynne.
Description: New York : Routledge, 2025. | Includes bibliographical
    references and index.
Identifiers: LCCN 2024025425 (print) | LCCN 2024025426 (ebook) |
    ISBN 9781032559827 (hbk) | ISBN 9781032559797 (pbk) |
    ISBN 9781003433231 (ebk)
Subjects: LCSH: Students—Psychology. | Anxiety. | Social isolation. |
    Behavioral assessment. | Communication in education. | Teacher-
    student relationships. | Inclusive education.
Classification: LCC LB1060.2 .T59 2025 (print) | LCC LB1060.2
    (ebook) | DDC 371.801/9—dc23/eng/20240715
LC record available at https://lccn.loc.gov/2024025425
LC ebook record available at https://lccn.loc.gov/2024025426

ISBN: 978-1-032-55982-7 (hbk)
ISBN: 978-1-032-55979-7 (pbk)
ISBN: 978-1-003-43323-1 (ebk)

DOI: 10.4324/9781003433231

Typeset in DIN
by Apex CoVantage, LLC

Access the Support Material: https://resourcecentre.routledge.com/speechmark

Contents

viii ■ *Contents*

Acknowledgements

Huge thanks to my amazing family, friends and colleagues who have provided invaluable advice and support, particularly to Alice, Alisa, Clare, Gill, Ginny, Jemma, Paula, Sarah, Tania and Tina for taking the time to read chapters and feedback with fabulous suggestions, thoughts and advice (and often for listening to and calming my anxieties along the way). Thank you also to my fantastic boss (at the time of writing), Nicki, who is one of the most supportive and inspirational people I know.

A massive thank you to my husband Paul for his chapter-reading, support and advice and for always being there when I need him and to my daughters Amelia and Elena for being fabulous in every way and making me proud every day. To my sister Emily, for her support, advice, love and friendship (and special mention to my nephew Jasper, who wants to be an author – always follow your dreams)! And, thanks to my Dad for all the on-going support and encouragement.

To Clare and Molly and everyone else at Taylor & Francis for their constant support and advice and for always being there with a supportive email.

Huge thanks to all of the staff in the schools I work in, for always embracing and implementing suggestions with enthusiasm, and for feeding back those that have been the most impactful for our anxious pupils.

Introduction

Children and young people are currently experiencing increased anxiety in schools. At the time of writing, 95 per cent of schools have seen an increase in pupil anxiety (Pickets, 2023). According to the World Health Organisation (2022), the COVID-19 pandemic triggered a 25 per cent increase in prevalence of anxiety and depression worldwide. Therefore, the subject of anxiety, is now more than ever, a crucial topic for school practitioners to reflect upon. With school anxiety and avoidance increasing, many children are facing feelings of isolation, which is negatively impacting their mental health and wellbeing as well as their attainment.

Anxiety is not always included in teacher training programmes or with on-going Continuing Professional Development (CPD) for school staff, neither is it always covered in parenting courses. Consequently, children displaying behaviours driven by high levels of anxiety are often misunderstood and labelled as oppositional, defiant, rude or uncooperative, leading to a lack of support, breakdowns in relationships and further difficulties for the person with anxiety, forming a vicious cycle.

This book outlines the causes and symptoms of anxiety and how it can impact individuals within the school setting. It draws upon my own experiences with anxiety and situational mutism, as well as the experiences of children and young people with whom I have worked. It provides a guide to support education staff to scaffold activities in a gradual way, which progressively aims to increase the pupil's confidence and participation and reduce their anxieties in a way that feels safe and supported. It provides indispensable tried and tested advice, ideas and strategies which can be implemented in a busy school system. It also offers advice to caregivers in terms of supporting pupils when they present with such anxieties around school, offering school staff and caregivers the tools to work collaboratively for the best outcomes.

Positive mental health and wellbeing is essential for pupils to succeed and flourish, socially and academically. The advice in this book

DOI: 10.4324/9781003433231-1

has pupils' Social, Emotional and Mental Health (SEMH) needs at the forefront and focuses on how to support them to reach their full potential within the school setting, by reducing anxiety for all pupils as well as providing for individual needs. It supports adults to recognise signs of anxiety, therefore enabling them to be in a better place to provide support, empathically and compassionately.

This book provides school staff with suggestions on how to foster positive relationships with pupils and families, increase safety cues and promote a sense of belonging as well as reduce anxieties to increase wellbeing. Such strategies lead to improved attendance, engagement and attainment as well as self-esteem and confidence. If school staff are armed with a range of ways to help remove stigma from mental health issues, alleviate anxieties, reduce stress, provide regulation and practical strategies to support, then pupils will leave school better equipped to recognise when they are finding things difficult and have embedded a bank of techniques to support them well into the future.

Information is presented sensitively and the book contains a range of supportive strategies and approaches including presentations of anxiety, language re-frames, regulation and coping techniques and explores how the brain works when under (real or perceived) threat. It, furthermore, provides specific information on social anxiety and situational mutism, school-based and separation anxiety and whole school approaches to reducing anxiety. The book includes case studies and examples, chapter take-aways, printable checklist reminders and signposts readers to further relevant and useful resources.

Having personal experience of social anxiety, commencing at a time when very little was understood about it, I know first-hand, how hard it can be to receive little help and to feel isolated and misunderstood. By understanding the communicative function of behaviours and seeing the person and drivers behind their actions, adults will learn to support and nurture their pupils with consistency, empathy and positivity. The impact that all school staff can have on supporting pupils through challenges and difficulties is immense. Greater understanding of need and support put in place to manage anxiety can make a huge difference which lasts a lifetime.

References

Pickets, D. (2023) Thesendcast.com: *How Schools Can Build Positive Wellbeing Among Students* Available at: https://www.thesendcast.com/how-schools-can-build-positive-wellbeing-among-students [Accessed 1.3.23]

World Health Organisation (2022) *COVID-19 Pandemic Triggers 25% Increase in Prevalence of Anxiety and Depression Worldwide* Available at: https://www.who.int/news/item/02-03-2022-covid-19-pandemic-triggers-25-increase-in-prevalence-of-anxiety-and-depression-worldwide [Accessed 16.7.23]

1
Anxiety

What is anxiety?

Anxiety is a sense of unease, a feeling of worry, being scared about something or fearing something bad is going to happen, which often presents as a range of physical symptoms and behaviours. Feelings of anxiety can range from mild to severe and depend upon on a person's propensity to cope, in that moment (NHS, 2022a, Willetts & Waite, 2014, p.7).

Stress and anxiety relate to an individual's internal reaction to the fear and distress triggered by a potential (perceived or real) threat, the person's ability to cope with that stress response for the time it needs to be tolerated and the protective factors surrounding the person. 'What worries, fears, and anxiety have in common is that they involve an expectation that something bad is going to happen, a particular way in which our bodies respond to this, and certain characteristic behaviours' (Creswell & Willetts, 2019, p.4).

Anxiety is the body's response to threat which has adapted, over time, to keep people safe from danger and help them to cope with unfamiliar situations. It warns a person to act, protect themself from danger or injury and helps them prepare for significant events or circumstances. Anxiety is the body's 'in-built warning system' (Star, 2020), the instinctive response system which triggers to protect from harm.

Therefore, a certain level of anxiety is a normal, healthy emotion which presents, at times, for everyone. In school, all pupils will experience increased anxiety and stress at certain points. This 'positive stress' can help them rise to a challenge, increase productivity or motivate them to work harder (to revise for exams, give a presentation to their peers, play in the sports team or act in the school play) without overwhelming them.

DOI: 10.4324/9781003433231-2

Sometimes, however, levels of stress or anxiety can become unmanageable, with people feeling anxious, frightened or panicked most of the time. 'Some people find it hard to control their worries. Their feelings of anxiety are more constant and can often affect their daily lives' (NHS, 2022a).

> [Anxiety] likes to call the shots and dictate what you can and can't do. It gets in the way of your sleep, might interfere with your eating, could interrupt your fun activities, and might not let you stop thinking about something.
>
> (Hutt, 2019, p.77)

Anxiety can, therefore, affect key aspects of day-to-day life, impacting sleep patterns, mental health and wellbeing, behaviour, attainment and relationships.

Support for pupils is not about removing all anxiety and stress, but about helping them to recognise their anxiety and how it presents for them, gradually increasing their ability to cope and understanding when it is having a negative or overwhelming impact, alongside providing them with strategies to cope more effectively during periods of increased stress.

The threat response

Anxiety activates the autonomous nervous system – the body's threat response or survival mechanism – which has developed, as humans have evolved over time, in order to keep them safe from threat. It is the automatic reaction or body's alarm system to help protect itself by sending it into fight (refusing, attacking, shouting or aggression), flight (running away or hiding), freeze (being unable to speak or move), fawn (people-pleasing, seeking to connect, being extremely helpful or compliant) or flop (becoming unresponsive, fainting or collapsing) when faced with a threatening situation. It is an essential response to protect people from danger and help them respond quickly to emergencies. The heart beats faster and blood is pumped to the muscles to provide the energy and adrenaline to allow someone to protect themself by running away from danger or fighting off a challenge.

However, the body can overreact to stressors which are not life-threatening. People who experience high and prolonged levels of anxiety can develop an overreactive stress response.

This response can become similar to a faulty smoke alarm system, triggering at the tiniest amount of burnt toast and refusing to switch off again. It means the body responds to everyday mild triggers or stressors as if it is in danger.

(Thynne, 2022, p.79)

'Think about anxiety like a bad guard dog. A good guard dog is supposed to bark when there is danger. However, when you have anxiety your mind and body "barks" at many things, whether they are dangerous or not' (Hutt, 2019, p.77). The body's response to threat is immediate and involuntary and anxiety can become problematic when the body signals that there is a threat, when in fact it is not in physical danger.

The threat response cannot distinguish between actual threat (a real danger to life, such as being faced by a sabre-toothed tiger or needing to get out of the way of a moving car), activities which may naturally heighten anxiety (such as an exam, job interview or needing to present in front of the class) and perceived threat (those things which cause unnecessary anxiety such as certain phobias, going to school or talking to a teacher). The body reacts to the perceived threat in the same way it would if it was faced with immediate danger so prepares to fight, flight or shutdown. Blood pumps to essential systems such as the heart, lungs, legs and arms and muscles, making the heart race and body feel tense or faint. Cortisol supresses the digestive system, increasing feelings of nausea or butterflies in the stomach.

When a person is anxious, the pre-frontal cortex, or the 'upstairs brain' (Siegel & Payne Bryson, 2012, p.38) (the rational, reasoning, regulating and thinking part of the brain) – goes offline. This is then taken over by the brainstem and limbic systems, or the 'downstairs brain' (Siegel & Payne Bryson, 2012, p.38) (the part of the brain responsible for safety and survival, and constantly on the alert for threat and danger). The individual is consequently rendered unable to think straight, process or express verbal information or regulate their feelings or behaviours. 'The destructive aspect of anxiety is that it makes a direct impact on the brain and undermines the higher-order thinking processes, so instead of being able to objectively weigh up decisions or critically evaluate a situation, it becomes personal' (Jennings, 2023, p.13).

'Fear and stress can restrict and constrict our thinking and our ability to process and reflect. They can make us react instead of reflect' Treisman (2021, p.160). This is true of pupils, but also of adults working with them, so staff wellbeing and reflection is essential. To manage anxiety, it is necessary to find ways of bringing the pre-frontal cortex back online, thus allowing for rational thinking, and to support the brain and body to distinguish between real and perceived threat; to fix the faulty smoke alarm system or train the bad guard dog! 'How we feel in a situation bears only an indirect relationship to the degree of risk present in that situation' (Bowlby, 1998, p.215). When a child's threat response has been activated, adults need to reassure them that they are safe and not under threat, while supporting them to soothe, through co-regulation and modelling pre-taught coping strategies (see Chapter 4).

Anxiety disorders

People can experience anxiety around a range of different issues, events and situations. 'Anxiety can come in different shapes and sizes. Some of us get anxious in response to a wide variety of things and some of us get anxious in response to things that are more specific' (Collins-Donnelly, 2013, p.26).

A person does not need to have a diagnosis to have anxiety and need support. However, a person may be diagnosed with a particular anxiety disorder if they have a certain type of anxiety or when their anxiety impacts negatively on their everyday activities, relationships or emotional wellbeing. Being aware of this can help staff to signpost pupils and caregivers towards appropriate help and advice and provide effective strategies to support them.

'Children and young adults (ages 10–25 years old) are at highest risk for developing anxiety disorders and almost one third of the child and adult population meets criteria for an anxiety disorder' (Michael et al., 2007). Anxiety disorders affect nearly 300,000 young people in Britain, they are estimated to affect 5–19 per cent of all children and adolescents and about 2–5 per cent of children younger than 12 in the UK (NHS, 2023). However, a much larger percentage of young people will go undiagnosed and will need support.

Anxiety disorders are characterised by excessive worry and avoidance that cause significant impairment across multiple domains of an individual's life (in the *Diagnostic and Statistical Manual of Mental Disorders*, a reference book on mental health and brain-related conditions by the American Psychiatric Association (2022)). 'There are different types of anxiety disorders, but they all share some common features, including a subjective feeling of discomfort or fear, behaviors of avoidance or escape, and physiological reactions such as sweating, nausea, and dizziness' (Minahan, 2018, p.74).

The following are different types of anxiety disorder.

Generalised Anxiety Disorder (GAD)

'People with GAD [Generalised Anxiety Disorder] feel anxious most days and often struggle to remember the last time they felt relaxed. As soon as one anxious thought is resolved, another may appear about a different issue' (NHS 2022a). The person rarely feels calm and experiences anxiety and intense worry, usually about a wide range of situations and issues, rather than one specific event. A person with GAD may feel constantly on edge and overwhelmed over a prolonged period of time. 'I worry that I won't do well at school and I will get bad marks. I worry that my friends will stop liking me. I worry about being late to school and getting into trouble' (Willetts & Waite, 2014, p.13).

Phobias

A phobia is heightened anxiety or extreme fear when faced with or thinking about a certain situation or item, which goes away if that situation or item is removed. It usually leads to avoidance of the situation or item which triggers the fear. Phobias become a problem when they start to impact on, and interfere with, day-to-day life.

Phobias are classed as either specific (previously called simple phobias) or complex. Specific phobias (which include spiders, the dark, water, needles, crowds and flying) may diminish on their own, as a child gets older. Complex phobias tend to be more restricting than specific phobias because they are often an entrenched fear about a particular situation and may continue for a prolonged period of time. Complex phobias include social phobias and agoraphobia (an intense fear of being in open places, crowds, leaving the home or being in a place from which escape is difficult).

Social anxiety (or social phobia) *(see Chapters 5 and 6)*

Social anxiety is an intense fear of engaging in social situations. A person may worry excessively about up-coming social interactions or dwell on past social experiences, as well as experiencing heightened fear within the moment itself.

Selective/situational mutism *(see Chapters 7 and 8)*

Selective or situational mutism is a form of social anxiety, which renders a person unable to speak within certain social situations or with certain people (particularly those who are unfamiliar).

Health anxiety

Health anxiety is when a person experiences excessive worry about becoming ill or about their health and safety for no apparent medical reason. Thoughts about illness may always be at the forefront of the person's mind and they may constantly predict the worst about their health. They may be on the look-out for signs and symptoms of illnesses and worry intensely about death. People may also avoid school or work and physical or social activities due to health concerns.

Health-related fear was a common response within the COVID-19 pandemic, with young people being recurrently warned of threats to the health of themselves and loved ones. For some, increased anxiety about health and germs continues. Health anxiety can sometimes be linked to Obsessive-Compulsive Disorder.

Obsessive-Compulsive Disorder (OCD)

Obsessive-Compulsive Disorder (OCD) is an anxiety-related condition where a person experiences repetitive, frequent, intrusive and unwanted obsessional thoughts, images or compulsions. Compulsions are repetitive behaviours or rituals which people feel compelled to carry out in order to prevent something bad happening or to prevent perceived harm. 'Such behaviours include avoidance of people, places or objects and constant reassurance seeking, sometimes the rituals will be internal mental counting, checking of body parts, or blinking' (OCDUK, undated). 'OCD involves getting scary thoughts or pictures in your head that keep coming back and are hard to stop and/or having to do the same thing over and over again to stop bad things happening' (Willetts & Waite, 2014, p.44). It can be very distressing and impact negatively on everyday life and on wellbeing.

Post-Traumatic Stress Disorder (PTSD)

Post-Traumatic Stress Disorder (PTSD) is caused by an extremely stressful, frightening or distressing event or events, such as abuse or assault, bullying, a single traumatic event such as a death, a traffic accident, a house fire, witnessing a loved one being hurt or prolonged separation from caregivers (NHS, 2022b; PTSDUK, undated). Essentially, any situation which is found traumatic by a person can cause PTSD. People may experience flashbacks and nightmares, low mood, isolation, shame and aggression. Symptoms may impact daily life and relationships (NHS 2022b).

PTSD may present differently in children than in adults, as adults are usually more able to verbalise their feelings and emotions. In children, it may present through a range of behaviours. PTSDUK (undated) categorises these under 'three main symptom clusters':

■ 'Re-experiencing trauma' – intrusive thoughts and flashbacks and recurring nightmares, re-living trauma through talking, writing and drawing.
■ 'Avoidance of traumatic triggers' – including people, places, events and things and emotional detachment or withdrawal.
■ 'Chronic physiological hyperarousal' – sleep disturbance, poor concentration, being easily distracted, feeling irritable, aggression, oppositional behaviours, difficulties regulating emotions or behaviours and hypervigilance to threat.

Separation anxiety *(see Chapters 10 and 11)*

Separation anxiety is the overwhelming fear of being away from key attachment figures, such as parents and caregivers. Distress presents at the thought of, or during the separation, often stemming from fear of permanent separation or fear for the safety or health of themselves or the loved one during the period of absence.

Panic attacks or panic disorder

Panic disorder is characterised by regular 'sudden attacks of panic or fear'. 'Someone with panic disorder has feelings of anxiety, stress and panic regularly and at any time, often for no apparent reason' and 'panic' is described as 'the most severe form of anxiety' (NHS 2020). People may experience sudden onset of chest pains, rapid breathing, racing heartbeat, headaches and shaking, which can last between five to twenty minutes (sometimes longer), during which time the person may feel like they are out of control or dying. The experience can be extremely distressing. Panic attacks often lead to anxiety between attacks and avoidance of certain situations, for fear of another attack, described as 'living in fear of fear' (NHS 2020).

Presentations of anxiety

School staff need to be aware of how anxiety can present in order to provide support and help young people to recognise, understand and begin to regulate their emotions. Anxiety is the most common form of Social Emotional and Mental Health (SEMH) difficulty experienced by young people, and over 5 per cent of children are likely to have an anxiety problem that gets in the way of their day-to-day life (Creswell & Willetts, 2019, p.20).

Anxiety can present in a variety of ways, which can be negatively perceived by adults and viewed as 'choice' behaviours which are within the pupil's control. In reality, the behaviour is the body's involuntary response to a perceived threat. Such 'fear behaviour' is 'plainly to serve a single biological function, namely protection' (Bowlby, 1998, p.113). 'When anxiety is underlying a student's behaviour, it can lead to inconsistent, seemingly overreactive behaviour that can be confusing to teachers' (Minahan, 2018, p.73). By recognising what activates a pupil's anxiety responses, understanding behaviour as communication and remaining curious about translating these behaviours, adults are better placed to provide support and help soothe those responses with empathy and compassion.

Behaviours which may be communicating heightened levels of anxiety could include increased fidgeting and moving around, lack of attention or focus on a task, refusal and work avoidance, opposition and defiance, verbal and physical aggression or violence and rage. As Jennings (2023, p.89) states, 'we don't want to admit we are scared, so we'll put on a show of strength'.

Using an iceberg analogy can be a useful means of understanding the communicative function of behaviour. The behaviour presentations or actions that are seen (aggression, refusal, defiance, lack of focus, avoidance, withdrawal, non-attendance, inflexibility) are merely the tip of the iceberg, whereas, under the surface, are all of the feelings and emotions which are driving those behaviours (activation of the threat response, anxiety, excessive fear, negative thoughts, physical sensations, unmet needs, shame, feeling overwhelmed). Adults need to be curious about what is hidden beneath the surface and what the behaviours are trying to communicate.

As the feelings that the pupil is experiencing are below the surface and not visible, it can be difficult to spot warning signs. Communication and collaboration with caregivers and pupils themselves are therefore essential, to intervene and provide timely support.

Everyone is unique and anxiety will present differently for each individual, however, there are some key symptoms to look out for. Anxiety presents through a person's physical sensations, through their thoughts and feelings and also through actions and behaviours.

Anxiety arises when you over-respond to fear or worry. It is physiological. Anxiety may cause uncomfortable bodily states, such as stomach pains or chest tightness, headaches, dry mouth, or hot palms. Anxiety also comes with a psychological component (distorted beliefs and/or negative expectations) and an emotional facet (fear, dread).

(Saline, 2023a)

Symptoms

A pupil with high levels of anxiety may experience

Physical symptoms	
■ Tiredness, trouble sleeping, restlessness and the inability to relax ■ Increased thirst ■ Headaches, stomach aches, nausea ■ Chest pains ■ Hair loss ■ Tinnitus ■ Clenching/grinding teeth ■ Exhaustion and burnout ■ Flashbacks ■ Tics ■ Inability to speak, going mute, stuttering or stammering ■ Shaking ■ Feeling hot and sweaty or cold and clammy ■ Rushing feeling in arms and legs	■ Rapid, shallow breathing ■ Increased heart rate ■ Butterflies or churning stomach ■ Increased need for the toilet ■ Clenched muscles, raised shoulders ■ Forgetfulness ■ Shutdown ■ Crying ■ Body-Focused Repetitive Behaviours (BFRBs) (e.g. hair-pulling, skin-picking, nail-biting, nose-picking, and lip- or cheek-biting) ■ Jumping or flinching ■ Freezing or looking blank ■ Weight loss or gain
Behavioural symptoms	
■ Emotional dysregulation ■ Fixations or compulsive behaviours ■ Perfectionism ■ Smoking, drinking, substance abuse ■ Self-harm or suicidal ideations ■ Panic attacks ■ Lack of motivation ■ Changes in eating habits ■ Social withdrawal ■ Trouble focusing or concentrating ■ Conforming and compliance ■ Acting the 'class clown' ■ Catastrophising ■ Talking and interrupting	■ Moving, fidgeting, fiddling, wandering, pacing, rocking, bouncing, tapping ■ Daydreaming or zoning out ■ Hiding or running away ■ Taking risks ■ Overachieving ■ Always being punctual or early ■ Being highly organised ■ Focusing on tiny details ■ Disengaging ■ Overthinking or overanalysing ■ Impulsiveness ■ Working extremely hard ■ Masking

(Continued)

Continued

■ Seeking approval, reassurance and connection ■ Difficulties distinguishing between fantasy and reality ■ Chewing on non-edible items such as clothing and pencils ■ Making noises (humming, tapping)	■ Increased absence ■ Procrastination ■ Using a voice which changes pace, pitch or volume ■ Engaging in 'baby talk' ■ Confabulation/memory errors ■ Hypervigilance
Internal symptoms/feelings	
■ Nervous or 'on edge' a lot of the time ■ Panic and fear ■ Being frozen or stuck ■ A sense of shame and blame ■ Low mood ■ Low self-esteem ■ Self-doubt ■ Obsessive, racing or negative thoughts ■ Loneliness ■ Needing to be in control	■ Trapped ■ Out of control ■ Hopeless ■ Lost ■ Unhappy ■ Overwhelmed ■ Rejected ■ Fear of failure and making mistakes ■ Dissociation (feeling disconnected from themselves or their surroundings)

By recognising the various presentations of anxiety and understanding the stress and sense of overwhelm which the pupil is experiencing, adults will be in a position to identify patterns, alleviate anxiety and provide appropriate support. They will then be able to explore ways of noticing and labelling these, to increase awareness and understanding for the pupil.

> As anxiety increases, the brain cannot effectively regulate behaviour and emotions because the ability to think logically and process information decreases. Therefore, by understanding that the behaviours are communicating a state of heightened distress or overwhelming anxiety, the negative behaviours will be reduced by reducing the stress.
>
> (Thynne, 2022, p.83)

All behaviour has a function; it is a form of communication, a means of meeting a need or a response to the environment. Behaviour which is driven by anxiety may be communicating that a pupil does not feel safe, needs to escape or take a break and requires support to regulate.

By helping pupils to understand anxiety – what it is, what it looks like and how it feels for them – adults can give them the tools to begin to manage their anxieties when, and even before, anxiety begins to affect the quality of everyday life, interactions, relationships and engagement.

Masking

Although some pupils will have a very outward display of anxiety and may become aggressive or withdraw, it can be difficult to recognise anxiety and stress in some pupils, particularly those with hidden symptoms or not presenting with extreme or externalised behaviours which are not tolerated in school. In fact, certain 'anxiety-driven' behaviours are encouraged in schools; perfectionism, high levels of organisation, hard work, high academic or sporting performance, compliance, being helpful and so on. However, often driving some of these aforementioned behaviours is an intense fear of failure or making mistakes, fear of being negatively judged or disapproved of by others and rejection sensitivity. A highly anxious pupil may be extremely successful, appear to be in control and maintain an outward sense of calm, while masking persistent feelings of fear, unease or worry.

Personal case study:

As a Year Leader in a large primary school, I always used to be amazed when people commented on how calm I was, particularly in times of stress (an Ofsted visit being one). I was genuinely perplexed, because I felt hugely anxious and sick most of the time and remember assuming everyone must know how I was feeling. I do know, on reflection, that anxiety for me mainly presents inwardly, with the outward presentation being people-pleasing, perfectionism and over-planning.

Anxiety presents in different ways and it seems a person can mask without even knowing they are masking!

Masking is when a person hides, camouflages or suppresses their emotions, behaviours or anxieties, presenting as 'fine' and aiming to 'fit in' socially. A person who is masking may act like the 'class clown', laugh at jokes they don't understand, use social scripts or talk incessantly to mask feelings of social anxiety. They may engage in social mimicry such as mirror facial expressions, act like their friend or a celebrity, or a person may pretend they like an activity, game or television programme to fit in socially. A perfectionist, or someone who is terrified of making mistakes, may be extremely compliant, spend hours on homework or preparing for presentations in order to produce the 'perfect' finished product. A person who needs to fidget and move may put all their energy into sitting still (at the expense of being able to concentrate on learning) for fear of being reprimanded or not fitting in.

Masking anxiety and suppressing emotions and symptoms can be exhausting, it may make people feel that they do not belong and lead to feelings of shame. Masking and high levels of anxiety, stress and feeling overwhelmed can lead to burnout and the inability to engage or become motivated academically, socially or physically, impacting negatively on mental health and wellbeing.

To provide support with masking in school, pupils need access to safe spaces, movement and sensory breaks, sensory tools and to be taught healthy coping strategies to relieve stress (see Chapter 4). They need positive relationships and safe adults who foster an ethos of acceptance and empathy, help them spot their early warning signs of anxiety and provide support. They need to know that difference and diversity is valued and they need a sense of belonging and connectedness.

Anxiety triggers in school (see also Chapters 9 and 10)

There are a variety of factors in school which may trigger anxiety, including:

- Separating from caregivers (see Chapters 11 and 12).
- Speaking in public or to unfamiliar people.
- Cold-calling (asking pupils to answer a question with no preparation or warning).
- Public praise and rewards.
- Reading aloud.
- Still or cross faces, closed body language, stern tone of voice.
- Sensory sensitivity to the environment: smells (dinner hall, bleach, perfumes, air fresheners, shampoos, changing rooms and toilets), crowds, loud, sudden or unexpected noises (raised voices, school bells, fire alarms, doors slamming) or sudden movements.
- Transitions and unexpected change (change to seating plan, changes to timetable or routine, new or unfamiliar adult in the

room). 'Uncertainty can be felt as overwhelming anxiety, and tolerating the uncertainty of not knowing becomes an unbearable threat' (Geddes, 2006, p.56).

■ Lacking understanding of a task or instruction.
■ Lacking a skill to complete or start a task.
■ 'Academic anxiety' (Cassady, 2009) (exams and tests, fear of making mistakes or failure, work is or feels too challenging).
■ Certain topics (Mother's/Father's Day, festivals, birthdays, *All about Me* topics, topics on war and evacuation, texts which include death and loss).
■ Relationship difficulties (with peers and/or staff).

Personal case study:

When I was 14, my family and I moved house and I inevitably had to start a new school and make new friends. I made some lovely friends, but struggled to feel accepted and liked by anyone out of my 'inner circle'. At the age of 15, I was physically sick most mornings before getting on the school bus. At the time, I had no idea what it was, so stopped eating breakfast and told myself I didn't like eating early in the morning, which seemed (superficially) to help.

The physical sickness subsided after leaving school, but the feelings of nausea continued (and still continue at times) well into adulthood.

I now recognise it as heightened anxiety. A lack of understanding meant a lack of recognition and therefore a lack of knowledge of how to help myself or where to go to for support. By the time I started university, my social anxiety was huge and I was situationally mute.

On reflection, I wonder if recognising and learning how to manage the physical symptoms may have helped?

Anxiety and learning

Anxiety can negatively impact a pupil's ability to learn effectively and reach their full potential. A person cannot learn in a state of heightened anxiety, as it impairs cognitive performance and reduces motivation, attention and processing. Activation of the threat response can inhibit executive functioning and negatively affect learning, concentration and focus, regulation and working memory, and can escalate to social, les-son or school avoidance. 'Anxiety specifically interferes with an aspect of executive functioning known as attentional control. This interference makes concentrating and switching attention from task to task more difficult for individuals high in anxiety' (Hunley, undated). Anxiety can make it difficult for children to take risks, complete tasks that they perceive as difficult or contribute to classroom discussions, leading to underachievement.

At times of heightened stress and anxiety, the pre-frontal cortex (the part of the brain responsible for logical, rational thought) goes offline, meaning that a pupil will not be able to think coherently. This will therefore make it difficult for them to follow instructions, engage in learning tasks, voice their opinions, express their emotions effectively or regulate their behaviours. People with high anxiety tend to have negative thought patterns, fearing the worst and have an intense fear of failing and being judged, which can all impact negatively on engage-ment and attainment. 'Anxiety can make your world grow smaller and smaller and your head becomes full of the things you can't do' (Knightsmith, 2022, p.175).

Anxiety and neurodiversity

Anxiety has a high comorbidity rate with diagnoses such as autism and Attention Deficit Hyperactivity Disorder (ADHD). Often people (par-ticularly girls) are diagnosed with anxiety prior to being given such a diagnosis. Anxiety can be increased for people who are neurodivergent because navigating a world which does not cater well enough for their needs can certainly heighten anxiety.

'In adults with ADHD, the rates of anxiety disorder approach 50% and symptoms tend to be more severe when ADHD is in the picture. This comorbidity contributes significantly to the prevalence of perfec-tionism in individuals with ADHD' (Saline, 2023b).

Nadeau et al. (2011) report that up to 80 per cent of autistic children 'experience clinically significant anxiety with high comorbidity rates for social phobia, Generalized Anxiety Disorder (GAD), Obsessive–Com-pulsive Disorder (OCD) and Separation Anxiety Disorder (SAD) having been observed'. They go on to state that autistic people with comorbid anxiety are at increased risk of displaying difficulties with regulating their behaviour, social avoidance and withdrawal from peer-centred activities, difficulties establishing and maintaining peer relationships and difficulties following teacher demands. It seems that labelling these diagnoses and differences as 'disorders' in no way helps reduce anxiety and a complete language reframe is needed to value difference and diversity and provide support for difficulties, with compassion, empathy and genuine acceptance.

For a person with a demand avoidant profile, one of the key traits is the anxiety-based need to avoid demands. However, anxiety for those with Pathological Demand Avoidance (PDA) may present differently than in other children.

> Anxiety of the PDA kind is less likely to cause someone to look nervous and to be withdrawn – especially in younger years. We may be more likely to chat away (distracting people or putting off doing things!) or if things have got really hard, it may be that shouting or violence sometimes takes over.
>
> (PDA Society, undated)

Furthermore, McMahon et al. (2019) suggest a link between anxiety and sensory processing difficulties. Increased sensory sensitivity can cause heightened emotional responses which are difficult to regulate, which, in turn, increases anxiety.

Anxiety and relational trauma

People who have experienced relational and developmental trauma often display heightened anxiety. Bombèr (2007, p.31–8) describes how anxiety can present for children with different insecure attachment styles. Behaviours may include compliance, helpfulness, perfectionism, connection-seeking, the need to be in control and hypervigilance.

People who have insecure attachments or have experienced relational trauma often have high levels of shame and low feelings of self-worth which can also increase anxiety.

Chapter take-aways

■ Anxiety is a fear or worry that something bad is going to happen and is the body's response to threat, which has adapted over time, to keep the person safe.
■ Anxiety becomes a problem when it starts to negatively impact everyday life, relationships, functioning and wellbeing and individuals may need to seek medical support.
■ Anxiety presents in a range of sensations and reactions, stemming from various triggers. Understanding the communicative function of behaviour is crucial in providing support.

Further signposting

Books

A Toolbox for Wellbeing by Tina Rae
Behaviour Barriers and Beyond by Rachel Thynne
Helping Your Child with Fears and Worries by Cathy Creswell and Lucy
    Willetts
Inside I'm Hurting by Louise Bombèr

Resources to share with pupils

All Birds Have Anxiety by Kathy Hoopmann
Can I Tell You About Anxiety? by Lucy Willetts and Polly Waite

Websites

Anna Freud *Seven Ways to Support Children and Young People Who
    are Worried* https://www.annafreud.org/schools-and-colleges/
    resources/7-ways-to-support-children-and-young-people-who-
    are-worried
Child and Adolescent Mental Health Service (CAMHS) https://www.
    oxfordhealth.nhs.uk/camhs/self-care/anxiety
Dr Russ Harris *The Happiness Trap: Evolution of the Human Mind* https://
    www.youtube.com/watch?v=kv6HkipQcfA
Mind *Anxiety and Panic Attacks* https://www.mind.org.uk/information-
    support/types-of-mental-health-problems/anxiety-and-panic-
    attacks/self-care
NSPCC (The National Society for the Prevention of Cruelty to Children)
    How to Help Children Suffering From Depression and Anxiety
    https://www.nspcc.org.uk/keeping-children-safe/childrens-
    mental-health/depression-anxiety-mental-health
NSPCC Post-Traumatic Stress Disorder (PTSD) https://www.ptsduk.
    org/ptsd-in-children-information-for-teachers
Teach Resiliency *The Anxiety Iceberg* https://phecanada.ca/programs/
    teach-resiliency/resources/iceberg-diagram

Podcasts

Mind *Anxiety and Panic Attacks* https://www.mind.org.uk/information-
    support/your-stories/mind-podcast-anxiety-and-panic-attacks
Pooky Ponders *Finding What Feels Safe: A Gentle Approach to Tack-
    ling Anxiety* https://www.creativeeducation.co.uk/explore-our-
    podcast-pooky-ponders

SENDcast *Supporting Anxiety and Trauma* https://www.thesendcast.com/supporting-anxiety-and-trauma

References

American Psychiatric Association (2022) *Diagnostic and Statistical Manual of Mental Disorders,* Fifth Edition, *Text Revision (DSM-5TR)* American Psychiatric Publishing

Bombèr, L. (2007) *Inside I'm Hurting – Practical Strategies for Supporting Children with Attachment Difficulties in Schools* Worth Publishing

Bowlby, J. (1998) *Attachment and Loss: Separation, Anger and Anxiety* Pimlico

Cassady, J. (2009) *Anxiety in Schools – The Causes, Consequences and Solutions for Academic Anxiety* Peter Lang

Collins-Donnelly, K. (2013) *Starving the Anxiety Gremlin – A Cognitive Behavioural Workbook on Anxiety Management for Young People* Jessica Kingsley

Creswell, C. & Willetts, L. (2019) *Helping Your Child with Fears and Worries* Robinson

Geddes, H. (2006) *Attachment in the Classroom* Worth Publishing

Hunley, S. (undated) *Executive Functioning and How It Relates to Anxiety* Available at: https://www.anxiety.org/what-is-executive-functioning-and-how-does-it-relate-to-anxiety [Accessed 23.6.23]

Hutt, R. (2019) *Feeling Better: CBT Workbook for Teens: Essential Skills and Activities to Help You Manage Moods, Boost Self-Esteem, and Conquer Anxiety* Althea Press

Jennings, S. (2023) *Managing Social Anxiety in Children and Young People – Practical Activities for Reducing Stress and Building Self-esteem* Routledge

Knightsmith, P. (2022) *Things I Got Wrong So You Don't Have To – 48 Lessons to Banish Burnout and Avoid Anxiety for Those who Put Others First* Jessica Kingsley

McMahon, K., Anand, D., Morris-Jones, M. & Rosenthal, M. (2019) A Path from Childhood Sensory Processing Disorder to Anxiety Disorders: The Mediating Role of Emotion Dysregulation and Adult Sensory Processing Disorder Symptoms *Frontiers in Integrative Neuroscience* 13: 22 Available at: https://www.ncbi.nlm.nih.gov/pmc/articles/PMC6629761 [Accessed 30.6.23]

Michael, T., Zetsche, U. & Margraf, J. (2007) Epidemiology of Anxiety Disorders *Psychiatry* 6: 136–142 Available at: https://www.sciencedirect.com/science/article/abs/pii/S1476179307000237 [Accessed 24.6.23]

Minahan, J. (2018) *The Behavior Code Companion: Strategies, Tools and Interventions for Supporting Students with Anxiety-Related or Oppositional Behaviours* Harvard Education Press

Nadeau J., Sulkowski M., Ung D., Wood J., Lewin A., Murphy T., May J. & Storch E. (2011) Treatment of Comorbid Anxiety and Autism Spectrum Disorders *Neuropsychiatry* 1(6): 567–578 Available at: https://www.ncbi.nlm.nih.gov/pmc/articles/PMC3809000 [Accessed 30.6.23]

NHS (2020) *Panic Disorder* Available at: https://www.nhs.uk/mental-health/conditions/panic-disorder [Accessed 12.5.23]

NHS (2022a) *Overview – Generalised Anxiety Disorder in Adults* Available at: https://www.nhs.uk/mental-health/conditions/generalised-anxiety-disorder/overview [Accessed 12.5.23]

NHS (2022b) *Overview – Post Traumatic Stress Disorder* Available at: https://www.nhs.uk/mental-health/conditions/post-traumatic-stress-disorder-ptsd/overview [Accessed 12.5.23]

NHS (2023) *Anxiety Disorders in Children* Available at: https://www.nhsinform.scot/illnesses-and-conditions/mental-health/anxiety-disorders-in-children#:~:text=Nearly%20300%2C000%20young%20people%20in,in%20children%20younger%20than%2012 [Accessed 29.6.23]

OCDUK (undated) *Introduction to Obsessive Compulsive Disorder* Available at: https://www.ocduk.org/ocd/introduction-to-ocd [Accessed 12.5.23]

PDA Society (undated) *Anxiety of the PDA Kind* Available at: https://www.pdasociety.org.uk/life-with-pda-menu/adult-life-landing/adult-life-by-pdaers-landing/anxiety-of-the-pda-kind [Accessed 30.6.23]

PTSDUK (undated) *PTSD in Children: Information for Teachers* Available at: https://www.ptsduk.org/ptsd-in-children-information-for-teachers [Accessed 29.6.23]

Saline, S. (2023a) *How to Stop Catastrophizing: A Guide for ADHD Worriers* Available at: https://www-additudemag-com.cdn.ampproject.org/c/s/www.additudemag.com/catastrophizing-worrying-negative-thoughts-adhd/amp [Accessed 7.7.23]

Saline, S. (2023b) *When Perfectionism Stems from ADHD: Challenging the Fallacy of "Not Good Enough"* Available at: https://www.additudemag.com/perfectionism-adhd-not-good-enough-anxiety [Accessed 7.7.23]

Siegel, D. & Payne Bryson, T. (2012) *The Whole Brain Child – 12 Proven Strategies to Nurture your Child's Developing Mind* Robinson

Star, K. (2020) *The Benefits of Anxiety and Nervousness* Available at: https://www.verywellmind.com/benefits-of-anxiety-2584134#:~:text=Built%2DIn%20Warning%20System,to%20react%20faster%20to%20emergencies [Accessed 9.2.24]

Thynne, R. (2022) *Behaviour Barriers and Beyond: Practical Strategies to Help All Pupils Thrive* Routledge

Treisman, K. (2021) *A Treasure Box for Creating Trauma-Informed Organizations* Jessica Kingsley

Willetts, L. & Waite, P. (2014) *Can I Tell You About Anxiety? A Guide for Friends, Family and Professionals* Jessica Kingsley

2

Safety, relationships and communication

Increasing feelings of safety

Pupils who endure states of high anxiety will often miss signs of safety, being hypervigilant and primarily focused on threat. Safety, therefore, often needs to be explicitly communicated to pupils. 'We need to convince the primitive parts of the child's brain that we are safe through providing repeated messages of safety through our interactions. We need to be Amygdala Whisperers' (Baylin, 2016).

By assuming someone who is anxious or dysregulated does not feel safe, the adult then becomes increasingly focused on alleviating the child's anxiety and helping them to feel both emotionally and physically safe. Children can only learn and engage when they feel secure, safe and calm. Schools need to become a safe base from which to learn, explore and interact socially. They need to be supportive, inclusive places, where all pupils are confident to express their worries and make mistakes. 'In essence, fear restricts and safety expands learning and relationships' (Treisman, 2017, p.10).

Porges (2022) emphasises the need for safety in his explanations of Polyvagal Theory: 'Feelings of safety play a fundamental role enabling humans not only to survive, but to thrive . . . When humans feel safe, their nervous systems support the homeostatic functions of health, growth, and restoration, while they simultaneously become accessible to others without feeling or expressing threat and vulnerability.'

DOI: 10.4324/9781003433231-3

■ 'Safety needs to be consistently communicated to pupils at all times throughout the school day, through every verbal and non-verbal interaction' (Thynne, 2022, p.63). A smile and a calm, prosodic tone of voice from adults, along with open, welcoming body language will help pupils to feel safe from the moment they walk through the school gate. 'Nonverbal cues – the look on your face, your eye contact, your tone of voice, your posture, the timing and intensity of your response – all offer enormous potential to quell raging emotions' (Siegel & Payne Bryson, 2020, p.164).

■ Up safety cues by smiling! Vulnerable and anxious pupils tend to interpret neutral faces as angry faces and are quicker to detect any negative changes in facial expression. 'When we are anxious we often stop differentiating between facial expressions, and everyone may be perceived as hostile and unfriendly' (Jennings, 2023, p.58). Berenson et al. (2009) found that people who presented with heightened rejection sensitivity (see p.114) showed changes in brain activity when they saw a face that displayed disapproval or looked as if it might reject them. Furthermore, brain changes during puberty and adolescence mean there is 'a period when young people lose their emotion reading skills and are more likely to interpret someone as being hostile when they are not' (Andrews, in Morgan with Costello, 2023, p.240). Smiling is a simple yet effective means of making someone feel safe; it reduces stress and reassures pupils that they are liked and valued, and quickly builds connections.

■ Anxious children can interpret harsh, raised voices or even neutral tones of voice as cross and hostile and need soft, prosodic voices to convey calm. 'Your tone can influence whether she moves further towards reactivity and frustration . . . or back into calm and control' (Siegel & Payne Bryson, 2020, p.164). Knightsmith (2022) recommends making our voices 'slow, low, low' (slow the pace down and use a quieter voice and a lower pitch) to convey a sense of calm when supporting children who are heightened.

■ Use open body language and get alongside a pupil to convey openness and approachability. Sitting down and getting down to a child's level or below their eyeline (if safe to do so) can immediately communicate safety and calm the threat response.

■ Increase feelings of safety and reduce anxiety by providing predictable, consistent routines, language and responses. Pupils feel less anxious when they know what to expect, so consistent approaches alongside powerful nurture are key. Consistency can be achieved by using the same visuals, vocabulary and predictable phrases as colleagues and caregivers in order to convey the same message and can be helpful in 'providing consistent structure and helping to lessen anxiety' (Thynne, 2022).

Building positive relationships

The importance of relationships between adults and pupils in schools cannot be overstated. Relationships and the way adults communicate with children are essential in building trust, developing positive well-being and reducing anxieties. 'Lack of relationship can hinder us, and good, stable relationships can enable us to grow' (Bombèr, 2007, p.60). As adults begin to foster positive relationships with their pupils, they become better placed to recognise their anxieties and thus provide appropriate support and help to reduce stress.

- Relationships are key in helping children to feel emotionally safe. The most supportive strategy for someone with anxiety is being in close proximity to a trusted, safe person, who understands them and can begin to help them to overcome their fears. 'When a child is in distress – when she's suffering emotionally or her nervous system is sending her into fight, flight, freeze, or faint – that negative state can be shifted by an interaction with a caregiver who shows up for her. She might still suffer, but at least she won't be alone in her pain.' (Siegel & Payne Bryson, 2020, p.154).
- Staff need to help pupils to look for patterns and triggers and provide support at their key times of stress. 'Checking in' with pupils at the end of the week 'can help reinforce school as a secure and safe place for them . . . A clear and individualised welcome into school on a Monday morning can help them settle back into a secure routine.' (MacDonald, 2019, p.54).
- Actively listen to understand the pupil's concerns (and reflect back to the pupil that you've listened) so that pupils trust that you have understood their anxieties and are there to support them to find a way forward. It is only by fully understanding what is triggering the anxiety for each individual that appropriate steps can be put in place to help alleviate this. Address any issues such as bullying or relationship difficulties to ensure the environment is, and feels, safe for the individual and that measures will be taken to ensure this continues, through regular check-ins with the pupil and increased monitoring, particularly at unstructured times. Identify, address and support with triggers, for instance, sensory sensitivities within the environment (such as over- or under-sensitivity to noise, light, touch or smell) and difficulties accessing the curriculum (see p.254).
- Pupils who are presenting with anxiety benefit from regular check-ins and support from trusted adults, particularly at key trigger times (such as lunch time, break times, transition times)

to provide a buffer and help them to soothe and regulate. Similarly, support to start a task and at intervals during a lesson can help a pupil to settle and refocus attention.

■ Find ways of maintaining relationships and connections over holidays or other periods of absence, such as by sending a postcard or email home, or sending the pupil home with a transitional object (see pp.231–2), such as the class mascot, a plant to care for or a journal to bridge the gap between home and school during the break. Communicate to pupils, on their return, that they have been 'kept in mind' (Bombèr, 2007, p.94), even when they have been away, for example, *I thought about you during the holiday as I saw an old steam train and it made me think of you and how much you love trains and Harry Potter.*

■ Take time to build relationships with pupils, engaging in attachment play such as den building, playing games, sensory play and other shared activities. 'When adults change their behaviour in response to a child's intense reactions, it can change the child's behaviour' (Siegel & Payne Bryson, 2020, p.152).

Positive communication

How staff communicate with pupils can make a huge difference to pupils' sense of wellbeing and belonging in school as well as their engagement and attendance.

■ Research has shown that neurodivergent pupils receive a much higher proportion of negative attention from adults than a neurotypical child. As adults we need to flip this and reframe language used into positives: talk about *anxiety, distress, overwhelm* and *dysregulation* rather than *inappropriate* or *challenging* behaviours (see also p.244).

■ 'A shift from traditional language to a trauma-informed description of vulnerable individuals can create compassion instead of blame, hope instead of hopelessness and connection rather than disconnection' (Beacon House, undated). Examples include:

■ *Inappropriate* or *negative* behaviour becomes *anxious* or *distressed* behaviour.

■ Rather than describing a pupil as *aggressive, defiant* or *refusing* describe them as having *activated their threat response,* is *in survival mode'* or *scared.*

- *Attention-seeking* becomes *attention-needing, connection-seeking* or *seeking reassurance.*
- *Withdrawn* is reframed as *cautious*, *rude* as *self-protective* and *not engaging* becomes *doesn't feel safe yet'* (Beacon House, undated).
- Use the phrases *brain differences* and *neurodivergent* rather than *disorder*.
- 'Reframe emotionally charged situations as opportunities to build children's ability to self-regulate' (Conkbayir, 2023, p.193).

■ Validate how difficult the pupil is finding the situation, however, aim to focus on the pupil's successes, finding solutions and moving them on, rather than the problem or anxiety. Acknowledge what is going well and build on those positive experiences. Aim for ten positive interactions for each (perceived) negative. Emphasise successes and steps towards success and 'catch the good'. Make a positive statement before any form of redirection, e.g. *I love how engaged you are in this task, it is great to see, just lower your voice for me for the next part of the lesson, thanks.*

■ Adapt and differentiate communication style for different pupils' needs, for example, use clear, direct, unambiguous language for literal thinkers and simple, single step instructions for those who struggle to retain longer steps. Visual communication helps alleviate anxiety for most people (see pp.52–3). 'Moments of extreme dysregulation are often preceded by a lot of verbal demands' (Elley with Morewood, 2022, p.102). Reduce verbal demands, particularly in times of heightened stress or anxiety and allow processing time.

■ Reframing demands and making suggestions can also be effective (particularly when pupils are using avoidance as a coping mechanism and when demands trigger heightened anxiety for them):

- *I wonder where we should start.*
- *Do you think you could . . .?*
- *Let me know where in the classroom you'd feel most comfortable.*
- *I wish there was someone here who could help me.*
- *Would that work for you?*
- *Which one would you like to do first?*
- *Let me know when you are ready to have a go.*
- *Any idea how to sort out all these toys on the floor so we don't fall over them all?*
- *You can do this in whichever order you think best.*

- *I am really interested in this, I wonder where we can find out more.*
- *I wonder what the next step would be.*
- *I'm wondering where the pencils are.*

- Anxiety often stems from feeling out of control. Offer two or three clear positive alternatives to increase a pupil's feeling of choice and autonomy, for example, *Where are you going to do your maths, here next to me, at your table with your friends or in your safe space?* or *Are you taking your hoodie off once we get in the classroom or are you going to do it now where it's a bit quieter?*
- Be aware that certain words can be a trigger for some children. For many pupils it is helpful to avoid the words *don't, no* and *that's wrong/a mistake*, where possible, as they can often cause a negative response and increase anxiety, particularly for those prone to rejection sensitivity, social anxiety or who fear being judged negatively. Try to reframe such interactions into a positive.
- Keep praise quiet, factual and specific when a pupil overcomes anxiety or makes little steps towards success. Use phrases such as, *I know it was difficult for you to step into the classroom with me today, well done for giving it a go* or *I noticed that you did your breathing before trying that question, well done.* 'Praise things within the pupil's control such as effort, persistence, attitude or behaviours for learning rather than correct answers or amount of work produced' (Thynne, 2022, p.84).

The PACE approach

The PACE (Playfulness, Acceptance, Curiosity, Empathy) approach, developed by Daniel Hughes (Bombèr & Hughes, 2013, pp.79–141) is a way of thinking, communicating and behaving when building genuine relationships with pupils. It aims to make pupils feel psychologically safe and emotionally connected, thus reducing stress and anxiety. It allows adults to establish emotional connection and begin to understand the emotional experience of pupils.

Using PACE supports adults to remain open and engaged when certain feelings may make pupils act defensively. It helps adults to make sense of the pupil and their behaviours within their individual emotional context in a way that is compassionate and non-judgemental. PACE encourages adults to slow down and reflect on the drivers behind the behaviours, making them better placed to provide empathic support.

'Connect and redirect: When a child is upset, connect first emotionally, right-brain to right-brain. Then, once the child is more in control and receptive, bring in the left-brain lessons and discipline' (Siegel & Payne Bryson, 2012). Behaviour is communication and once a pupil feels that their level of emotion has been connected with, they can stop displaying that emotion through behaviour and begin to engage the rational, articulate, problem-solving areas of their brain.

Playfulness

A playful approach and attitude can reduce anxiety and fear for pupils in a way that is safe and non-threatening. It is a means of building connection by bringing a sense of lightness, fun, laughter and happiness to interactions. It's not necessarily about engaging in games or playing with the pupils, although play is an essential component in learning and relationship-building, but it is about reciprocal joy in relationships, showing that you like and value the pupil to build their sense of self-worth.

Adults adopting a playful approach can be particularly helpful when working with pupils who have experienced relational trauma. It builds trust and overcomes 'blocked trust' (Baylin & Hughes, 2016) – where past experiences have subconsciously taught defensiveness and to put up barriers against forming new relationships in order to avoid feeling vulnerable, rejected or helpless. 'If we are too serious, our verbal and nonverbal cues communicate danger to our students who have been hurt, and they remain wary. If we can be more playful in our interactions, we communicate that problems can be overcome' (Phillips et al., 2020, p.51).

Playful interactions strengthen neural pathways, inhibiting the threat response, helping both parties to stay open and engaged rather than becoming defensive and can help diffuse situations and reduce escalations in behaviours. Laughter releases oxytocin and reduces stress and anxiety, allowing for higher level, rational thinking and learning to take place. 'Being playful reduces feelings of anxiety and stress as pupils are more relaxed and feel safe in relationship' (Thynne, 2022. p.83).

Engaging pupils in playful interactions also teaches them to regulate emotions which may feel more positive (such as excitement, happiness or pride) which, in turn, will help them begin to regulate more stressful emotions. Taking a playful stance can expand a pupil's window of tolerance and build resilience.

Playfulness case studies:

- Jessica did not want to come in from the playground. The adult responded playfully, *Ah well, I'm going in, off I go* and did a silly walk the wrong way with an exaggerated 'bump' into the hedge.
- TJ was refusing to engage in his writing, saying that he was a cat and cats can't write. The adult responded playfully, *Ah, I wonder if there are any writing cats, perhaps they would use their tails, paws or mouth. I might look up writing cats later and see if there are any, or you might be the first ever writing cat. We'd have to get you a certificate and pop you on Britain's Got Talent.*
- Jeremy was not engaging in his maths task. The adult got another sheet and engaged playfully, *Right, I will have to do this myself then, 4x4, easy, 8. Next, 10x6, even easier 424. I am a maths genius.*

Acceptance

Unconditional acceptance creates psychological safety and a sense of belonging while reducing feelings of shame and rejection. It involves acceptance of the pupil's internal experience – their thoughts, feelings, wishes, beliefs and hopes. Respecting the pupil's emotions and demonstrating that they are accepted and valued as an important member of the school community increases their sense of self-worth.

Actively communicating acceptance does not imply accepting behaviours, it is accepting the drivers behind the behaviours, even when the behaviours themselves need addressing, by separating the behaviours from the person, and avoiding negative labelling (*challenging, disruptive, naughty, misbehaving, defiant* . . .). It involves correction alongside connection. For example, an adult can accept that the pupil is anxious but not accept the throwing of chairs or running away (see also Emotion Coaching, p.33). It is about understanding rather than blaming with the focus on the pupil's feelings, instead of on their behaviour, in order to soothe and regulate. It involves finding ways of validating emotions, communicating understanding and accepting the emotions behind the behaviours.

Through being met with genuine acceptance, the pupil learns to trust that adults understand their thoughts, feelings and wishes and have their wellbeing at the heart of the relationship. They learn that mistakes don't rupture the relationship and repair is possible. Feeling judged and criticised decreases a person's sense of safety and increases shame and is often at the heart of social anxiety. Once a pupil feels genuinely accepted they have the capacity to change their behaviour and to accept themselves. As a child feels safer, there is less need for reactive-defensive behaviours.

Acceptance case study:

■ James told the adult that she was always picking on him and didn't like him. In her response, she accepted and validated his feelings before gently trying to change his perception; *It must be hard to feel that I don't like you. I am sorry you feel that way and I will try and be better at showing how much I like and value you. Are there any times that maybe you feel that I do like you? Remember when we played basketball yesterday? I really enjoyed that.*

Some useful phrases to convey acceptance:

Help me to understand . . ., I get it . . ., Let me see if I have this right . . . (Bombèr, 2020, p.204)

That sounds tough. . ., I care . . ., Thank you for letting me know, . . .,

This seems tricky at the moment; shall we take a break and have another look a bit later?,

It sounds as if . . .(repeat what they have said back to them).

Curiosity

Curiosity involves taking a genuine interest, wanting to understand and know more about the pupil, their experience within the world, their motivators, what is important to them and interests them, what helps them (and what doesn't). It is impossible to understand the drivers behind individual behaviours without being curious. It is impossible to improve behaviour without knowing the driver.

It will be necessary to slow down, take a step back, observe and get to know the pupils, to respond and reflect rather than react. Curiosity, with acceptance, enables a child to make sense of behaviour without shame and fear. When adults model thinking and curiosity it encourages pupils to start to be curious themselves and helps them learn to self-reflect. 'If we're curious, it will support our pupils to develop curiosity about themselves, other people and the world we share' (Bombèr, 2020, p.205).

Adults can be curious by tentatively wondering and imagining aloud, showing an active interest in a pupil's experience by engaging in calming and connecting commentaries and noticing what might be happening for the pupil.

Curiosity case studies:

■ Dimitri had become dysregulated and the class were removed from their classroom as he was tipping tables and chairs and throwing equipment. Once he had calmed, the adult responded, *It seems you were having a difficult time just now, I wonder what was going on for you. Let's see if we can figure this out together.*

■ Georgia had run out of the classroom into the playground. The adult spoke to her, *What happened just then? I was wondering if you might have felt a bit overwhelmed by all of those maths questions and just needed to get away. I was really worried as I didn't know where you were. Perhaps there might be a place you can go to next time you feel like that, so you can get away, but I know you are safe. What do you think?*

Some useful phrases:

Are you ok? I'm worried about you, What's happening?, I might be wrong, but I just wondered if you might be feeling . . ., Do you think . . ., I wonder if you are a bit anxious with a new teacher in the room. I am here with you.

Empathy

The importance of empathy cannot be emphasised enough. 'An empathic relationship is powerful, as it facilitates brain growth and emotional development' (Bombèr, 2007, p.84). Empathy and compassion (rather than sympathy and pity) are needed in interactions with all pupils, particularly those who are vulnerable or highly anxious. Empathy involves being able to see things from the pupil's point of view and communicating true understanding of their motivators and stressors. Adults need to listen to and validate the pupil's perspective and understand that different people have different experiences and views of the world. When adults have empathy for a pupil, they create strong connections and trust. Empathy communicates understanding and helps the pupil to feel safe and explore their emotions with others.

Empathy involves the adult putting themselves in the pupil's shoes and understanding behaviour as communicating an emotion, need or response to the environment. It enables a child to face anxious thoughts and to collaboratively find a way forward. It helps pupils to make sense of their behaviours (and those of others). Empathy involves careful attunement to the changing states of the other person and is 'the antidote to shame' (Brown, 2012).

Empathy conveys that all emotions are accepted and normal, even though the responses may need regulating, and is an effective form of co-regulation, helping pupils to make sense of their strong emotions. Being empathic teaches pupils to show empathy and care towards others. To be able to empathise, a child first needs to have experienced empathy regularly, they can then begin to feel compassion and develop their own sense of empathy.

Empathy case study:

■ Georg did not want to stop playing with the trainset and kept shouting 'No, no, no'. His key adult empathised, *I can see you really don't want to stop playing with this trainset at the moment. You are really enjoying playing with it. I would be cross too, if I had to stop doing something I was really enjoying. Let's take a photo of the trainset to remind us both that you can come back to it later.*

Some useful phrases:
I understand why you are annoyed, I know you were looking forward to that.
You really are upset!
It seems like you are having a tough time at the moment.
I understand, I would feel that way too if . . .

When pupils are presenting with behaviours which are being driven by intense emotions such as anxiety, they can be soothed, regulated and calmed much more quickly and effectively by adults who are empathic, compassionate and kind than by being sanctioned, isolated and rejected by the adults around them. This approach also supports pupils to have longer periods of calm and reduces the intensity of the anxiety over time.

Recognising and validating emotions

It is important that pupils are provided with a variety of different means to communicate and that the discussing of emotions becomes the norm.

- Pupils need the opportunity to explore and express their emotions in a variety of ways. Suggestions include role play, small world play, puppets, stories, journal writing, creative arts, using visual supports such as a stress scale or emotions cards, playing games such as emotions Jenga, etc. alongside a trusted adult, who is there to listen and provide support.
- Many pupils need to be given the words to help them to understand and manage their emotions. Adults need to 'name it to tame it!' (Siegel & Payne Bryson, 2012, p.27) and help pupils to recognise and notice their anxiety symptoms. 'Having a reflective adult to help you find words for feelings is a stress-regulating activity. This means it can release calming chemicals in the brain' (Sunderland, 2015, p.16). Noticing and naming a pupil's feelings can help them feel soothed, understood and support them to regulate. 'It seems that naming the anxiety out loud reduces the build-up of stress' (Bombèr, 2007, p.89).
- Take fear and anxiety seriously and avoid dismissing or minimising pupils' fears, but rather validate their feelings to help them, over time, to understand and reflect on their emotions and begin to regulate them, using phrases such as *I imagine you might be feeling . . .?* It is important for adults to acknowledge (rather than dismiss), validate and empathise with the pupil's perspective in that moment (even if it differs from their own), before reassuring them, problem-solving or trying to move them on. For example, if a child says, *Nobody likes me*, their perspective can be validated by a response such as, *It must feel really difficult to feel like nobody likes you. I can understand why that would make you feel like you don't want to be here. Are there any times when you feel like people do like you? I know I like spending time with you and I miss you when you are not here.*
- Emotion Coaching enables adults to label and validate emotions, supporting pupils to begin to recognise, understand, regulate and express their feelings and anxieties.

Emotion Coaching uses moments of heightened emotion and resulting behaviour to guide and teach the child and young person about more effective responses. Through empathetic engagement the child's emotional state is verbally acknowledged and validated, promoting a sense of security and feeling 'felt'. This activates changes in the child's neurological system and allows the child to calm down, physiologically and psychologically.

(Emotion Coaching UK, undated)

Emotion Coaching accepts all emotions as normal and natural and enables adults to set expectations for behaviours, as necessary, and problem-solve together. For example, *I can understand why you are feeling angry. Put the chair down, it's not safe. Let's go out and throw a ball together instead and we can talk about how we can sort this out.*

- For pupils who struggle to share and regulate their emotions, starting with more positive feelings can be effective initially, such as, *I wonder if you are really proud of that work, you have a big smile on your face* or *I wonder if you are very excited about your birthday, you are bouncing up and down in your seat as we talk about it.*
- Adults need to be aware of and reflect on their own emotions in order to remain regulated themselves, recognise their own triggers and then co-regulate and provide support in a calm way.

Belonging and connectedness

Fostering a sense of belonging and connectedness in school is essential, as it shows all pupils that they are welcome, important and accepted, which is crucial when reducing anxiety in the school setting.

Reflection opportunities:

- How do pupils know that they belong in my class/school/the playground?
- How are pupils welcomed into my class/school?
- How are diversity and difference celebrated?

■ Positive, trusting relationships are essential when it comes to improving school attendance, increasing engagement and attainment and fostering wellbeing. 'In the classroom, the relationship between young people and their teachers is the most significant factor in terms of whether they have a sense of school belonging' (Riley, in Morgan with Costello, 2023, p.176).

■ Engage in 'getting to know you' activities, such as putting the pupils into groups to make the longest list of things they all have in common, stand in the circle if you are wearing blue, if you have a brother, if you have been to Scotland, etc. to show that we all have similarities and differences.

■ Welcome each pupil with a positive greeting. Implement predictable routines or a unique daily ritual, such as a word of welcome, a song or play list, a hand shake or a regulating or movement activity. Smile and connect at the beginning and end of each lesson. 'A simple positive greeting can have an impact on all of the things we want to improve: learning, behaviour and, most of all, belonging' (Finnis, 2021, p.19).

Belonging case study:

Every morning, Mr J put a fun riddle, challenge or *thunk* on the board for a discussion. At the end of the day the class would come back to it and discuss it before leaving for the day.

Reflection opportunity:

■ How might this activity support the pupils' sense of belonging and connectedness?

Relationships with caregivers

Building positive, sensitive relationships and engaging in collaborative approaches with caregivers helps alleviate pupil anxiety. By seeing that caregivers and school staff are 'on the same page' and have a consistent approach and a shared partnership, pupils trust that their best interests are at heart. 'Collaboration and honesty are fundamental for good outcomes' (Elley with Morewood, 2022, p.57).

■ Aim to build sincere, trusting, reciprocal connections with caregivers from the start.

- Regularly share the positives – everything you admire about the pupil, what they excel at and their positive coping strategies to build rapport before discussing concerns or strategies. Send regular, positive communications home (ensuring that there are considerably more positive interactions and messages than negative).
- Be aware of the language used and reframe behaviours positively (see pp.24–5) when talking to and about children.
- Be aware of caregiver anxieties and listen empathically to their concerns and experiences and to those of the pupil themselves, in order to gain shared understanding and develop a consistent approach. Encourage caregivers to share information, particularly what works well and the pupil's strengths as well as their dislikes, things to avoid and areas that they are currently finding difficult. 'Carers are the experts in their own children . . . Working closely means you get the best of both areas of expertise – surely a win win?' (Elley with Morewood, 2022, p.57).

Peer relationships

Positive peer relationships can significantly affect a pupil's sense of belonging and connectedness and therefore reduce their sense of anxiety, both in school and outside of school. Conversely, when relationships 'go wrong' and pupils struggle to make and maintain appropriate relationships with their peers, it can negatively impact their sense of wellbeing and increase anxiety.

- In school, adults may need to help pupils to build, develop and manage peer relationships and may need to help pupils to navigate changes in friendship groups (particularly evident at transition to secondary school). Take time to foster positive peer-to-peer relationships and interactions through activities which promote teamwork and collaboration, for instance, setting up clubs of shared interests, teaching structured games in small groups and buddy and playground leader systems.
- Teach what positive relationships look like. Prioritise friendship by focusing on and acknowledging 'kindness' through friendship 'recognition boards' (Dix, 2017, pp.24–5).
- Support with group work and be wary of pupils needing to get into pairs, groups or teams independently (as this creates unnecessary anxiety for many). Take the time to gradually teach the skills involved in working in a pair/team and ensure each member is clear about their role within the group.

Restorative approaches and relational repair

Children need support to repair and restore relationships (with adults and peers) when there has been a relationship rupture or sense of disconnect. Anxious pupils, particularly those with social anxiety, with rejection sensitivity or with negative or catastrophic patterns of thinking, may struggle to make and maintain friendships. When there is a falling out, they may need support to put it right and to understand that relationships can be repaired. 'The positive relationships that you form with pupils depends on a restorative approach being your default mode' (Dix, 2017, p.125).

'Collaborative problem-solving' (Greene, 2014) helps pupils to feel a sense of ownership and reduces anxieties around consequences, as it increases their feelings of control. It reduces the chance of further shame, as the adult works with the pupil to come up with solutions and supports them to repair and restore relationships, using empathy and acceptance.

- By remaining curious and commenting aloud, exploring with the pupil what should happen following an incident, the pupil can begin to put things right in a way that feels comfortable, supported and safe. A supportive adult can help them repair relationships in a way which does not induce further shame, by commenting *X looks sad, I wonder what we can do to put a smile back on their face?* Together they may come up with visual suggestions such as making a sorry card or drawing them a picture or engaging in 'random acts of kindness' (Bombèr, 2020), such as inviting them to play a game, helping them with some learning or helping to repair something that has been broken, etc.
- Restorative conversations can help pupils to begin to understand the perspective of other people and the impact of their behaviours on others. 'Restorative Practices provide a structure for students to heal broken connections, express their feelings, and rebuild relationships with trusted adults so that they can move forward in a supported and positive way' (Pathways to Restorative Communities, 2021).
- Be self-reflective and apologise if it goes wrong. Adults often make pupils apologise to them or to each other but can be reluctant to apologise themselves. However, modelling and offering genuine apologies can considerably help when building and repairing relationships. 'Apologise when apologies are needed and seek to understand, in times of calm, what went wrong and what we could do differently next time' (Knightsmith, 2022, p.211).

Case study:

Atalia was working calmly with her key adult. The adult told her it was nearly time for her reward as she was doing so well. Once the task was completed, Atalia tidied up, as requested and then threw her pencil case across the room. Her key adult used a raised voice, 'Atalia, stop, you won't get your reward if you act like that'. Atalia was then dysregulated and couldn't go back into the classroom for the rest of the day as she was so distressed.

Having reflected, the key adult told her line manager that it was her fault, she shouldn't have raised her voice, but she was shocked and didn't want Atalia or anyone else to get hurt. The line manager asked if the adult had said this to Atalia. She hadn't.

The next day, the key adult met Atalia (who was anxious about seeing her and coming into school) with an apology and empathised with Atalia's feelings, *Atalia, I am so sorry, you must have been shocked and scared when I used a big voice. I was worried someone was going to get hurt but I shouldn't have raised my voice. I am sorry I made you feel that way, I will try to do better next time.* Atalia visibly relaxed and replied, *It's alright Miss, I shouldn't have chucked my pencil case either,* and both were able to carry on with their day together.

Staff relationships

- Staff need to be self-reflective and self-aware. They need to rec-ognise and attune to their own states, triggers and emotions and develop coping strategies to move themselves back into an open and engaged state to be in a position to support pupils to remain regulated, open and engaged. If staff are anxious and dysregulated, pupils will soon pick up on it and become more anxious themselves. Both anxiety and calm are contagious – a dysregulated person cannot calm a dysregulated person.
- Adults will need to work collaboratively. Key adults who work with pupils will have observed different patterns and triggers and will be able to share strengths and successes as well as strategies which have worked well.
- Staff need to model positive relationships and interactions to pupils through the way they communicate with pupils, caregivers and colleagues.

Chapter take-aways

- Children need to feel safe in order to learn and reduce feelings of anxiety.
- Adults need to increase safety cues for pupils and building genuine, positive relationships in school is paramount.
- Positive communication is essential.
- Relationships and relational repair need to be taught and modelled.

Further signposting

Books

After the Adults Change: Achievable Behaviour Nirvana by Paul Dix
Attachment Play: How to Solve Children's Behavior Problems with Play, Laughter, and Connection by Aletha Jauch Solter
Behaviour Barriers and Beyond by Rachel Thynne
Know Me to Teach Me by Louise Bombèr
Independent Thinking on Restorative Practice: Building Relationships, Improving Behaviour and Creating Stronger Communities by Mark Finnis
Settling to Learn by Louise Bombèr and Dan Hughes
When Adults Change Everything Changes by Paul Dix

Websites

DDP Network *What is Meant by PACE?* https://ddpnetwork.org/about-ddp/meant-pace
Emotion Coaching UK *What is Emotion Coaching* https://www.emotion coachinguk.com
Touchbase *Trauma Recovery for All Ages* https://touchbase.org.uk

Videos

Dr Pooky Knightsmith *How to Promote Belonging & Connection at School* – https://www.pookyknightsmith.com/video-how-to-promote-belonging-connection-at-school

References

Baylin, J. (2016) *The Neurobiology of Trust Building: On Being a Social Buffering Amygdala Whisperer* Available at: https://ddpnetwork.org/library/neuro biology-trustbuilding-social-buffering-amygdala-whisperer-jon-baylin [Accessed 22.7.23]

Baylin, J. & Hughes, D. (2016) *The Neuro-Biology of Attachment-Focused Therapy: Enhancing Connection & Trust in the Treatment of Children & Adolescents* Norton

Beacon House (undated) *What We Say Comic 1* Available at: https://beaconhouse.org.uk/wp-content/uploads/2019/09/What-We-Say-Comic-1.pdf [Accessed 23.6.23]

Berenson, K. R., Gyurak, A., Ayduk, O., Downey, G., Garner, M. J., Mogg, K., Bradley, B. P., & Pine, D. S. (2009) Rejection Sensitivity and Disruption of Attention by Social Threat Cues. *Journal of Research in Personality* 43(6): 1064–1072 https://doi.org/10.1016/j.jrp.2009.07.007 [Accessed 22.5.24]

Bombèr, L. (2007) *Inside I'm Hurting: Practical Strategies for Supporting Children with Attachment Difficulties in School* Worth Publishing

Bombèr, L. (2020) *Know Me to Teach Me – Differentiated Discipline for Those Recovering from Adverse Childhood Experiences* Worth Publishing

Bombèr, L. & Hughes, D. (2013) *Settling to Learn – Settling Troubled Pupils to Learn: Why Relationships Matter in School* Worth Publishing

Brown, B. (2012) *Listening to Shame* Available at: https://www.ted.com/talks/brene_brown_listening_to_shame/transcript?language=en [Accessed 13.7.23]

Conkbayir, M. (2023) *The Neuroscience of the Developing Child – Self-Regulation for Wellbeing and a Sustainable Future* Routledge

Dix, P. (2017) *When the Adults Change, Everything Changes: Seismic Shifts in School Behaviour* Independent Thinking Press

Elley, D. with Morewood, G. (2022) *Championing Your Autistic Teen at Secondary School – Getting the Best from Mainstream Schools* Jessica Kingsley

Emotion Coaching UK (undated) *How Does Emotion Coaching Work?* Available at: https://www.emotioncoachinguk.com/what-is-emotion-coaching [Accessed 28.7.23]

Finnis, M. (2021) *Independent Thinking on Restorative Practice: Building Relationships, Improving Behaviour and Creating Stronger Communities* Independent Thinking Press

Greene, R. (2014) *The Explosive Child: A New Approach for Understanding and Parenting Easily Frustrated, Chronically Inflexible Children* HarperCollins

Jennings, S. (2023) *Managing Social Anxiety in Children and Young People – Practical Activities for Reducing Stress and Building Self-esteem* Routledge

Knightsmith (2022) *ANXIETY/ANGER – Using Slow-Low-Low to Calm Things Down* Available at: https://www.youtube.com/watch?v=x9Aqzln739o&t=6s [Accessed 22.3.23]

MacDonald, I. (2019) *Teen Substance Use, Mental Health and Body Image: Practical Strategies for Support* Jessica Kingsley

Morgan, F. with Costello, E. (2023) *Square Pegs: Inclusivity, Compassion and Fitting In – A Guide for Schools* Independent Thinking Press

Pathways to Restorative Communities (2021) *The Role of Restorative Practices in Trauma-Informed Schools* Available at: https://www.pathways2rc.com/news/2021/4/15/the-role-of-restorative-practices-in-trauma-informed-schools [Accessed 13.7.23]

Phillips S., Melim D. & Hughes D. (2020) *Belonging – A Relationship-based Approach for Trauma-informed Education* Rowman & Littlefield

Porges, S. (2022) Polyvagal Theory: A Science of Safety *Frontiers in Integrative Neuroscience* 10 May doi: 10.3389/fnint.2022.871227 Available at: https://www.frontiersin.org/articles/10.3389/fnint.2022.871227/full   [Accessed 30.12.23]

Siegel, D. & Payne Bryson, T. (2012) *The Whole Brain Child* Robinson

Siegel, D. & Payne Bryson, T. (2020) *The Power of Showing Up* Scribe Press

Sunderland, M. (2015) *Conversations that Matter – Talking with Children and Teenagers in Ways that Help* Worth

Thynne, R. (2022) *Behaviour Barriers and Beyond* Routledge

Treisman, K. (2017) *Working with Relational and Developmental Trauma in Children and Adolescents* Routledge

Safety, relationships and communication checklist

STRATEGY	COMMENTS
Increasing feelings of safety	
Consistently communicate safety through verbal and non-verbal interactions	
Provide predictable, consistent routines, language and responses	
Building positive relationships	
Relationships are key in helping children feel safe	
Help pupils look for patterns and triggers and provide support at these times	
Actively listen to understand	
Be consistent in approaches and responses	
Start each day positively	
Provide regular check-ins	
Maintain connections over periods of absence	
Take time to build relationships	
Positive communication	
Reframe language into positives	
Validate feelings before moving pupils on	
Differentiate communication	

(Continued)

Continued

STRATEGY	COMMENTS
Reframe demands, as necessary	
Offer positive choices to increase sense of control	
Awareness of language which may trigger defensiveness	
Use factual, specific praise to reward effort, persistence and attitude	
The PACE approach	
Use playfulness to distract and reduce defensiveness and to build relationships	
Convey constant, unconditional acceptance of the child, their emotions and their experiences	
Remain curious to understand the child's emotions and behaviours	
Respond with empathy and understanding	
Recognising and validating emotions	
Provide a range of ways for pupils to explore and express their emotions	
Take anxiety seriously. Name and notice feelings and validate these to increase understanding	
Use Emotion Coaching techniques	
Reflect on own emotions and triggers	

(Continued)

Continued

STRATEGY		COMMENTS
Belonging and connectedness		
Positive relationships are essential and time needs to be given to building these with adults and peers		
Consider daily routines to increase sense of belonging		
Relationships with caregivers		
Aim to build sincere, trusting relationships from the start		
Regularly share positives and successes		
Reframe language into positives		
Be aware of caregiver anxieties		
Peer relationships		
Support pupils to build, maintain and restore positive relationships		
Teach and recognise positive friendships		
Support paired or group work		
Restorative approaches and relational repair		
Wonder aloud to support pupils to repair and restore relationships		
Facilitate restorative conversations		
Be prepared to apologise		
Staff relationships		
Be self-reflective and attune to own emotions		
Work as a team of key adults		
Model positive relationships		

3
Alleviating anxiety

Understand and recognise anxiety

Anxiety symptoms can often become exacerbated over time and can be even more frightening for an individual and harder to regulate, if they are not understood or recognised. The first step to beginning to manage anxiety is to name and identify it – what it is, what triggers it and how it presents for the individual (physically, behaviourally and physiologically) (see pp.11–12) and to teach children how to begin to recognise these signs for themselves.

- Label anxiety and explore its symptoms for individual pupils. Provide commentaries, noticing when they are becoming anxious and what may be making them feel that way (see p.82), to help them begin to notice and understand their feelings.
- Help to explain why people may present in this way when anxious (activation of the threat response and how the brain works when under stress). By teaching pupils about anxiety, it's evolutionary function and the brain's response to threat, they have increased understanding and are then better able to recognise it (see pp.4–5). Siegel and Payne Bryson (2012, pp.38–41) introduce the 'upstairs' and 'downstairs' brain (see p.5); a useful concept for teaching pupils the basics of how the brain works when it is going into survival mode. Once pupils begin to understand this, they can then be supported and taught strategies to move from their 'downstairs' brain to their 'upstairs' brain and calm the anxiety by exploring a range of regulating strategies (see chapter 4).
- Teach pupils to recognise and extend their 'window of tolerance' (Siegel, 2020) – the optimal zone in which a person operates to

DOI: 10.4324/9781003433231-4

effectively manage and cope with their emotions. When they move outside their window of tolerance the threat response is triggered. The window of tolerance changes from moment to moment, depending on stressors present at that given time.

■ If pupils do not yet have the vocabulary to explain where and how the anxiety is presenting, body mapping can help them to identify the physical symptoms of their anxiety (see p.82). Alternatively, pupils could use a doll or a soft toy to indicate where in the body they may feel the anxiety. They can then perform 'body checks' (Minahan 2018, p.93) to identify their emotions and begin to learn when they need to use a regulating strategy.

■ Each pupil is unique and different things work for different people. It is important to know the pupil well and build up a positive relationship (see Chapter 2) in order to get to know what works (and doesn't work) for them. Collaboration with pupils themselves, caregivers and other key adults will be essential.

■ Key adults will need to provide regular check-ins with anxious pupils, find patterns and establish trigger points and help pupils begin to pre-empt these and put supportive strategies in proactively, particularly at times of increased stress such as exams and key transitions.

■ Wearing a fitness tracker can be an effective way of alerting pupils to an increased heart rate and allow them to implement timely regulation strategies.

Strength-based approaches

If we champion our kids and show everyone what we love about them, other carers form their initial impressions based on the upside and are more likely to respond better to the challenges . . . To start positive and *believe* positive is pretty important . . .

(Elley with Morewood, 2022, p.43)

This is also true of pupils in school. Adults need to focus on all pupils' strengths and champion their successes.

■ Use strength-based approaches and value successes within a broad range of subjects. Encourage pupils to share their talents, strengths and passions to boost self-esteem. 'If you tell a child they aren't good at something, they will live up to the label and eventually give up' (Carter, in Morgan with Costello, 2023, p.72). It is, therefore, crucial to celebrate pupils' strengths and tell them what they are amazing at.

■ 'Anxiety erases memories of success' (Saline, 2023), so it is important that staff regularly notice, remind pupils of and focus on their strengths and successes as a starting point to build on, rather than focusing on difficulties and problems. Help pupils focus on skills and coping mechanisms they already have and use those skills to begin to face situations which trigger anxiety. Focus on positives and praise small steps towards success.

■ Provide pupils with roles and responsibilities to increase their confidence, self-esteem and sense of belonging. This can also decrease anxiety by providing a focus and distraction.

■ Avoid negative labelling and talk openly and positively about mental health to reduce stigma and myths around anxiety. Aim to provide at least ten positive comments for each (perceived) negative.

■ When somebody cannot cope with stress, the ability to regulate diminishes. By positively reframing language used around behaviour and regulation (see pp.24–5), adults are more readily able to provide support, without judgement.

A dysregulated child is too frequently mislabelled as being *challenging* or *naughty*, or *pushing an adult's buttons*, *attention-seeking* and, perhaps more commonly, as having a *tantrum*. Such terms are dismissive of the child's psychological state during moments of dysregulation and serve to emotionally distance the adults from the child, while doing nothing to practically support them to regain equilibrium.

(Conkbayir, 2023, p.17)

Reframing patterns of negative thinking (see also Positive self-talk pp.88-9)

'Children with anxiety tend to think in negative and critical ways, overestimate the likelihood of bad things happening, focus on things that go wrong, underestimate their ability to cope and expect to be unsuccessful' (Stallard, 2009). They need support from adults to reframe these thought patterns.

Patterns of negative thinking often appear automatically and feed into the anxiety cycle. Becoming aware of these negative thoughts, labelling them and beginning to challenge them can help pupils towards awareness and help reduce anxiety. Examples of patterns of negative thinking include; *I'm so stupid*, *Nobody likes me*, *I'm such a failure* or *I can't do this*.

When we get stuck on a thought, it can lead to ruminating about the past or worrying about the future. It can be really hard to get unstuck from certain thoughts and focus on the moment. These thoughts are probably not helping us and can actually make us feel worse.

(Hutt, 2019, p.18)

By helping a pupil to notice and change their thoughts, adults can help them to notice and change their anxiety.

- Pupils need adults to help them begin to notice and identify their negative thoughts and begin to reframe them into more realistic or positive ones, before they spiral out of control. The first step is to help pupils to become aware of their negative thoughts, when they pop into their heads and label them as that or as 'thinking errors' (Hutt, 2019, p.20), MindWell Leeds (undated) states that 'recognising your ANTs (Automatic Negative Thoughts) is the first step to challenging them'.

  'Reframing thoughts is a way to change your perspective. Reframing gets you unstuck from your thought, decreases the emotional intensity the thought may have caused, helps you change unwanted behaviours related to the thought, and can free you from spending so much time focusing on one topic' (Hutt, 2019, p.39). Reframe language into positives to help pupils to recognise their strengths rather than weaknesses. 'When I'm in a *what-if* spiral, I shift my thinking to *what could go right?*' (Saline, undated).

- Eisen & Engler (2006, p.72) suggest it can be helpful to gather past evidence to help disprove negative automatic thoughts by asking questions:

  - *Has this ever happened in the past?*
  - *If so, when was the last time it happened? How bad was it?*
  - *How many times has it happened?*

Personal case study:

As I was voicing out loud that I had done something wrong and was *such an idiot* (or words to that effect) one of my colleagues stopped me and told me to speak to myself like I'd speak to my best friend. This really resonated with me and now, every time my inner voice tells me something negative, I stop, reframe it and talk to myself as I would talk to my best friend. I stop the *I'm such an idiot* in its tracks and tell myself *I have just made a mistake, it could happen to anyone*. When I hear my children saying something negative, I now tell them to speak to themselves like they would their best friend.

Reflection opportunities:

- How could this simple piece of advice help pupils to recognise and change their negative thinking patterns?
- How could this help alleviate anxiety?

- Once pupils can notice negative thoughts, they can be taught ways to reframe or move on from them. Hutt (2019, p.19) advises to 'imagine your thoughts as clouds in the sky. You are lying in the grass and your focus is on the blue sky. You don't move with the clouds, you just watch your thoughts on clouds as they move across the sky.'
- Anxiety can distort a person's sense of reality and increases catastrophising when dwelling on an incident or predicting what may happen in the future. Often if a pupil experiences one bad event during the school day (such as falling over and hurting their knee), then the whole day is perceived as bad. Adults need to help pupils who are catastrophising to look for positives as well, for example, *Yes, you did hurt your knee, that was really painful for you. Before that you were having such a lovely day, you were playing with X in the playground and you did that beautiful painting this morning that you were so proud of.* 'You can learn to unravel these perceptions and stop catastrophizing. To start, identify if a worry is productive or toxic' (Saline, undated). Teach children to 'think like a problem-solver' (Eisen & Engler, 2006, p.67) to help them recognise and change their negative and catastrophic thoughts.
- Aim to foster a sense of gratitude, such as name three things you are grateful for today. Research has shown that gratitude reduces negativity and helps develop a positive outlook. Model gratitude by thanking them for acts of kindness and telling them why you are grateful.

Teaching and learning

Anxiety often leads to lack of focus or difficulty starting and completing activities.

> Avoidance of a task, an inherent, protective response to a stressor, is the flight part of the fight-flight-or-freeze anxiety response. This anxious response is escape-motivated and could be the result of the student's anxious thinking (*I am horrible at this! I stink at math*).
>
> (Minahan, 2018, p.44)

Dopamine is 'the key neurochemical for learning' the production of which is 'under the control of the emotional brain' (Curran, in Morgan with Costello, 2023, p.234). To help anxious pupils become emotionally ready to learn, staff need to ensure that they feel safe and supported. By alleviating anxieties around learning tasks and teaching pupils coping and regulating strategies they become calmer and more able to engage and settle into their learning.

■ Create a calm, predictable learning environment, where it feels safe and pupils are encouraged to take risks in their learning, to make and learn from their mistakes (see pp.130–2) and to seek positive means of asking for help.

■ Schools need to ask themselves if the curriculum is somehow contributing to, maintaining or increasing anxiety. It is necessary to monitor and evaluate the pupil's engagement with the curriculum, identify any barriers to engagement and provide appropriate scaffolding, support and adaptive teaching. Pupils need to feel a high level of success and sense of achievement alongside feeling suitably interested and challenged.

■ Aim to incorporate the pupil's interests and ensure that they understand the purpose of what they are learning, feel that it is relevant to them and meets their needs and abilities. Increase engagement by introducing activities which promote 'flow state' (Csikszentmihaly, 1990), those tasks that are just challenging enough to stretch pupils and avoid them becoming bored, but not so difficult that they feel overwhelmed or anxious.

■ Help anxious pupils to start a task by offering adult support (ensuring the pupil understands the instructions before moving away). 'Anxious students often have difficulty coming up with an idea to write about and have problems with organization, editing, spelling (especially for perfectionist students), grammar, and punctuation' (Minahan, 2018, p.82). Aim to change a pupil's negative perceptions and help them to feel successful in their learning, by providing visual supports such as checklists and reminders, sentence starters, vocabulary banks, etc.

- Allow anxious pupils to preview work and pre-teach key vocabulary, skills and concepts to alleviate anxieties around starting or engaging in lessons. 'Preparation is the key to reducing anxiety – for everyone' (Elley with Morewood, 2022, p.26). Have clear expectations, use concrete examples and model each step to ensure understanding.
- Provide regular check-ins to ensure understanding, refocus attention and provide positive encouragement and feedback.
- Alleviate anxieties and cognitive load by providing one question at a time. 'Reduce processing demands in the classroom and provide clear structures or plans for each task' (Rae, 2023). Breaking learning down into smaller chunks, presented in checklists for pupils to refer back to, helps to refocus their attention on the task, allowing them to see the progress that they are making towards completion. It also helps to make work look and feel achievable.
- Aim for shorter bursts of learning, followed by a quick movement break, such as completing two questions then going and sharpening two pencils. Either provide them with a break card, or include the movement breaks on a task checklist. 'Small escapes from work are important too; having an alternative activity on hand for those moments when the work feels impossible or before anxiety levels start to rise' (Moon, in Fricker, 2023, p.137).
- Asking for help can induce anxiety and pupils may need to be given more discreet means of asking for help than the traditional 'hands up' system (see p.127). Teach pupils what to do whilst they are waiting for help, are struggling to get started on a task or when they have finished, as this is a time when anxiety often increases. Pupils may use a doodle pad, read a book, use playdough or have an activity pack of word searches, dot to dots, sudoku, etc. or use their sensory box, do a job or do one of their movement tasks.
- Praise processes, applying skills, effort and attitude rather than outcome or correct answers.
- Avoid public calling out or displaying of test results as it increases anxiety. For those who are struggling in that area, it reduces self-esteem, reinforces cycles of under-achievement and sense of failure and increases shame. For those who often do well, are perfectionists or fear making mistakes, it can increase performance anxiety and lead to further stress and perfectionism.

- Avoid tests in the first few days back after a holiday and focus on re-establishing relationships.
- Multisensory approaches, where possible, can reduce anxiety, help learners to retain information, provide movement and increase engagement and understanding, as well as making abstract concepts more concrete and accessible.
- Feeling a sense of control over a situation can significantly reduce anxiety. Allow pupils to feel that they have choices and increase sense of ownership and control over tasks, where possible. For example, provide two or three options around where to sit, what pen/colour paper to use, which order to complete a task, a choice of tasks based on the same learning objective or opportunity to complete three, four or five questions.
- Executive function (the mental processes needed for working memory, regulation, concentration and attention, planning, organising and completing tasks, time management and flexible thinking) diminishes in times of stress. Help pupils develop executive function by teaching organisation skills such as creating and using checklists, modelling how to use their planner, timetable and calendar, teaching emotional regulation strategies, implementing clear and predictable routines, breaking tasks down into smaller chunks, providing visual reminders and employing regular movement breaks.
- Provide reasonable adjustments around homework, which can increase anxiety for pupils who are struggling to engage, who are masking in school and need to reset when they get home and those who fear making mistakes. Practical, fun tasks and those which teach life skills or encourage random acts of kindness can increase engagement. Homework clubs provide support and can be effective for those struggling to complete home learning tasks.

Visual supports

Visual supports can reduce anxiety for everyone as they help with information retention and can be referred back to. They also increase clarity, and can provide structure and predictability for transitions and changes. Visuals help improve understanding, avoid frustration and allow for processing time, they also increase independence for pupils.

- Present timetables visually to share exactly what is going to happen throughout the day.

- Rules and routines should be made clear through visuals such as a reminder of behaviour expectations. A visual noise thermometer, for example, can clearly convey expectations of voice volume at a given time (useful for many pupils, as this expectation can change throughout the day depending on the adult or the task).
- Visuals such as stress scales and calm cards can be useful to check in on how pupils are feeling and to remind them of helpful regulating strategies.
- Social Stories™ (Gray, undated) can be used to help pupils to plan for an up-coming situation or activity that may be causing anxiety or concern, for example an exam, school trip or a social event.

Step-by-step approaches

Step-by-step approaches aim to support pupils to increasingly overcome specific anxieties by breaking them down into small, graduated steps, supported by trusted adults. When things seem daunting or overwhelming they can be accomplished very gradually with the right support. Step-by-step approaches build confidence and help reduce the feelings of overwhelm. They help pupils to develop a sense of control over the situation, while feeling safe and supported.

An analogy could be helping someone to begin to overcome a fear of spiders.

Personal case study:

I was terrified of spiders (I am still not particularly keen on them). However, I didn't want my fear to be 'inherited' or mimicked by my children, so I knew I had to do something about it. My step-by-step plan is outlined below:

1. Look at cute pictures of spiders.
2. Look at pictures and videos of small spiders.
3. Touch a picture of a small spider.
4. Look at pictures and videos of large spiders and tarantulas.
5. Touch the pictures of large spiders.
6. Look at spiders outside on their webs.
7. Try to overcome negative thinking about spiders – begin an inner monologue about how magnificent their web is, begin to look at the markings on the spiders. Research

what spiders are useful for and how they help the environment. (Spiders are actually pretty amazing; according to
Conversation.com (2020) the oldest recorded spider died
at the age of 43 and was killed by a wasp sting rather than
old age, and the last human death from a spider was in
Australia over 40 years ago).

8. Gently pick up little spiders and pop them out of the house,
   when necessary.
9. Gently pick up slightly bigger spiders in a tissue and pop
   them out of the house,.
10. Use a glass and piece of cardboard to get larger spiders out
    of the house. (I am never going to be able to pick those big
    ones up in my bare hands, but look how far I have come!)

My children know that I am still not that keen on spiders in the
house, but they also see me modelling calming strategies (normally taking a few over-exaggerated deep breaths and engaging
in some positive self-talk – *OK, I can do this, it's only a spider.*

Reflection opportunity:

■ How can this analogy help when making step-by-step plans
  for anxieties in school?

'Teachers are in a great position to provide children with opportunities
to face their fears gradually so that they can overcome those fears'
(Creswell & Willetts, 2019, p.295). Establish the trigger to the anxiety
and plan small steps to help decrease that anxiety, in a way which feels
achievable and safe.

■ Try not to avoid a fear because avoidance reinforces the anxiety
  cycle, thus increasing future anxiety. Instead provide support,
  scaffold and intervene early. Start from where the pupil feels
  comfortable and with what they can already do. Plan small steps
  or increments so each step feels tolerable and achievable. Create an 'I can cycle' (Knightsmith, 2021) by building up tiny steps,
  which feel achievable and comfortable. This shows the pupil that
  they can feel successful and can then build on that success. For
  example, a child who is anxious about attending school may, as a
  first step, walk to school with a trusted adult and look at it through
  the gate on a day when it is closed.

Only move onto the next step, when the pupil is truly comfortable with the one they are currently working on. Aim to gradually build on each step with small increments to support pupils to feel safer. If necessary, each step can be broken down even further.

- When creating step-by-step plans, decide together what success may look like for each step and how that success will be measured. Often, 'just having a go is an achievement' (Creswell & Willetts, 2019, p.297). At each step, focus on and note all the successes and what has gone well (any small steps towards success, rather than those that have gone wrong). Be prepared to go back to previous steps, if anxiety is particularly high.
- Make a plan when the pupil is calm and problem-solve together to come up with the next step, to increase their sense of ownership and control. 'Starting with situations that are less scary, you work your way up to facing things that cause you a great deal of anxiety' (AnxietyCanada, undated). Coping strategies, positive thoughts and rewards can be referred to in the plans.
- Plans can be presented in a variety of different ways, such as a written step-by-step plan, an Exposure Ladder (see further signposting p.67) or by ordering a set of statements to determine which aspects generate the most (and least) anxiety. They can also be represented pictorially or creatively (see p.133).
- Some pupils may feel less overwhelmed if presented with just one step at a time, rather than focussing on the final goal. 'Letting go of the big picture and instead thinking of just the very first thing that needs to happen to set you in the right direction can help you make a start' (Knightsmith, 2022, p.177).
- Use pre-taught coping strategies prior to and alongside each step (see Chapter 4), to help reduce some of the physiological presentations of anxiety that the pupil may experience, and help them to feel calmer and in control.
- Hope for the best while planning for the worst. It can be helpful to ask the pupil what their biggest fear is for a certain situation, and then try to rationalise it, by thinking logically about how likely it is and plan for that 'worst case scenario'.

Do if and then planning – actually planning for the worst can help. Write your worries down about engaging with the situation and plan what you'd do in each eventuality. Having a plan you can enact if needed can often bolster your confidence to go ahead.

(Knightsmith, 2022, p.189).

In a way, learning to manage anxiety is a lot like exercise – you need to 'keep in shape' and practise your skills regularly. Make them a habit! This is true even after you are feeling better and have reached your goals.

(AnxietyCanada, undated)

Environmental adaptations

A welcoming, calm, inclusive and nurturing environment is essential for all pupils to feel safe. The school can support pupils to thrive, but if that school environment is not right for an individual, it can increase anxieties and stress. Alexander Den Heijer observed, 'When a flower doesn't bloom you fix the environment in which it grows, not the flower'. However, so often in school we try to make the pupil fit the environment, rather than adapt the environment to fit the child.

By understanding behaviour as communication, adults are able to support pupils and alleviate anxieties. For example, pupils who are overwhelmed by sensory information may move and fidget or wander or find it difficult to focus their attention on a task and seem easily distracted, pupils who are highly anxious may appear defiant, aggressive or rude. It is important to establish what it is about the environment or space that is causing anxiety or sense of overwhelm and then seek to provide support and implement adjustments.

- Be aware of pupils' sensory sensitivities and stressors. It will be necessary to reduce sensory overwhelm and 'minimise external stressors' (Elley with Morewood, 2022 p. 112). Calm, neutral colours are usually effective. Pay attention to smells (perfumes, foods, cleaning products), sounds, visual distractions (such as flickering lights, twirling shiny displays, clutter, etc.). Help the pupil to plan ahead to avoid sensory overload (by avoiding busy corridors and noisy canteens or providing sensory supports such as ear defenders for the noise sensitive). Staff need to try to ensure the environment works for the pupil. Sensory audits can be helpful here. Provide access to quieter, calmer spaces to help pupils to reset or decompress.
- Provide safe spaces and exit strategies, available for all pupils, when they are feeling overwhelmed and experiencing high levels of anxiety. Teach pupils how, and when, to use these to alleviate anxieties, avoid becoming overwhelmed and to reset when necessary. 'A truly calm and quiet place in school to retreat to when the classroom or playground gets too much is invaluable . . . To be

truly effective, escape needs to be totally unconditional and available on demand' (Moon, in Fricker, 2023, p.137).

∎ Implement a careful seating plan for anxious pupils to increase their feelings of safety, allowing pupils to communicate where they feel safe within each room. Some pupils may feel safer at the back of the class, near the wall, so they have a view of the whole room, some may need to be near the door to use their exit strategy, some may feel safe in proximity to the teacher or trusted peer, others will feel safer in a quieter area of the room away from distractions. It is important to know the pupil well, maintain predictability and pre-warn of any up-coming changes to the seating plan.

∎ Use the outdoor area, where possible (see p.99) and bring the outside in – introduce plants and nature into the classroom. Plants can improve mood and reduce stress (Lee et al., 2015) and can provide pupils with jobs to boost their self-esteem (watering, repotting, planting, growing from seed), improve academic performance (Daly et al., 2010), improve air quality and be great transitional objects (one class of Reception pupils all took a baby spider plant home for the holidays).

Unstructured times

Unstructured times of the school day can often be a source of high anxiety at school and can be difficult and overwhelming for many pupils. During break and lunch times pupils often have less adult support or less access to familiar adults. Many find it difficult to navigate social interactions and relationships successfully. The environment can become overwhelming for many pupils, with different smells, increased crowds, increased noise, etc.

∎ Provide quieter places for pupils to eat their lunch in a smaller group. This may help them to regulate over lunch time and set them up to be more successful for the rest of the day.

∎ Offer zoned activities, smaller groups and teach and rehearse structured games. Minahan (2018, p.70) suggests teaching 'cooperative games' rather than 'competitive games' as many pupils find the latter 'anxiety-provoking and frustrating'.

∎ Provide access to activities for pupils with shared interests, or encourage older pupils to set up clubs themselves, based on their own interests.

- Anxious pupils need access to safe places and faces to reset when they feel overwhelmed, at break times as well as in the class-room. 'Establish a safe space for children who need a more nur-turing environment at playtime and lunchtime. Make sure there is somewhere for them to go and someone who has time for them' (Dix, 2017, p.123). Ensure pupils know where to go, and who and how to ask for help at break times.
- Pupils need to feel a sense of social safety so need clear expecta-tions and routines at unstructured times as well as other times of the school day. Reinforce these with visual reminders. They may not generalise their learning from one area of school to another and may need rules and routines specifically taught in each area.
- Consider access to alternative toilets or changing areas, if this causes anxiety.
- Buddy or playground leader systems can be supportive, with pupils receiving support from peers.

Supporting transitions

Uncertainty and change (particularly unexpected change) can cause huge anxiety for many children. Transitions need to be carefully planned for all children, not only those who display anxiety as they tend to be anxiety-inducing for everyone, so the more manageable, safe and predictable these are the better. When adults pay careful attention to transitions and changes 'the child's anxiety levels may stay relatively stable because he or she feels that there is a sense of predictability and there is, therefore, an element of control' (Bombèr, 2007, p.114).

The key to successful transitions is to minimise anxiety, increase sense of control and build trusting relationships. Adults need to inter-vene proactively to help pupils to manage transitions. Change and unfamiliarity heighten anxiety, so the more adults can communicate and share with the pupils so they know what to expect the better.

Supporting pupils to manage transitions, breaking them down into smaller steps and teaching a range of coping strategies is essential. 'The keys to success in any transition . . . are preparation, managing expectations, involving all the relevant people and thinking of it as a journey rather than a destination' (Morgan with Costello, 2023, p.179).

Transition into school *(see also Chapters 10 and 12)*

Transition into school sets the tone for the whole day. 'If it is not han-dled sensitively, the beginning of the school day can prove to be a potent "trigger time" of heightened anxiety for children with attachment diffi-culties' and 'can bring up very strong feelings, as there is often a deep terror of possible loss or abandonment' (Bombèr, 2007, p.116).

- Smile, welcome the pupils in, ensure their first moments in school are positive (issues such as punctuality, uniform, missing homework, etc. can be sorted out with a trusted adult later in the school day, when the pupil is settled and calm).
- Aim for consistent and predictable boundaries, routines and responses from adults. 'Children need to know what's expected of them. They need to know what's okay, and what's not. It helps them feel that the world is predictable and safe' (Siegel & Payne Bryson, 2020, p.173).
- Consider transitional objects to bridge the gap between home and school (see pp.231–2).
- Pre-warn, as soon as possible, of any changes of people, places or the physical environment, such as changes to seating plans, dis-plays, wall colour, etc. (providing photographs where appropriate).

Case study:

Tyler was a Y10 student. After a half term break, the flooring in the entrance to the Y10 block had been changed from blue carpet to black and white tiles. Tyler couldn't get through the door and became very distressed. He threw his bag down and walked away.

Reflection opportunity:

- How could Tyler have been supported with this change?

Suggestions:

- Pre-warn of the up-coming changes.
- Look at photographs or the actual tiles.
- Use a Social Story™ (Gray).

Transitions in and around school

- Carefully plan how to manage each transition within the day. Sup-port executive function by teaching organisation and planning and preparing pupils for change. Use timers, warnings or count-downs, clearly mark endings and prepare pupils for transitions, giving sufficient time for pupils to complete tasks. For many, leaving something unfinished can be a trigger. Using memory cards (Bombèr, 2007, pp.120–1) or taking photographs of an activity can remind pupils that they can return to the task later, helping to support them tolerate stopping and moving on from a high interest activity.

■ Use visual supports (see pp.52–3) and provide an individual, portable visual timetable or *Now and Then* board for anxious pupils, include photographs of places and adults, where possible, so that they know exactly what to expect. Use 'change' or 'oops' cards to fore-warn of any unexpected changes to the school day and show pupils that unexpected changes to routine are normal and can be tolerated. 'You could use a " 'change" visual symbol and add this to a timetable. Even if a change happens last minute, you can use this symbol to reassure children that "change" is part of that daily routine' (SparkleAppeal.org, undated). 'Children who can anticipate what to expect throughout the day, often have an easier time self-regulating' (Brukner, 2014, p.90).

■ Simple one-way systems can help alleviate congestion in corridors, thus reducing stress at transition times.

■ Teach pupils how to wait, and include a 'wait tool' or activity (e.g. heavy work activity such as wall press or palm press), to help pupils to remain regulated, before, during or after transitions.

■ Make transitions as predictable as possible by introducing specific routines or rituals around these. Use consistent language to reduce processing time and increase feelings of safety and belonging. Including multi-sensory cues such as music or dimming the lights at key transition times can be effective. Brukner (2014, p.90) suggests using 'one calm song . . . during all transitions [to] improve motor planning, organization, and time management skills'. Knightsmith (2023) suggests 'mood flip music' to support transitions. Carefully choose the music or playlist depending on the mood which is required, for example, up-beat music when moving from a calm to active activity and calming music when moving from an active to calm activity. Increase predictability by using the same playlists each time.

■ Monotropism – a cognitive theory of autism (Murray et al., 2005) – is the focus of attention on one particular interest at a time, with difficulty diverting attention away from that interest in order to refocus onto another activity. Similarly, some pupils, particularly some neurodivergent pupils may enter a 'flow' state (Csikszentmihaly, 1990) a mental state where someone becomes fully immersed in, and hyperfocused on, an activity. 'Transitioning from a hyperfocused, high-dopamine-reward activity to a lower-dopamine one requires a lot of impulse control, emotional regulation, and metacognition' (Saline, 2022). Understanding this theory and these states can help adults to recognise how pupils may have difficulty and need support and alternative approaches when switching attention away from one activity and moving onto another.

■ Provide sufficient time to finish tasks and warnings to move on. For pupils who hyperfocus, once they are in their flow state, they may find it very difficult (and detrimental to the task) to suddenly have to stop. Flexibility around transitions, at times, can be supportive, for example, letting the pupil finish their maths, before moving on to the next task, if they are engrossed or struggle to leave things unfinished. Planning activities which can be achieved by the pupil in the allocated time is important.

■ Support pupils when moving from a high interest or preferred activity to an activity that they are less keen on (such as moving from break times back to class or from reward time back to a learning task) by providing 'soft landings' in between. Ideas include providing a calming, grounding or creative activity between tasks (such as a colouring task or breathing activity when moving from computing to writing) or providing jobs for pupils struggling to come in from break time (such as carrying a box of equipment in from the playground or giving the books out when they arrive back in the classroom).

■ Support generalisation – teach rules and routines in different areas of the school and with different adults, as some pupils will not transfer the knowledge and skills learned in one environment, or with one adult, to the next.

■ Be aware of sensory sensitivities which may present at transition times. Pupils who struggle in crowded corridors may benefit from accessing these at quieter times, or wearing ear defenders or carrying a fidget tool. Consider abolishing or muffling loud school bells (which can cause anxiety and sensory overwhelm for those with auditory sensitivities, can retraumatise and distress those who have suffered from adversity and trauma) and opt for quieter transition signals.

■ Whole class regulation activities can help all pupils to reset and calm after alerting activities, for example, whole class stretching, yoga, seat presses, mindfulness or breathing techniques after break time and before settling to a learning task.

■ Provide a brief relational check-in to co-regulate and focus attention on a task following transitions.

- Minimise transitions where possible, or use them as productive movement breaks, such as asking key pupils to carry a box of equipment in after PE, or whole class activities such as stretch, calf raises, play *Simon Says* or do ten wall presses while waiting in the line.
- Transitional objects within school can be useful if a pupil works with a different adult, such as looking after a key adult's special pen or eraser to 'keep them in mind' (Bombèr, 2007, p.94) while they are not with them (see p.232).

School trips and off-timetable days

- Pre-warn and plan as much as possible by looking at websites and photographs of places to be visited. Caregivers may choose to familiarise pupils with a place in advance (if possible and practical).
- Provide anxious pupils with roles and responsibilities, such as helping to set up for sports day or having a clipboard and ticking off equipment, helping to plan the route using map apps, and map out where lunch will be eaten and where the toilets are, or being photographer for the day.
- Provide a visual timetable or plan of the day, including photographs of key adults, coaches and meeting points. Social Stories™ (Gray) can be effective in helping prepare pupils.
- Look at photos of similar off-timetable days from previous years so that pupils know what to expect.
- Folders of predictable, familiar, achievable activities to engage in at times of heightened stress (on the coach, while waiting for lunch or during 'off-timetable days') can help to calm pupils (crosswords, mindful colouring, dot to dots, pencil mazes, colour by numbers, etc.) as can using coping strategies.

Transitions to new classes and unfamiliar adults

- A positive transition process involves time and commitment from adults. It is important that existing and new staff work collaboratively and communicate effectively with each other, pupils and caregivers to create transition plans which share strengths and successes, triggers and strategies which work (and those that don't) to help the pupil to regulate.
- Fear of the unknown increases anxiety. Rather than focusing on all the up-coming changes, look at and list all the things which will stay the same or remain similar for the pupil. Keep as many

effective routines, rules and structures in place as possible, such as visual timetables, 'recognition boards' (Dix, 2017, p.24), *Now and Then* boards, sensory boxes and anxiety scales. 'Schools that feel safer are those that contain their pupils within a predictable environment where changes are minimal and explained in advance' (Moon, in Fricker, 2023, p.136).

■ Increase familiarity by visiting new areas of school with trusted adults and encourage pupils to run errands to and take messages to new classrooms and be in charge of taking photos for the other pupils.

■ Prioritise relationship building. Key adults from new year groups should aim to build relationships as soon as possible, in person, ideally, but virtually if that is not possible.

■ Create profiles for pupils to share the things that they are good at, things that help them (and don't help them) and their coping strategies in school.

■ Send reminders home during the holidays, such as photographs of key adults and places, timetables and maps of the school or new year group areas. Maintain contact over holidays by sending an email or postcard and sending a transitional object home.

■ Share a clear, detailed plan and expectations for the first day and discuss where the pupil may feel safe sitting and who they feel safe with. Ensure that pupils know rules, routines, where to put bags, etc. and where to access key equipment, safe spaces and key adults (and walk through this if necessary).

■ Try to maintain an existing friendship in each new class, or ensure a plan is in place to help foster new friendships early on to ease anxieties (through playing games in small groups, buddy systems and careful seating plans).

■ Where possible, encourage previous key adults to continue to check-in with anxious pupils.

■ Have a familiar, trusted adult check-in with the pupil at the beginning of the school day and at regular points during the day and at home time for the first week and beyond, as necessary.

Transitions to new schools

'Specific peaks in non-attendance appear to emerge at transition points in the life of school-age children' (Pelligrini, 2007), particularly around key phase changes, such as entry into Early Years and when moving from primary to secondary schools. Transition to a new school, therefore, needs careful consideration and planning in order to minimise anxieties for all. Relationships with key adults and becoming familiar and confident within the environment are key.

- Collaboration between schools is essential for a successful transition, with positive working relationships being developed, over time, where possible. Share information, including where the pupil's strengths lie and what is already working well, as well as where they may need support. Create a transition booklet for the pupil to share all the things that they are good at and things that help them (and don't help them) and their preferred coping strategies in school.
- Prepare the pupils in advance and involve them as much as possible in the transition process. Work collaboratively and communicate effectively with caregivers, actively listen to their concerns and provide support and reassurance, where possible.
- Have a careful plan in place to manage goodbyes, such as making memory books (Bombèr, 2007, p.281–2), year books or cards and taking class photos to record memories for the pupils to take with them.
- Use positive language and avoid inadvertently increasing stress and negativity around transitions, by making negative comments such as *You won't be able to do that in big school.* or *That behaviour won't be tolerated in Year 7* which will increase anxiety about moving on.
- Familiarise pupils with the new setting in advance by looking at the website, plans, photos and timetables and visit the site for school fairs, concerts, clubs, open days, etc.
- Share concerns with trusted adults, ask questions and receive answers in advance (possibly by email). Encourage pupils to voice their anxieties and have key adults in the new setting answer *what if . . .?* questions to normalise and help alleviate worries and prevent unnecessary anxiety prior to starting a new school.
- Share a clear plan and expectations for the first day and provide timetables and simple maps. Walk through with pupils, where they need to go, pointing out key areas such as the form room, library, canteen, playground, hall, toilets, changing rooms, sensory room and where to find key adults they can go to when they feel anxious or overwhelmed.
- Prioritise relationship building. Ensure a plan is in place to help foster new friendships early on to ease anxieties through buddy systems and careful seating plan, playing games or engaging in small group activities. Encourage various means of

communicating and sharing experiences which do not always focus on talking and are inclusive of all pupils' needs.

■ Provide calmer areas for new year groups to access, such as quieter playgrounds, an indoor space and lunch clubs just for their year group, a separate cafeteria or lunch trolley, safe adults to go to when they feel overwhelmed, quieter times to transition around the school (e.g. five minutes before the rest of the school). Where possible, minimise transitions for new year groups.

■ Provide clear visual cues and signage around the school so pupils can easily navigate the site with minimal fear of getting lost. One-way systems can reduce overwhelm in crowded corridors.

■ Consider buddy systems with pupils in older year groups, particularly at break and lunch times.

Enhanced transitions to new settings

Implement enhanced transition plans for anxious pupils, particularly those with a history of school anxiety.

■ Aim for pupils to become as familiar as possible with their new setting. The timing is important, as if started too early it can induce further anxiety. Look at websites, plans, photos and timetables. Plan the route to and from the new setting and walk it through in advance. Look at the school site from outside, while it is quiet.

■ Plan an increased number of personalised visits to the school, starting at quieter times, with a familiar adult. Take photographs for transition presentations or booklets (to provide them with a job, sense of purpose, distraction and to build self-esteem). Provide virtual tours where face-to-face visits are difficult or impossible. Visit the school again towards the end of holidays with key staff – when it is quiet – to walk through routines, become familiar with the environment and re-establish relationships with key adults.

■ Provide uniform and equipment checklists and discuss any adjustments needed. Encourage pupils to try on the uniform, shoes and PE kit and become comfortable with them at home before attending the new school.

■ Positive and regular collaboration between the existing and new setting and caregivers is supportive, and helps alleviate anxieties for adults as well as young people. Allocate a key adult from the new setting as a point of contact for the pupil and caregivers (including a photograph to take home to aid memory). Share any previous anxieties, particularly those involving school-based anxiety, engagement or relationship difficulties, along with key trigger points, how anxiety presents for the individual, effective coping techniques and supportive strategies. Ideally, the key adult should aim to build a relationship with the pupil in their current setting, or otherwise, remotely or by email/phone, before the pupil attends the new school. Alternatively, if meeting in the new setting, meet initially on a less formal basis, such as by playing a game, engaging in attachment play activities, watching funny video clips, having a drink and snack together, with safe, familiar key adults alongside, to build up rapport and connection.

■ A transitional object (see p.232) from their new class to take home over the holidays (such as the class soft toy mascot) can help to bridge the gap between school and home.

■ Provide access to safe spaces and key adults during the day and also at unstructured times, walk through safe spaces in advance and ensure the pupil knows how to use them.

■ Teach and rehearse coping strategies regularly, when the pupil is calm.

■ Provide a *meet and greet* from a key adult and establish a consistent predictable routine for the mornings. Have a familiar, trusted adult check-in with the pupil at the beginning of the school day and at regular points (particularly trigger times). Check in with the pupil at the end of the day to help them reset, address any concerns, also draw their attention to all the positive things that happened in the day.

Chapter take-aways

■ The key to supporting pupils to manage anxiety is to help them to recognise their anxiety and how it presents for them.

■ Supported, gradual step-by-step plans can help pupils to gradually face their fears in a safe way which is not overwhelming.

■ Key aspects of school, such as changes to routine, transitions, the environment and unstructured times, can heighten anxiety. Staff need to be proactive and put in support to minimise anxiety at key trigger times.

Further signposting

Books for adults

Behaviour Barriers and Beyond by Rachel Thynne
Helping your Child with Fears and Worries by Cathy Creswell and Lucy Willetts

Resources to share with pupils

Brave Every Day by Trudy Ludwig

Cards Against Anxiety by Pooky Knightsmith

Feeling Better: CBT Workbook for Teens – Essential Skills and Activities to Help You Manage Moods, Boost Self-esteem and Conquer Anxiety by Rachel Hutt

I Am Stronger than Anxiety: Children's Book about Overcoming Worries, Stress and Fear by Elizabeth Cole

Ruby Finds a Worry by Tom Percival

Starving the Anxiety Gremlin by Kate Collins-Donnelley

What to Do When You Worry Too Much: A Kid's Guide to Overcoming Anxiety by Dawn Huebner

Websites

Charlie Waller Trust *Lesson Idea: Steps to Help Anxiety* https://4123326. fs1.hubspotusercontent-na1.net/hubfs/4123326/.OCR/Campai gns/RT05%20Mental%20Health%20Awareness%20Week%20 2023/OMD10892-Mental-Health-Awareness-Week-Lesson-Plan-A4-0.pdf

Creative Education Training Course *Plan an Effective Transition for Your Students*– https://www.creativeeducation.co.uk/courses/plan-an-effective-transition-for-your-students

Dr Pooky Knightsmith *Anxiety Exposure Ladder* https://www.pookyk nightsmith.com/download-anxiety-exposure-ladder

Dr Pooky Knightsmith *Checklist to Help Spot Anxiety Triggers* https:// www.pookyknightsmith.com/download-my-anxiety-triggers-worksheet

Dr Pooky Knightsmith *Energy Boosters vs Drainers* https://www.pookyk nightsmith.com/download-emotional-boosters-vs-drainers

Dr Pooky Knightsmith *Transition Tips* https://www.pookyknightsmith. com/download-classroom-tips-for-transition-chart

Mindwell-leeds.co.uk *Automatic Negative Thoughts (ANTs) and Unhelp-ful Thinking Styles* https://www.mind.org.uk/information-support/ tips-for-everyday-living/relaxation/relaxation-exercises/#. WbFe_nnf0mQ

Touchbase Transition Guides (primary and secondary) https://touch-base.org.uk/new-guide-for-transition-back-to-school/ and https:// touchbase.org.uk/secondary-school-guide-to-collective-recovery

Young Minds Resilience Cards (primary) https://www.youngminds.org. uk/shop/product/resilience-cards-primary--YMRC-P

Young Minds - Resilience Cards (secondary) https://www.young minds.org.uk/shop/product/resilience-cards-secondary-pack--YMRC-S

Podcasts

Dr Pooky Knightsmith *Using Transition Activities to Move Between Activities, Places or People* https://www.pookyknightsmith.com/podcast-transition-activities

Sendcast.com *Focus on What They Can Do, Not What They Can't with Joanne Jones* https://www.thesendcast.com/focus-on-what-they-can-do-not-what-they-cant

Videos

Dr Pooky Knightsmith *ANXIETY/ANGER – Using Slow-Low-Low to Calm Things Down* https://www.youtube.com/watch?v=x9Aqzln739o&t=6s

Dr Pooky Knightsmith *Creating an 'I Can' Cycle to Support Anxious Children* Available at: https://www.youtube.com/watch?v=cY75yxfcDX8 [Accessed 7.7.23]

SEL Sketches *Upstairs and Downstairs Brain* https://www.youtube.com/watch?v=dk1Nt-xnSGI

References

AnxietyCanada (undated) *Self-Help Strategies for Social Anxiety* Available at: https://www.anxietycanada.com/sites/default/files/adult_hmsocial.pdf [Accessed 23.5.23]

Bombèr, L. (2007) *Inside I'm Hurting – Practical Strategies for Supporting Children with Attachment Difficulties in Schools* Worth Publishing

Brukner, L. (2014) *The Kids' Guide to Staying Awesome and in Control – Simple Stuff to Help Children Regulate Their Emotions and Senses* Jessica Kingsley

Conkbayir, M. (2023) *The Neuroscience of the Developing Child – Self-regulation for Wellbeing and a Sustainable Future* Routledge

Conversation.com (2020) *Don't Like Spiders? Here are 10 Reasons to Change Your Mind* Available at: https://theconversation.com/dont-like-spiders-here-are-10-reasons-to-change-your-mind-126433 [Accessed 22 March 2023]

Creswell, C. & Willetts, L. (2019) *Helping Your Child with Fears and Worries – A Self-Help Guide for Parents* Robinson

Csikszentmihalyi, M. (1990) *Flow: The Psychology of Happiness* Random House

Daly, J., Burchett, M. & Torpy, F. (2010) *Plants in the Classroom Can Improve Students' Performance* Available at: https://interiorplantscape.asn.au/wp-content/uploads/2016/04/Plants-in-the-classroom-can-Improve-Student-Performance-Report-2010.pdf [Accessed 22.7.23]

Dix, P. (2017) *When the Adults Change, Everything Changes: Seismic Shifts in School Behaviour* Independent Thinking Press

Eisen, A. & Engler, L. (2006) *Helping Your Child Overcome Separation Anxiety or School Refusal: A Step-by-Step Guide for Parents* New Harbinger Publications

Elley, D. with Morewood, G. (2022) *Championing Your Autistic Teen at Secondary School – Getting the Best from Mainstream Schools* Jessica Kingsley

Fricker, E. (2023) *Can't Not Won't: A Story About a Child Who Couldn't Go to School* Jessica Kinglsey

Gray, C. *Social Stories™* Available at: https://carolgraysocialstories.com [Accessed 24.2.24]

Hutt, R. (2019) *Feeling Better: CBT Workbook for Teens: Essential Skills and Activities to Help You Manage Moods, Boost Self-Esteem, and Conquer Anxiety* Althea Press

Knightsmith, P. (2021) *Creating an 'I Can' Cycle to Support Anxious Children* Available at: https://www.youtube.com/watch?v=cY75yxfcDX8 [Accessed 7.7.23]

Knightsmith, P. (2022) *Things I Got Wrong So You Don't Have To – 48 Lessons to Banish Burnout and Avoid Anxiety for Those Who Put Others First* Jessica Kingsley

Knightsmith, P. (2023) *Using Transition Activities to Move Between Activities, Places or People* Available at: https://www.pookyknightsmith.com/podcast-transition-activities [Accessed 29 June 2023]

Lee M., Lee J., Park B. and Miyazaki Y. (2015) Interaction with Indoor Plants May Reduce Psychological and Physiological Stress by Suppressing Autonomic Nervous System Activity in Young Adults: A Randomized Crossover Study *Journal of Physiological Anthropology* 34 Available at: https://doi.org/10.1186/s40101-015-0060-8 [Accessed 18.2.24]

Minahan, J. (2018) *The Behavior Code Companion: Strategies, Tools and Interventions for Supporting Students with Anxiety-Related or Oppositional Behaviours* Harvard Education Press

MindWell Leeds (undated) *Challenging Negative Thinking* Available at: https://www.mindwell-leeds.org.uk/myself/exploring-your-mental health/depression/challenging-negative-thinking [Accessed 22.3.23]

Morgan, F. with Costello, E. (2023) *Square Pegs – Inclusivity, Compassion and Fitting In: A Guide for Schools* Independent Thinking Press

Murray, D., Lesser, M. & Lawson, W. (2005) Attention, Monotropism and the Diagnostic Criteria for Autism *Autism*, 9: 139–156 Available at: https://pubmed.ncbi.nlm.nih.gov/15857859 [Accessed 24.2.24]

NHS (2020) *Social Anxiety (Social Phobia)* Available at: https://www.nhs.uk/mental-health/conditions/social-anxiety/#:~:text=Social%20anxiety%20is%20more%20than,before%2C%20during%20and%20after%20them [Accessed 1.2.23]

Pelligrini, D. (2007) School Non-attendance: Definitions, Meanings, Responses, Interventions *Educational Psychology in Practice*. 23(1): 63–77. Routledge Available at: https://schoolrefuserfamilies.files.wordpress.com/2018/01/pellegrini.pdf [Accessed 24.2.24]

Rae, T. (2023) *Therapeutic Tools to Support Wellbeing in Schools* Available at: https://worldofeducation.tts-group.co.uk/dr-tina-rae-therapeutic-tools-to-support-wellbeing-in-schools [Accessed 12.7.23]

Saline, S. (2022) *Flow State vs. Hyperfocus: On Channeling Your Unsteady ADHD Attention* Available at: https://www.additudemag.com/flow-state-vs-hyperfocus-adhd

Saline, S. (2023) When Perfectionism Stems from ADHD: Challenging the Fallacy of "Not Good Enough" Available at: https://www.additudemag.com/perfectionism-adhd-not-good-enough-anxiety [Accessed 7.7.23]

Saline, S. (undated) *How to Stop Catastrophizing: A Guide for ADHD Worriers* Available at: https://www-additudemag-com.cdn.ampproject.org/c/s/www.additudemag.com/catastrophizing-worrying-negative-thoughts-adhd/amp [Accessed 7.7.23]

Siegel, D. (2020) *The Developing Mind* Guilford Press

Siegel, D. & Payne Bryson, T. (2012) *The Whole Brain Child – 12 Proven Strategies to Nurture Your Child's Developing Mind* Robinson

Siegel, D & Payne Bryson, T. (2020) *The Power of Showing Up – How Parental Presence Shapes Who Our Kids Become and How Their Brains Get Wired* Scribe

SparkleAppeal.org (undated) *Supporting Children and Young People with Anxiety and Worry: A Toolkit to Help Support Children with a Disability or Developmental Difficulty with Their Anxiety and Worry* Available at: https://www.sparkleappeal.org/ckfinder/userfiles/files/sparkle%20anxiety%20toolkit.pdf [Accessed 22.7.23]

Stallard, P. (2009) *Anxiety – Cognitive Behaviour Therapy with Children and Young People* Routledge

Alleviating anxiety checklist

STRATEGY	COMMENTS
Please also refer to Chapters 2 and 4	
Understand and recognise anxiety	
Label anxiety and explore its symptoms by noticing aloud	
Teach how and why anxiety may present	
Teach pupils to recognise and extend their window of tolerance	
Help pupils to recognise their physical symptoms through body mapping	
Build positive relationships and work collaboratively	
Key adults should provide regular check-ins, find patterns and establish triggers and provide support	
Strength-based approaches	
Use strength-based approaches and value successes within a broad range of subjects	
Focus on positives and praise small steps to success	
Provide pupils with roles and responsibilities to increase their self-esteem and sense of belonging	
Avoid negative labels and provide ten positives for each (perceived) negative	
Reframe language into positives	

(Continued)

Continued

STRATEGY	COMMENTS						
Reframing patterns of negative thinking							
Support pupils to identify and begin to reframe negative thought patterns							
Aim to foster a sense of gratitude							
Teaching and learning							
Create a calm, predictable learning environment where it feels safe to take risks and make mistakes							
Evaluate any barriers to engagement within the curriculum. Do pupils feel a high level of success as well as challenge?							
Support anxious pupils to start a task							
Preview/pre-teach vocabulary, concepts or skills, if necessary							
Regular check-ins							
Break tasks into smaller chunks, presented in a checklist. Include movement breaks							
Provide help cards and teach pupils what to do while waiting for help or struggling to get started							
Praise processes, applying skills, effort and attitude rather than outcome or correct answers							
Avoid public calling out or displaying of test results							
Use multi-sensory approaches							
Provide choices							
Help develop executive function							

(Continued)

Continued

STRATEGY	COMMENTS
Reasonable adjustments around homework	
Visual supports	
Visual timetables, rules and routines	
Stress scales and calm cards	
Social stories™	
Step-by-step approaches	
Start from where the pupil feels comfortable. Provide support, scaffold and intervene early to plan small steps	
Do 'if and then' planning	
Collaborate and decide what success may look like	
Environmental adaptations	
Awareness of sensory sensitivities and reduce sensory overwhelm	
Safe spaces and exit strategies – pre-taught and rehearsed	
Careful and considered seating plan	
Use the outside environment	
Unstructured times	
Smaller, quieter places to eat	
Zoned activities and clubs	
Access to safe spaces and safe faces	
Clear expectations and routines	
Consider alternative toilets or changing areas as necessary	

(Continued)

Continued

STRATEGY	COMMENTS
Transitions into school	
Buddy systems	
Always aim for a positive start to each day for every pupil	
Consistent boundaries, routines and responses	
Transitional objects	
Pre-warn of changes	
Transitions in and around school	
Carefully plan each transition and support executive function	
Use visual supports	
Teach pupils how to wait and to use 'wait tools'	
Make transitions as predictable as possible	
Provide time to finish tasks and give warnings. Be aware of hyperfocus and provide some flexibility and 'softer landings'	
Be aware of sensory sensitivities at transition times	
Provide settling or regulating activities following transitions and check-in to focus attention	
Minimise transitions or make them into productive movement breaks	
Transitional objects from key adults	
School trips and off-timetable days	

(Continued)

Continued

STRATEGY	COMMENTS
Pre-warn, plan and use visual supports. Provide roles and responsibilities	
Provide predictable activities where possible and teach coping strategies	
Transitions to new classes/adults	
Collaboration and communication to create transition plans	
List things that will remain the same	
Become familiar with new areas of school	
Prioritise relationship building	
Create profiles	
Send visual reminders home and share clear expectations	
Aim to maintain existing positive relationships	
Transition to new schools	
Collaboration and communication to create transition plans	
Plan and prepare pupils and include them as much as possible	
Carefully manage goodbyes	
Careful use of language	
Increase familiarity with new setting	
Prioritise relationships and provide a means to express worries	
Share clear expectations and provide visual supports	
Provide safe spaces	
Plan and provide enhanced transitions for key pupils	

4

Regulating and coping strategies

What are coping strategies?

Regulating and coping strategies can help people to manage and reduce their anxiety and begin to take control of its symptoms, providing them with 'a toolkit to use for in-the-moment stress' (McMillan, 2023). Self-regulation is the ability to manage behaviours, thoughts and emotions. It 'helps us to remain calm and attentive and helps us to respond, rather than react' (Conkbayir, 2023, p.2).

Regulating strategies can be used with all children at different points throughout the day. They may be effective on arrival, after break times and before or after periods of inactivity to support pupils become settled and ready to learn. They can be used before and after particularly stressful times such as exams or presentations or especially exciting times, such as before and on return from a school trip. They are helpful for everyone, particularly those pupils who mask in school, and can help prevent stress levels from building up and becoming overwhelming.

Regulating strategies reduce anxiety and support pupils to become emotionally ready to learn. 'When we calm the child's body physiologically, their calm body sends calming messages to their brain (brain-gut interactions). As a result, the frontal lobes can start to function again' (Sunderland, 2015, p.157).

DOI: 10.4324/9781003433231-5

Co-regulation and modelling

Before pupils can learn to self-regulate, they need to be taught how to do so and have experienced a trusted adult alongside them.

> Pupils who are overwhelmed and struggling to regulate their emotions will need co-regulation before they can begin to regulate themselves. Children will not be able to self-regulate if they have not had their emotions attuned to and soothed in infancy.
>
> (Thynne, 2022, p.34)

Repeated experience of co-regulation gradually leads to self-awareness and self-regulation.

When a child is anxious or dysregulated, the adult's response can calm them or heighten their anxiety further. Co-regulation helps pupils to calm, in the moment. When children are highly anxious and become dysregulated, their pre-frontal cortex or 'upstairs brain' (Siegel & Payne Bryson, 2012) (the part of the brain responsible for executive function, rational and logical thought and emotional regulation) goes 'offline'. The limbic system (emotional) and brainstem system (survival) 'downstairs brain' (Siegel & Payne Bryson, 2012) then take over. 'When kids have flipped their lids, they need someone . . . to step in and co-regulate so they can move back to the harmony of integration and regain control of their emotions, bodies and decisions' (Siegel & Payne Bryson, 2020, p.155).

- ■ Pre-teach and regularly rehearse a range of regulating strategies, when the pupil is calm and comfortable. The aim is for them to become embedded so that the pupil naturally begins to use them (with support and modelling initially) when they are becoming dysregulated.
- ■ Rather than telling a pupil to calm, model using pre-taught calming strategies alongside the pupil, in moments of dysregulation, emotional overwhelm or when they are presenting with behaviours which may indicate heightened anxiety, with the aim of them mirroring. For example, if a pupil is becoming dysregulated, sit down close by and model using a pre-taught calming strategy (such as playdough, sketching, breathing, tapping), whilst also slowing down your breathing, taking deeper breaths, dropping your shoulders, and using a 'slow, low, low' voice (Knightsmith, 2022b) (see p.22). Pre-learned breathing strategies give you a go-to script to work through which can be a real help in moments

when the child's anxiety has the potential to be catching. Roll out your favourite breathing strategy and allow the child to catch your calm instead (Knightsmith, undated).

■ Regularly model strategies, such as using a 'calm bag', using a stress tool or massaging hand cream into the hands to relax, for example, *This board is not working, I am going to just do my breathing exercises so I don't get too frustrated with it. Join in with me and we can calm together* or, *Ooh, I can feel my heart beating a bit faster than usual and my voice went louder than I like, let's all do some chair presses to help us to reset.*

■ Use visual reminders, such as a stress scale, to help pupils recognise and manage their emotions. Encourage pupils to photograph their preferred (pre-rehearsed) coping strategies (to increase sense of ownership). Present these alongside the stress scale, as a visual reminder to refer to, as soon as those anxious feelings begin. Review and evaluate these regularly to monitor which strategies work best for the individual.

Case study:

Peter (aged 4) became dysregulated. He was shouting and throwing equipment and then ran out of the door and was running around the playground in the rain. Mr A followed him, asking him to come in. Peter started laughing and running faster, with Mr A following.

Mrs B arrived to support and sat in the undercover space, where she could see him and started playing with the Duplo (one of Peter's favourite activities). She invited Mr A to join her, which he did. Mrs B talked to Mr A (so Peter could hear), while they played; *Oh dear, Mr A, you look wet and cold, let's take some deep breaths together out of that rain and have fun playing with this Duplo until you feel a bit better. This is fun isn't it? I love building with the Duplo.* The adults talked about building towers together and used exaggerated gestures and voices so that Peter could hear and see what was going on. Very soon, he came over and joined them and quickly regulated by engaging in an activity that he found calming.

Reflection opportunity:

■ How and why do you think modelling, a calming and diverting activity, supported Peter to regulate?

■ 'Weave regulating tasks and activities throughout the day, every day as this soothes the nervous system and eventually calms the survival response' (Beacon House, 2020). Coping strategies are most impactful when taught and rehearsed regularly, while the pupil is calm, in a playful, non-stressful environment. 'Children can learn to control their bodies, thinking and emotions. They just need to be taught in positive, fun ways' (MacKenzie, 2015, p.viii). They require a trusted adult, who can attune to the pupil's needs, support them through co-regulation and transfer that learning to different situations and environments.

Case study:

Suzy, aged 7, was eager to please adults in school. While sitting at her desk, she often appeared quite anxious. She displayed a lot of movement when asked to sit at her desk and struggled to concentrate. She had built up a trusting relationship with Mrs M, the pastoral support worker. Mrs M noticed and wondered aloud with Suzy – *Suzy, I have noticed that when you are asked to sit at your table, you sometimes get very wiggly. Some people who need to move a lot while they learn find these wobble cushions can help.* Mrs M showed Suzy the wobble cushion and they looked at it together, exploring both sides. Mrs M explained that one side is bumpier than the other and that the bumpy side is useful if she is feeling tired and needs waking up a bit. Mrs M modelled sitting on the cushion and then Suzy had a turn, sitting on both sides and was also shown how to cover it with a blanket to make it less bumpy, if it started to feel uncomfortable. They both had a go at sitting with the wobble cushion on the chair and moving from side to side with their feet on the floor. Suzy agreed that she may like to try the cushion in the classroom.

Mrs M went into class with Suzy, while no other children were in there and they spoke to the teacher. Suzy showed the teacher the wobble cushion and explained what it was for. Mrs M and Suzy put it on Suzy's chair and checked that her feet could still touch the floor comfortably. Mrs M explained that, at times, Suzy may want a break from the wobble cushion altogether, *After a while you may want to put it to the side, or Jo might like to try it, or you could hold it and squeeze it in your arms, or pop it behind your back, you could even take your shoes off and pop it under the table so that you can put your feet on it.*

Mrs M then checked in on Suzy more regularly than usual, to see how she was getting on with the cushion. Suzy said that she liked being *allowed to move while I work.*

Reflection opportunities:

■ How did Mrs M support Suzy to use the wobble cushion effectively?
■ What might have happened if Suzy had just been given the cushion with no modelling, exploration or explanation?

■ Through co-regulation, adults can gradually support pupils towards increased self-awareness. Helping pupils to become mindful of their individual calmers and stressors will help them begin to understand when to use their coping strategies. Everyone is unique and different pupils need different things. Work with pupils to explore what works best for them and when. What works may change from day to day or over time so explore and rehearse a range of calming strategies with pupils regularly.
■ To co-regulate and when teaching regulation strategies a trusting relationship is essential. Teaching regulation strategies can be an ideal opportunity to engage in the playfulness of the PACE approach (see pp.27–8). Playfulness and laughter can help relaxation and relieve some of the physical symptoms of stress, help build connections and trust and support emotional regulation. Interactive play ideas include (Bombèr, 2020, p.181):

■ Thumb wars
■ Passing balloons to each other
■ Popping bubbles on different body parts
■ Building towers.

Further ideas include:

■ Try not to laugh games
■ Mirror faces
■ Would you rather . . .?
■ Clapping or drumming patterns
■ Jumping while balancing bean bags on different body parts.

Recognise dysregulation

Before pupils can self-regulate, they will need to be taught to spot their triggers as well as the physical signs that they are becoming anxious and dysregulated.

Many pupils will find it difficult to understand their emotions and behaviours. They may not know how to switch from one emotional state to another and will need teaching, support and modelling. In order to learn to regulate, pupils need trusted adults to attune to their needs and changing emotions, to support them to soothe and reflect through co-regulation and noticing aloud. Some pupils may not recognise the emotions which they are experiencing and will need adults to explicitly 'name it to tame it' (Siegel & Payne Bryson, 2012, p.27). They may not yet know what calm feels or looks like. Noticing their emotions and providing commentaries can help pupils to begin to understand and regulate their feelings and behaviours (see p.30).

- Adults need to notice and attune to the child's emotions to spot early signs of dysregulation and anxiety. It is important to understand the behaviour presentations which may be driven by anxiety (see p.11–12). Intervene early by checking in with the pupil, commenting aloud, modelling and engaging in a regulating activity such as a breathing or grounding technique or providing a movement break, job or distraction.
- Noticing what is happening within their bodies helps children develop strategies to manage the anxiety (Zandt & Barrett, 2021, p.75). Teach pupils to spot the physical signs that they may be becoming dysregulated or anxious, to increase their self-awareness, by sensitively noticing aloud, such as, *I can see that your fists are clenched and your head has gone down, I wonder if you are worried about starting this writing? Let's go and throw a ball while we think of some ideas.*
- Encourage pupils to think about how they tend to feel physically when they become anxious (Collins-Donnelley, 2014, p.151) and support them to 'anticipate' and 'accept physical feelings as a normal part of experiencing anxiety' and 'appreciate a lack of connection between physical feelings and actual illness' (Eisen & Engler, 2006, p.78–9). Physical changes which occur in the body can be identified through body mapping: encourage the pupil to draw on an outline of the body to indicate where they feel their anxiety, such as drawing butterflies in the stomach or scribbling on the hands if they clench their fists.

■ Help pupils to spot patterns and stressors, and provide support, increase their sense of control and rehearse coping strategies beforehand. For example, *We're going into the canteen now, I know that can be a bit overwhelming for you at times. We can go together a bit earlier than the others if you like, or you can go to the front of the line with your friend. Choose a stress tool to pop in your pocket and squeeze it too. If it all gets too much, come to the inclusion room, like we practised.*

Suggestions to support pupils to regulate

When the threat response is activated, pre-learned regulation strategies and co-regulation help pupils to feel safe and return to a state of calm. Beacon House (2019) recommend 'brainstem calming activities' which need to be:

■ 'Relational (offered by a safe adult)
■ Relevant (developmentally matched to the child rather than matched to their actual age)
■ Repetitive (patterned)
■ Rewarding (pleasurable)
■ Rhythmic (resonant with neural patterns)
■ Respectful (of the child and family).'

Normalise the use of regulation and coping strategies by teaching the whole class how to do them and implementing them regularly. Each week pupils could try out and practise a different regulating activity. Produce visual reminders of each technique to display around the room.

Breathing techniques

Deep breathing is one of the most effective ways to support a pupil to regulate when they are anxious. 'Breathing strategies are a fantastic way to calm things down. When we take control of our breathing, it slows down the physical anxious response (so our heartrate slows and we start to feel a little calmer' (Knightsmith, undated).

Teach pupils to breathe in through the nose and out through the mouth, while concentrating on their breath. Teach and rehearse a range of breathing techniques so pupils can choose their preferences (links to further information on these strategies can be found on p.101):

- **Finger breathing**: hold up one hand and spread out the fingers. Use the index finger of the other hand to slowly trace up and down the fingers and thumb of the upheld hand. Whilst tracing up the fingers, breathe in slowly through the nose, and whilst tracing down the fingers breathe out slowly through the mouth. This is this is effective because it also uses the sense of touch and is visual.
- **Box breathing**: use a finger to trace the sides of an imaginary square in front of the body. Cross the midline with your finger. Breathe in for four, hold for four, breathe out for four, hold for four. Swap hands and repeat as necessary.
- **Finger candles breathing:** hold up one hand and spread out the fingers. Pretend each finger is a candle on a birthday cake. Take a deep breath in and breathe out to 'blow out' the imaginary candle on your thumb and each finger in turn. Children can also 'blow out the candles' on an adult's hand. A sense of playfulness can be added by pretending the fingers are the 'magic' relighting ones, and the adult's fingers could pop back up to be 'blown out' again. Repeat as necessary.
- **Lazy 8 breathing:** draw a large imaginary sideways 8 with your finger. Breathe in deeply while crossing your midline, breath out as you trace the shape. Repeat with a finger from the other hand.
- 'Try challenging your child to breathe as quietly as they possibly can – this breathing is likely to be slow and deep, just what you are trying to encourage' (Willetts & Creswell, 2007, p.240).
- **Blow bubbles:** picture the anxiety in a bubble and blow it away.
- **Sing** or play a woodwind instrument.
- **Blow a feather or ping pong ball through a straw**.

Sensory tools

- Create regulating boxes with pupils (a box of items to help the pupil to self-soothe and manage their anxiety). Decorate the outside of the box with items that the pupil finds calming, such as pictures of pets, favourite places, soothing fabrics, pom poms, etc. Bombèr (2020, p.178) suggests purses/pencil cases or toiletry bags rather than boxes for older pupils. Trial a variety of sensory tools for a range of senses with the pupil and let them choose which they would like to include. Ideas include fiddle tools (such as tangles, marble pushes), toys that are manipulative, squeezy, squashy or stretchy toys, textured toys, scented playdough, lip balm, hand cream (gain permission from home and check for allergies). Alternatively make a glitter jar and include comforting smells (fabric sprayed with a parent's perfume/aftershave or washed with familiar washing powder) and mindful colouring.

■ Explore using the sensory tools in ways that combine the senses, for example, vanilla playdough would be tactile and use the sense of smell, adding glitter introduces a visual element, a textured ball that lights up would be tactile and visual, a scented, chewy pencil topper provides proprioceptive oral feedback and uses the olfactory sense, scented kneadable erasers are functional, tactile and use the olfactory sense.

■ Holding a transitional object (see pp.231–2) can increase feelings of safety and reduce anxiety, for example, cuddling a soft toy from home, stroking a piece of velvet in a pocket, holding a little gem stone, a squishy toy or a fidget tool.

■ Create a regulation station or a 'sensory tool box' for the whole class (Brukner, 2014, p.83) including items for a range of senses.

■ Have an easy-to-grab collection of calming tools to use if a dysregulated pupil leaves the room. Bombèr (2020, p.178) suggests 'SOS bags', containing a range of calming and regulating items. By modelling and engaging with the contents of the bag, 'the pupils will come and join you as they can sense this is a safe interaction and that whatever you have will soothe their dysregulation'.

Case study:

A Special Educational Needs Coordinator (SENCO) has given members of staff a bum bag each. They are small and portable and each one contains a 'set of basics' and then they are personalised for key children, for example, one key adult has hand cream and lip balm for her pupil, as these are the pupil's 'go to' regulating tools.

Focusing fiddle tools

Many people cannot sit still and actively listen at the same time and need to fidget to aid relaxation, regulation, concentration and learning. Some forms of fidgeting can be distracting in the classroom setting so it is important to find something quiet that works for the pupil without disturbing others. Referring to them as *focusing fiddle tools* rather than *fiddle toys* can help remind pupils of their purpose. Set clear guidelines around their use, explaining what they are, how they can help and when and how they should be used (including where to put them when they are not being used).

■ There is a range of commercial focusing fiddle tools such as marble pushes, tangles, fidget cubes, stress balls, squishies, thinking putty, hand exercisers, sensory pencil grips, fidget pens/pencil toppers, sensory rulers and fidget rings. However, playdough, Blu Tack® or art pom poms can be useful (cheaper) options. A piece of velvet or tactile fidget strip on the under-ide of the table may be effective as they are discreet and can be less distracting.
■ Providing doodle pads, teaching note-taking skills or giving copies of presentations to highlight and annotate can give pupils a sense of purpose and support listening while allowing movement and increasing focus.

Grounding techniques

Grounding techniques are simple activities that help pupils to focus on the present moment and distract them from anxious or overwhelming thoughts, thus helping them to calm and relax.

■ Look around and name all the green things you see/all the things beginning with 'b', etc.
■ Say a name/city for each letter of the alphabet.
■ Name an item for each colour of the rainbow.
■ **5-4-3-2-1**: name 5 things you can see, 4 you can touch, 3 you can hear, 2 you can smell, 1 you can taste.
■ List your favourite foods, songs, films, books . . .
■ Write a reflective journal.
■ Place socked feet on a wobble cushion.
■ **Be a tree**: 'There's nothing more grounded than a tree! Teach your student to feel his or her connection with the ground by imaging him/herself as a tree' (PTSDUK, undated). Encourage pupils to focus on their feet and toes on their ground, their back stabilising them as trunk, feel and move their arms as the branches. 'Simply noticing their bodies and feeling their connection with the room helps kids feel grounded!' (PTSDUK, undated). Balancing on one leg in a yoga tree pose can help focus negative or racing thoughts.

- **Object focus**: provide items with different textures and colours – 'these could be sensory items, colourful rocks, snow globes . . . Students can hold an item in their hands and tune in all of their focus to the item. Notice the colours. Notice the textures. How does it feel in my hand? How does it feel when I squeeze it? What colours do I see? Just notice everything there is to notice about the item!' (PTSDUK, undated).
- **Stomp, stomp, blow**: 'stomp the left foot, stomp the right foot and then exhale deeply. Continue this pattern of stomp, stomp, blow, stomp, stomp, blow, stomp, stomp, blow. Feel the connection of feet with the floor. Blow away anxious thoughts' (PTSDUK, undated).

Cross the midline

The more communication there is between the right and left hemispheres of the brain, the easier it is to process information, be creative, apply logic, problem solve, perform tasks and regulate emotions. Crossing the midline (the imaginary line down the centre of the body) can be grounding, regulating and help pupils to reset.

- Pass a stress ball from one hand to the other across the midline to integrate the left and right hemispheres of the brain. Try to pass it up and down and behind the back, under the knees and roll it under one foot and then the other.
- Pop bubbles on different body parts, alternating from left side to right side.
- Hold the right fist against the left palm to the far right of the body, slowly use the fist to push the palm to the left side, providing some resistance with the palm. Repeat with a left fist and the right palm at the left side of the body and push to the right.
- Give yourself a hug while breathing deeply and calmly.
- Arm pretzels – place arms straight out in front, palms back to back, cross hands over at the wrist, so palms are facing each other. (Clapping (awkwardly) a few times at this point can be grounding and focusing). Interlace the fingers and twist your arms down and in towards the chest. Hold and repeat.
- Touch your left ear with your right hand and your right ear with your left hand. Breathe, hold, repeat.
- Bring your left knee up to touch your right elbow and vice versa. Repeat.
- Dance!

Positive self-talk

People with high anxiety are likely to have negative thinking patterns and tend to have a low sense of self-esteem and a more negative view of themselves and the world around them.

■ Adults can teach pupils positive self-talk and help them to recognise and change their negative thought patterns. 'Positive self-talk can have a big impact on how we think and feel. Over time, engaging in more positive self-talk can help reduce stress, improve self-esteem, increase motivation, inspire productivity, and improve overall mental and physical health' (Pathway2Success, 2017). Positive self-talk can help pupils to regulate their thoughts, emotions and behaviours and support them to cope in situations which provoke anxiety.

■ Pupils need support to understand that these thoughts are exactly that – thoughts – rather than facts. Separating thoughts from facts can be very helpful in overcoming anxiety. The first step is to establish what those negative thoughts are and to recognise them when they appear (see p.48).

■ Eisen & Engler (2006, p.77) suggest asking *What's the best thing that could end up happening?* in order to help steer children away from negative or catastrophic thinking and help them to visualise coping and success.

■ Pathway2Success (2017) suggests that adults 'discuss the benefits to positive self-talk. Be open about what self-talk is and how it helps. Kids, and especially teens, might be sceptical about why they should change their thinking at first . . . but you have to change your words before you can really change the silent thinking in your head'.

■ Teach children to 'try to let go of the negative voice by saying the opposite'. 'For example, when the words "I can't do this" pop into their head, adults need to teach the pupil to recognise these thoughts and then change them to "I can do this". Repeat the positive statement in your head several times' (Jennings, 2023, p.59).

■ Teach pupils to use positive self-talk by rehearsing positive affirmations or mantras – 'specific, simple statements that you repeat to yourself (often) to provide yourself with encouragement or motivation' (He's-extraordinary.com, undated). Create affirmations which are positive and easy to remember, such as *I can stay calm, I've got this* or *I am good enough*. AnxietyCanada (2023) suggest the following coping statements:

- *If I get anxious, I will try some calm breathing.*
- *I just need to do my best.*
- *People cannot tell when I am feeling anxious.*
- *This has happened before and I know how to handle it.*
- *My anxiety won't last forever.*

He's-extraordinary.com (undated) suggest:

- *This took courage and I'm proud of myself for trying.*
- *I may not be able to control this situation, but I am in charge of how I respond.*
- *It's okay to feel how I feel. Emotions are normal, and this will pass.*
- *Sometimes things don't go according to plan, but there are plenty of positives; I won't let this ruin my day.*
- *There is always a solution; I just haven't thought of it yet.*
- *This is hard, but it's challenging me to try my best.*
- *If I can't overcome this obstacle on my own, I can ask for help.*

- Once the positive statements have been chosen, pupils can be creative about how they display them. They can be written in journals, on pebbles, lollipop sticks, paper hearts, paperchains or bookmarks. Pupils could design badges, coasters, tea towels, magnets or posters. They could write them and pop them in a box or scrapbook to read at a later date or make a positive affirmation 'tree' and write the statements on the 'leaves'.
- Adults need to teach, rehearse and model positive self-talk for pupils.

'Anxiety likes to control your behaviour but using techniques to manage your thoughts and face challenging situations can give you back control' (Hutt, 2019, p.83).

Mindfulness

Mindfulness ('the practice of bringing your attention to your body in the present moment') can decrease stress and anxiety and improve overall physical and mental health and emotional wellbeing (Hanratty, 2017). Mindfulness aims to help a person become more self-aware, feel calmer and less stressed and become more able to choose how to respond to and cope with thoughts and feelings (Mind, 2021). Mindfulness-based activities involve noticing, accepting and paying attention to sensations and emotions in the here and now.

Mindfulness-based activities can include:

- Meditation 'sitting quietly to focus on your breathing, thoughts, sensations in your body or things you can sense around you. Try to bring your attention back to the present if your mind starts to wander' (Mind, 2021).
- Yoga.
- Positive visualisation of people, places or images.
- Body scanning – move your attention slowly through different parts of your body. 'Start from the top of your head and move all the way down to the end of your toes. You could focus on feelings of warmth, tension, tingling or relaxation of different parts of your body' (Mind, 2021).
- Gratitude activities such as taking photos of, drawing or writing down three things that you feel grateful for.
- Watching a visual timer, lava lamp or sensory bottle.

Movement and exercise

'Being physically active releases positive endorphins. This makes children feel more relaxed and overall happier' (Psychreg, 2021). Movement is regulating for most people, having the 'potential to decrease nervous-system arousal' and '[soothe] the body and the emotions it experiences' (Siegel & Payne Bryson, 2020, p.180–1). Exercise can help to alleviate anxieties, calm emotions and improve behaviour.

- Implement short movement or sensory breaks regularly throughout the day, particularly before or after pupils are expected to sit for prolonged periods of time. 'Teachers often confuse breaks with rewards, but students with anxiety need breaks as preventative accommodations' (Minahan, 2018, p.58). Regular movement breaks help pupils to focus and concentrate, increase memory retention, reduce stress and anxiety, decrease feelings of overwhelm and regulate emotions.
- Engaging in regular physical exercise such as yoga, dance, sports, skipping, hula hooping and climbing are all effective ways of helping pupils to regulate. Knightsmith (2022a, p.94) suggests finding an exercise that is 'fun' and 'builds connection with others'.
- Use transition times to move in a variety of different ways – stomp, march, skip, giant strides, tip toe. Use lining up time to engage in wall presses, shoulder rolls, fist clenches, calf raises, etc.

> **Case study:**
>
> Demi (aged 5) struggled with coming to school in the mornings and didn't want to go into the classroom. She was invited to join Sensory Circuits each morning with a key adult, who met her at the door. She helped set up the activities with the adult, and then two other children joined them. Demi enjoyed the activities, which started with something energetic, fun and alerting, such as bouncing the ball into a target and running back. She then moved on to the next activity, which was more calming such as balancing on a beam, or moving along the climbing wall. The final activity was relaxing, such as listening to quiet music in the calm tent or mindful colouring. Once Demi got used to this new routine, it helped her to calm in the mornings and she was able to access the classroom with her key adult settling her to learn.

- 'The difference between tension and relaxation can be demonstrated by pretending to be two different characters . . .: one who is very stiff and another who is very floppy' (Willetts & Creswell, 2007, p.240). The examples given include a robot and a rag doll and a breadstick and a jelly.

'In seat' movement activities

'In seat' movement activities can be carried out at the table, whilst seated and can include:

- Chair presses – sit on a chair and place palms on chair by sides. Push on your arms to lift your body.
- Sharpen pencils (manual sharpener).
- Hole punch or staple paper.
- Wobble cushion (see case study, p.80).
- Under desk pedal exerciser or foot roller.
- Weighted lap pad or shoulder pad.
- Resistance band around the chair legs, to push feet against.
- Arm and hand massage (use hand cream to add a sensory element), swap hands/arms.
- Flex feet at the ankle.
- Fist clench and hand stretch.

- Muscle tense and untense – start at the feet and then move up the body, to thighs, core, fists, biceps, chest, head and face – tense the muscles for 3–5 seconds and then unclench slowly and relax for ten seconds and repeat. 'The idea is when your child tenses and then relaxes his muscles, he will release his anxiety and frustration' (Eisen & Engler, 2006, p.83).
- Shoulder rolls.
- Stretching.
- Bend down on the chair, leaning forward and touch your toes.
- Use a wobble stool, gym ball, gym ball chair or Zuma® rocker.

Proprioceptive input (heavy work)

Proprioceptive input (heavy work) refers to activities which provide resistance and input to the muscles and joints such as pushing, pulling, stretching, carrying or lifting. It helps pupils to feel centred, provides them with sensory input, can help increase attention and focus, decrease defensiveness and be calming and regulating. Heavy work activities include:

- Hanging and climbing.
- Using chin up bars.
- Floor or wall presses (stand arm's length from a wall, place hands on the wall and in a controlled way, bend elbows until nose is almost touching the wall and repeat). Alternatively, be playful and try to 'push' the wall to 'make the classroom bigger'.
- Carrying objects such as books or a box.
- Jumping on a trampoline or trampette.
- Pressing and squeezing playdough.
- Rolling or throwing a weighted ball on the ground.
- Battle ropes.
- Gardening – digging, raking, planting, sweeping, watering the plants, pushing a wheelbarrow.
- Pushing a gym ball along the floor and up the wall.
- Star jumps.
- Sitting on a gym ball or using a space hopper.
- Pulling and stretching a resistance band.
- Squatting and lunging.
- Wearing a back pack (particularly when moving around the school or on the way to and from school).
- Oral input, including sensory snacks (see alerting and calming activities pp.94–5), chew tools such as of necklaces, bracelets and chew pencil toppers, drinking through a straw or sports bottle.

Vestibular input

Vestibular input is changes in position, direction or movement and contributes to a sense of balance and coordination. It can help increase attention and focus and be calming and regulating for pupils. Vestibular input activities include:

■ Using wobble boards.
■ Balancing on alternate legs – try bending, touching opposite ears (to cross the midline), putting hands in the air.
■ Using balance beams.
■ Using tummy scooter board.
■ Using a rocking chair.
■ Playing on swings and slides.
■ Spinning giant balance tops.
■ Riding scooters and bikes.
■ Rocking over a gym ball on tummy.
■ Spinning or pushing along on a wheeled chair.
■ Jumping and turning.
■ Action songs such as 'Head, Shoulders, Knees and Toes'.
■ Climbing ropes or rope ladders.
■ Doing obstacle courses and games involving running and changing direction.
■ Rolling on mats or down a slope.

Jobs and errands

Jobs and errands provide quick movement breaks and can boost self-esteem. Jobs that include heavy work are particularly effective. Ideas include:

■ Tidying or sorting the book corner, cloakroom or boxes of equipment.
■ Holding the door open.
■ Watering the plants.
■ Stacking or putting out the chairs.
■ Giving out equipment.
■ Updating the visual timetable.
■ Taking a box of equipment to a different area of the school.
■ Pushing the lunch trolley.
■ Cleaning the tables or whiteboard.
■ 'Work experience' with the site manager/in the canteen/IT suite/office staff (sweeping, gardening, pushing a wheelbarrow, unpacking the photocopy paper).

Whole class movement

Whole class movement activities can be useful for helping all pupils to regulate and focus and prevent anxious pupils from feeling singled out. They can be topic-related or stand-alone activities such as:

- 'Sit down/stand up' – teacher says a fact – if it is correct, sit down, if it is false, stand up.
- Post questions on the walls around the room, pupils move to each question and write their answers on a clipboard.
- Stand in a circle, throw a beanbag to each other – the person holding the beanbag can answer/speak.
- Give each pupil a question or an answer/two phrases that match/two words that make up a compound word, etc. and they need to walk around and find their 'partner'.
- Have a one-minute dance off.
- Stand, stomp and shake.
- Add actions to rhymes, texts, poems, songs and stories.
- Stand and clap/march/tap whilst chanting multiplication tables, the periodic table, number bonds, etc.
- Play *Simon Says . . .* or *Follow the Leader*.
- Doing Stormbreak activities (see 'Further signposting').

Calming and alerting strategies

Pupils will need alerting at times (when they are withdrawn, lethargic, bored or losing focus) and at other times need calming (when they are angry, frustrated or excited). Each person is different and will need to explore what is calming and alerting for them personally.

- Alerting or re-energising activities tend to be those that are quick and high energy such as spinning, running, turning and twisting. Alerting breathing techniques tend to have an extended inhale and quicker, stronger exhale. Crunchy sensory snacks such as bread sticks or apple and carrot batons and anything cold such as drinking ice-cold water or sucking an ice pop tend to be alerting. Scents or flavours, such as peppermint, citrus, cinnamon and eucalyptus, and anything sour or spicy also tend to be alerting.
- Calming activities tend to be slower paced, heavier and rhythmic such as linear movements, rocking, balancing, hanging and

climbing. Calm breathing techniques tend to involve slow inhales followed by an elongated exhale. Chewy sensory snacks such as dried mango, raisins and chewy cereal bars tend to be calming, as do warm drinks. Lavender and vanilla scents tend to be calming.

Performing arts

Participating in creative and performing art activities can help reduce pupil anxiety and stress and increase self-confidence.

- 'One of the most helpful ways to move children from these super-high anxiety states, to their calmer "thinking brain", is patterned, repetitive rhythmic activity' (Beacon House, 2019) such as clapping or playing percussion instruments. This can integrate both sides of the brain and be grounding. Research has indicated that group drumming sessions over 6–10 weeks can reduce depression, anxiety and social resilience (Fancourt et al., 2016). Drumming can also be an effective way of releasing tension and expressing negative emotions.
- Playing an instrument can be relaxing and reduce stress, increase focus and calm anxiety.
- Create energising and calming play lists. Research has indicated that listening to music reduces the stress hormone cortisol, which can calm the threat response.
- Writing songs and raps and composing music can be a fun, creative, positive way of releasing emotions and feelings.
- 'Singing releases endorphins that reduce stress and anxiety levels, allowing students to switch off from the outside world' (Psychreg, 2021).
- Similarly, dancing can release feel-good chemicals in the brain, reducing cortisol, which helps reduce stress and anxiety.
- Drama and dramatic play can help pupils to express emotions, provide a sense of release and escape and build confidence, increase collaboration and help develop empathy. Role-play or puppets can help children explore powerful emotions and learn effective regulation skills. 'Using puppets allows you to discuss emotions in a safe and fun way, which can help reduce anxiety and stress around emotional topics' (Leicestershire County Council Early Years SEND Team, 2023).
- Music and drama therapy sessions can be supportive.

Case study:

Aniq was struggling to remain in the classroom, often becoming dysregulated. His engagement in lessons had declined and he completed very little learning. Staff were very concerned about his lack of self-esteem and low feelings of self-worth. He refused to go into the playground as he felt that he had no friends, and if he did play football with his peers, he was concerned that he would 'lose it, hurt them and get into trouble again'.

Aniq was invited to music therapy in school. Having never played an instrument, he discovered a love and flair for the piano. At the end of the year, Aniq was singing and playing the piano in assemblies. His confidence began to grow and many of his anxious behaviours were no longer presenting.

Cognitive breaks

- Colouring – MacDonald (2019, p.126) describes 'how powerful this simple strategy can be . . . to manage overwhelming feelings. It means being able to get absorbed in something which has a definable start and end, something which can be quite sensory in terms of going from black and white to full colour, and most importantly something which can wholly distract us from whatever it is that is causing distress.'
- Creative and craft activities.
- A mindful sensory bottle, liquid motion timer or glitter jar.
- Modelling clay, playdough.
- Writing poetry or stories.
- Sorting, stacking, building, connecting or threading.
- Crosswords, dot to dots, sudoku, word searches, puzzles.
- Engaging in special interests.

School pets

- Interacting with a school pet can reduce stress and anxiety (University of Lincoln, 2022) and increase serotonin and dopamine levels, which are calming and relaxing and increase feelings of wellbeing. As well as decreasing anxiety, interacting with pets can build self-confidence and encourage playfulness.

Exit strategies and safe spaces

■ Pupils who are feeling overwhelmed by sensory information or anxieties will need access to a quiet space or sensory room to regulate and reset. Create safe spaces *with* the pupils to provide a sense of ownership. Ask pupils to choose (from a limited selection) what they would like to go into their safe space such as cushions, soft toys, fleece blankets, fairy lights and sensory tools. 'It is worthwhile finding out from children and young people what makes them feel relaxed and whether there are familiar objects they would like to see in the space' (Jennings, 2023, p.16). Read books and play games in there, when the pupil is calm, to ensure that the space genuinely feels safe. Pay attention to what and who are in the space and tailor them to the pupil's needs. Teach and rehearse when and how to use the safe space effectively.

■ At times of heightened stress and anxiety, the ability to think logically and to verbalise emotions diminishes. Support needs to be given to provide pupils with an effective means of communicating in times of stress. Provide pupils with some form of pre-agreed and rehearsed exit strategy, such as a signal, gesture, leaving an item or exit card on their desk (allow them to decorate or choose a picture to go on the card, to give a sense of ownership). Ensure pupils are taught and regularly rehearse how and when to use their exit strategy.

■ Using an exit card and then standing outside the classroom alone can increase anxiety. Pupils need to know what to do when they leave the classroom, such as going to a safe place and safe adult, using the sensory room, going for a walk or using their pre-taught breathing technique and doing ten wall presses. Include visuals of the chosen strategy on the reverse of the exit card, as a reminder.

Explore alternative behaviours

'A person's emotional state can completely change when the body moves vigorously. Anger, frustration, tension and other negative emotions are released so that emotional balance can return' (Siegel & Payne Bryson, 2020, p.181).

■ When pupils are regularly feeling and displaying big emotions such as frustration, anger or anxiety and communicating these through their behaviours (kicking, hitting, biting, screaming, throwing, etc.), they need to be taught alternative behaviours, when they are calm. These alternative behaviours should then be rehearsed and role-played regularly over time in a fun, playful way, so that they become embedded.

Bombèr (2007, p.203) suggests 'the general rule is to match the behaviour with another activity that uses the part of the body that they are using inappropriately'. She goes on to give the example of a child who used to spit at times of heightened anxiety being given bubbles to blow. Other examples include encouraging the pupil who is throwing equipment to go outside and throw beanbags at a target or 'wet sponges to hurl against the fence' (Kranowitz, 2005 p.269). If a child is jumping and stamping, teach them to stomp on bubble wrap or use the trampette instead. If a pupil is up-ending tables and chairs, tell them to go and throw a weighted ball onto the floor or use battle ropes. If they are presenting with aggression, let them use the punch bag or pummel playdough. If they are running or hiding, teach them to use a safe space. If they rip up their work or displays off the wall, let them rip up cereal boxes as an alternative. Someone who gets louder may benefit from using a 'screaming space' in the playground (Kranowitz, 2005, p.269).

■ Regularly engage in such activities when the pupil is calm, so that they become embedded and natural, as a means of releasing stress and tension.

■ Ask the pupil to take a photo of their preferred strategies, when they are calm, to use as a reminder to access them in times of stress, when the 'upstairs' brain goes off-line and it becomes difficult to think rationally.

■ Knightsmith (2023) suggests a 'write and rip' or 'create and destroy' activity if pupils are struggling to let go after an incident has been resolved and it is affecting focus and learning. The pupil would be given the opportunity to write about what has happened and then rip it up, or create a playdough image of the incident and then destroy it. Be sure to arrange a time for pupils to talk about any big feelings if they need further support. However, this is a cathartic and visual way of helping pupils to let go of grudges and move on, where appropriate.

■ Use Emotion Coaching (see pp.32–3) to remind pupils of these alternative behaviours in the moment and to set expectations on behaviour with empathy. Scripts can be helpful, particularly when emotions are running high on both sides (and the adult and pupil's 'upstairs brain' (Siegel & Payne Bryson, 2012) is going offline), such as, *X, I can see you are really cross right now, let's go and stomp on some bubble wrap and talk* or *I can see that you are really cross at the moment, but I am not for hitting. Let's go and throw some bean-bags and you can be cross safely.*

Access the outdoor environment

Being in nature can have positive effects on children's physical and mental health and emotional wellbeing. Studies have shown that green spaces can lower levels of stress and reduce anxiety and act as a buffer for children against life's stress and adversity (Wells & Evans, 2003).

Regulating activities in the outdoor area can include:

- Nature trails, minibeast hunts or mindfulness walks.
- Engaging with animals; walking the dog or feeding the birds.
- Gardening, growing plants, fruit and vegetables.
- Learning outside the classroom – sharing a book under a tree, sand/water play, phonics or number 'treasure' hunts, drawing and painting, taking photographs, painting or writing poetry outdoors.
- Building a bug hotel or a bird table.
- Picnics.
- Sports and exercise.

Teaching and learning

- Pupils need to be taught a range of regulating and coping strategies when they are calm, and these should be rehearsed regularly so that they become natural and embedded. Regulation strategies need to be planned into the curriculum and general ethos of the school rather than used as a motivator or reward. 'The key aspect for the school environment is to ensure the availability of the coping strategy and that those relevant staff are also made aware so that the young person is not denied the opportunity to access or use the coping strategy when relevant' (Johnson, 2024, p.38).
- Model, teach and rehearse coping strategies to the whole class, as part of the regular classroom routine. All pupils will benefit from these life skills and those who are anxious will not feel singled out. 'Self-regulation is the greatest gift we can give to children' (Conkbayir, 2023, p.6). Strategies can then be practised more regularly with individuals or small groups as necessary. Pupils will often then go on to model strategies to each other in times of stress.

Chapter take-aways

- Teaching pupils a range of regulating and coping strategies can help them begin to manage their anxiety.
- Regulating and coping strategies need to be practised regularly, when the pupil is calm, so they become embedded.
- Initially, and at times of heightening anxiety, strategies will need to be modelled and pupils will need co-regulation before self-regulation.
- Teaching strategies to the whole class supports all pupils and prevents individuals from feeling singled out.

Further signposting

Books

Inside I'm Hurting – Practical Strategies for Supporting Children with Attachment Difficulties in Schools by Louise Bombèr

Know Me to Teach Me – Differentiated Discipline for Those Recovering from Adverse Childhood Experiences by Louise Bombèr

Managing Social Anxiety in Children and Young People – Practical Activities for Reducing Stress and Building Self-esteem by Sue Jennings – Nesting and breathing (pp.21–8)

Raising a Sensory Smart Child by Lindsey Biel and Nancy Peske

The Neuroscience of the Developing Child – Self-Regulation for Wellbeing and a Sustainable Future by Mine Conkbayir

The Out of Sync Child by Carole Kranowitz

Resources

A Therapeutic Treasure Deck of Grounding, Soothing, Coping and Regulating Cards (Therapeutic Treasures Collection) by Dr Karen Treisman

Cards Against Anxiety by Dr Pooky Knightsmith

Resources to share with pupils

Help! I've Got an Alarm in my Head: How Panic, Anxiety and Stress Affect Your Body by K.L. Aspden

Tam's Journey by Amanda Peddle

The Healthy Coping Colouring Book and Journal: Creative Activities to Help Manage Stress, Anxiety and Other Big Feelings by Dr Pooky Knightsmith

The Kid's Guide to Staying Awesome and in Control: Simple Stuff to Help Children Regulate their Emotions and Senses by Lauren Brukner

Websites

Anna Freud *Let's Talk About Anxiety* Animation and Teacher Toolkit https://www.annafreud.org/resources/schools-and-colleges/lets-talk-about-anxiety-animation-and-teacher-toolkit

Beacon House *Developmental Trauma Resources* https://beaconhouse.org.uk/resources

Emotion Coaching UK *Resources for Professionals, Parents and Carers* https://www.emotioncoachinguk.com/resources-for-professionals-parents-carers

Hamish and Milo *Calm Me – Helping Children with Anxiety* https://hamishandmilo.org/wellbeing-emotion-themes/calm-me-helping-children-with-anxiety

PTSDUK *PTSD in Children: Information for Teachers* https://www.ptsduk.org/ptsd-in-children-information-for-teachers

Stormbreak https://www.stormbreak.org.uk/our-programmes

Breathing exercises

Coping Skills for Kids *Using Shapes to Teach Deep Breathing* https://copingskillsforkids.com/blog/using-shapes-to-teach-deep-breathing

Dr Pooky Knightsmith *Box Breathing Technique* https://www.youtube.com/watch?v=JYytiS0ymZg

Dr Pooky Knightsmith *Five Finger Breathing* https://www.pookyknightsmith.com/download-five-finger-breathing

Dr Pooky Knightsmith *Simple Breathing Strategies* https://www.pookyknightsmith.com/wp-content/uploads/2022/11/Simple-Breathing-Strategies.pdf

Relaxation exercises

Dr Karen Treisman *Free Videos to Support Relaxation and Emotional Regulation* www.safehandsthinkingminds.co.uk/covid-anxiety-stress-resources-links

Elemental Health *In the Moment Stress Busters* https://www.ehe.org.uk/resource-centre

Glow Scotland *Emotional Regulation Activities for Children and Young People* https://blogs.glowscotland.org.uk/er/public/healthierminds/uploads/sites/18270/2020/06/22132034/Emotional-Regulation-Activities-for-Children-and-Young-People.pdf

Lincolnshire Behaviour Outreach Services *Toolkit for Regulation* https://www.family-action.org.uk/content/uploads/2020/07/Toolkit-for-Regulation.pdf

Coping strategies

Childmind.org *How to Change Negative Thinking Patterns* https://childmind.org/article/how-to-change-negative-thinking-patterns

Coping Skills for Kids *Strategies for Calming Anxiety* https://coping-skillsforkids.com/calming-anxiety

Dr Karen Treisman *An Introduction to a Sensory, Soothing, Regulating, Calming, Grounding Box* https://www.youtube.com/watch?v=9XyxqWiqLk0

Mentalhealthcenterkids.com *Positive Self-Talk* https://mentalhealthcenterkids.com/blogs/articles/positive-self-talk

Dr Pooky Knightsmith *Anxiety Coping Statements* https://www.pookyknightsmith.com/download-coping-statements

Social Emotional Workshop *Teaching Kids to Tame Negative Thinking* https://www.socialemotionalworkshop.com/how-to-tame-negative-thinking

Podcasts

Dr Mine Conkbayir *The Vital Importance of Self-Regulation* https://mineconkbayir.co.uk/self-regulation-in-early-years-education

Dr Pooky Knightsmith *Negative Self-Talk* https://www.pookyknightsmith.com/video-negative-self-talk

Pooky Ponders *Co-Regulation Ideas* https://www.pookyknightsmith.com/podcast-co-regulation-ideas

SENDcast *Arousal and Self-Regulation* https://www.thesendcast.com/arousal-and-self-regulation

SENDcast *The What and Why of Compassionate Co-Regulation* https://www.thesendcast.com/the-what-and-why-of-compassionate-co-regulation

References

AnxietyCanada (2023) *Helpful Thinking* Available at: https://www.anxietycanada.com/articles/helpful-thinking [Accessed 17.5.23]

Beacon House (2019) *Brainstem Calmers* Available at: https://beaconhouse.org.uk/wp-content/uploads/2019/09/Brainstem-Calmer-Activities.pdf [Accessed 19.12.19]

Beacon House (2020) *Parenting a Child with a Sensitive Fight Response* Available at: https://beaconhouse.org.uk/wp-content/uploads/2020/12/Parenting-a-child-with-a-sensitive-fight-response.pdf [Accessed 12.10.23]

Bombèr, L. (2007) *Inside I'm Hurting – Practical Strategies for Supporting Children with Attachment Difficulties in Schools* Worth Publishing

Bombèr, L. (2020) *Know Me to Teach Me – Differentiated Discipline for Those Recovering from Adverse Childhood Experiences* Worth Publishing

Brukner, L. (2014) *The Kids' Guide to Staying Awesome and in Control – Simple Stuff to Help Children Regulate their Emotions and Senses* Jessica Kingsley

Collins-Donnelley, K. (2014) *Starving the Anxiety Gremlin: A Cognitive Behavioural Therapy Workbook on Anxiety Management for Young People* Jessica Kingsley

Conkbayir, M. (2023) *The Neuroscience of the Developing Child – Self-Regulation for Wellbeing and a Sustainable Future* Routledge

Eisen, A. & Engler, L. (2006) *Helping your Child Overcome Separation Anxiety or School Refusal: A Step-by-Step Guide for Parents* New Harbinger Publications

Fancourt, D., Perkins, R., Ascenso, S., Carvalho, L.A., Steptoe, A. & Williamon, A. (2016) *Effects of Group Drumming Interventions on Anxiety, Depression, Social Resilience and Inflammatory Immune Response among Mental Health Service Users* Available at: https://www.ncbi.nlm.nih.gov/pmc/articles/PMC4790847 [Accessed 15.7.23]

Hanratty, J. (2017) *Mindfulness in Schools: What's Next?* Available at: https://www.nationalelfservice.net/treatment/mindfulness/mindfulness-in-schools-what-next/ [Accessed 21.6.23]

He's-extraordinary.com (undated) *Positive Self-Talk for Kids – Teach Your Child to Say "I Can" Instead of "I Can't"* Available at: https://hes-extraordinary.com/positive-self-talk-for-kids#:~:text=Positive%20Self%2DTalk%20Statements,-Here%20are%20a&text=I%20am%20a%20work%2Din,normal%2C%20and%20this%20will%20pass [Accessed 17.5.23]

Hutt, R. (2019) *Feeling Better: CBT Workbook for Teens: Essential Skills and Activities to Help You Manage Moods, Boost Self-Esteem, and Conquer Anxiety* Althea Press

Jennings, S. (2023) *Managing Social Anxiety in Children and Young People – Practical Activities for Reducing Stress and Building Self-esteem* Routledge

Johnson, S. (2024) *All About SEMH: A Practical Guide for Secondary Teachers* Routledge

Knightsmith, P. (2022a) *Things I Got Wrong So You Don't Have To: 48 Lessons to Banish Burnout and Avoid Anxiety for Those Who Put Others First* Jessica Kingsley

Knightsmith, P. (2022b) *ANXIETY/ANGER – Using Slow-Low-Low to Calm Things Down* Available at: https://www.youtube.com/watch?v=x9Aqzln739o&t=6s [Accessed 22.3.23]

Knightsmith, P. (2023) *Using Transition Activities to Move Between Activities, Places or People* Available at: https://www.creativeeducation.co.uk/explore-our-podcast-pooky-ponders [Accessed 29 June 2023]

Knightsmith, P. (undated) *Simple Breathing Strategies* Available at: https://www.pookyknightsmith.com/wp-content/uploads/2022/11/Simple-Breathing-Strategies.pdf [Accessed 15.5.23]

Kranowitz, C. (2005) *The Out-of-Sync Child. Recognizing and Coping with Sensory Processing Disorder* Tarcher Perigee Books

Leicestershire County Council Early Years SEND Team (2023) *The Effectiveness of Puppet Play & Storytelling to Promote Children's Social and Emotional Development* Available at: https://resources.leicestershire.gov.uk/sites/resource/files/2023-03/Puppet-play.pdf [Accessed 19.5.23]

MacDonald, I. (2019) *Teen Substance Use, Mental Health and Body Image: Practical Strategies for Support* Jessica Kingsley

MacKenzie, H. (2015) *Self-regulation in Everyday Life: A How-to Guide for Parents* Wired Fox

McMillan, A. (2023) *Ange McMillan's Profile Page* (LinkedIn) [Accessed 29.6.23]

Minahan, J. (2018) *The Behavior Code Companion – Strategies, Tools and Interventions for Supporting Students with Anxiety-Related or Oppositional Behaviors* Harvard Education Press

Mind (2021) *Mindfulness* Available at: https://www.mind.org.uk/information-support/drugs-and-treatments/mindfulness/mindfulness-exercises-tips/#:~:text=Mindful%20moving%2C%20walking%20or%20running,the%20different%20smells%20around%20you [Accessed 21.6.23] © Mind. This information is published in full at mind.org.uk

Pathway2Success (2017) *How to Teach Positive Self Talk* Available at: https://www.thepathway2success.com/how-to-teach-positive-self-talk [Accessed 17.5.23]

Psychreg (2021) *Many Ways Performing Arts Improve Children's Mental Health* Available at: https://www.psychreg.org/performing-arts-mental-health/#:~:text=Studies%20have%20shown%20that%20singing,world%20and%20enjoy%20the%20activity [Accessed 21.6.23]

PTSDUK (undated) *PTSD in Children: Information for Teachers* Available at: https://www.ptsduk.org/ptsd-in-children-information-for-teachers [Accessed 29.6.23]

Siegel, D. & Payne Bryson, T. (2012) *The Whole Brain Child* Robinson

Siegel, D. & Payne Bryson, T. (2020) *The Power of Showing Up: How Parental Presence Shapes Who Our Kids Become and How Their Brains Get Wired* Scribe

Sunderland, M. (2015) *Conversations that Matter – Talking with Children and Teenagers in Ways that Help* Worth Publishing

Thynne, R (2022) *Behaviour Barriers and Beyond – Practical Strategies to Help All Pupils Thrive* Routledge

University of Lincoln (2022) *New Study Finds Dogs May Reduce Stress Levels in Children* Available at: https://news.lincoln.ac.uk/2022/06/17/new-study-finds-dogs-may-reduce-stress-levels-in-children [Accessed 24.8.23]

Wells, N. & Evans, G. (2003) Nearby Nature: A Buffer of Life Stress among Rural Children *Environment and Behavior* 35(3): 311–330 Available at: https://ltl.org.uk/wp-content/uploads/2019/02/nearby-nature.pdf [Accessed 21.6.23]

Willetts, L. & Creswell, C. (2007) *Overcoming Your Child's Shyness and Social Anxiety – A Self-Help Guide Using Cognitive Behavioural Techniques* Robinson

Zandt, F. & Barrett, S. (2021) *Creative Ways to Help Children Manage Anxiety: Ideas and Activities for Working Therapeutically with Worried Children and Their Families* Jessica Kingsley

Regulating and coping strategies checklist

STRATEGY		COMMENTS
Please also refer to Chapter 2		
Co-regulation and modelling		
Co-regulate, pre-teach and rehearse regulating strategies		
Model pre-taught coping strategies when a pupil is becoming dysregulated		
Model using a range of calming strategies in the classroom		
Use visual reminders		
Rehearse coping strategies regularly when calm and allow pupils to choose what works best for them		
A trusted relationship is essential		
Recognise dysregulation		
Notice and attune to emotions and spot early signs of dysregulation		
Teach pupils to spot physical signs of anxiety		
Help pupils to spot patterns and stressors		
Suggestions to support pupils to regulate		
Normalise using regulation and coping strategies by teaching them to the whole class		
Use visual reminders		

(Continued)

Continued

STRATEGY	COMMENTS
Breathing techniques	
Teach a range of breathing techniques	
Sensory tools	
Create regulating boxes or whole class regulation stations	
Explore using tools in ways that combine the senses	
Hold transitional objects	
Model calming strategies with the aim of pupils mirroring	
Focusing fiddle tools	
Explore a range of fiddle tools to help the pupil to focus	
Doodle pads, note-taking or annotating presentations can encourage movement and give a sense of purpose	
Grounding techniques	
Teach a range of grounding techniques	
Cross the midline	
Teach pupils a range of activities which cross the midline	
Positive self-talk	
Teach positive self-talk and how to recognise and change anxious or negative thought patterns	
Separate thoughts from facts	

(Continued)

Continued

STRATEGY	COMMENTS
Display positive thoughts creatively	
Model and rehearse using positive self-talk	
Mindfulness	
Engage in a range of mindfulness activities	
Movement and exercise	
Implement regular movement breaks	
Encourage regular exercise	
Use transition times to incorporate different movements	
Teach a range of 'in seat' movement activities	
Provide proprioceptive and vestibular input	
Provide jobs and errands to encourage movement	
Implement whole class movement breaks	
Calming and Alerting Strategies	
Be aware of activities which are calming and alerting and use appropriately	
Performing arts	
Repetition and rhythmic activities can be calming and grounding	
Playing instruments, singing and listening to music can be regulating	

(Continued)

Continued

STRATEGY	COMMENTS
Cognitive breaks	
Dancing and drama can help with the expression of emotions	
Implement regular cognitive breaks	
School pets	
Interacting with animals can reduce stress	
Exit strategies and safe spaces	
Provide access to safe spaces when pupils are feeling overwhelmed	
Explore alternative behaviours	
Teach a range of alternative behaviours regularly when the pupil is calm	
Provide visual reminders	
Use Emotion Coaching or empathy scripts	
Access the outdoor environment	
Provide a range of regulating activities outside	
Teaching and learning	
Teach regulating strategies regularly. Plan these into the curriculum and model using them	

5

Social anxiety

What is social anxiety?

Social anxiety is an intense fear of interacting with and being watched or judged by other people in certain situations (particularly crowds, group activities or performing in school or college). 'It's not a phobia of being in social situations, it's being terrified of how people are going to perceive you' (Bubrick, in Ehmke, 2023). It can often lead to avoidance of certain social activities or scenarios and a heightened sense of isolation. Feeling 'constantly negatively judged' by others 'can lead to feelings of inadequacy, inferiority, embarrassment, humiliation and depression' (Jennings, 2023, p.11).

Social anxiety is more than being shy or introverted, it is debilitating and 'paralizing' (Goodman in Consiglio, 2023). 'It's a fear that does not go away and affects everyday activities, self-confidence, relationships and work or school life. Many people occasionally worry about social situations, but someone with social anxiety feels overly worried before, during and after them' (NHS, 2023).

People with social anxiety often fear:

- Social situations, events and activities.
- Being scrutinised by others.
- Appearing nervous or anxious in front of others.
- Being judged, criticised, disliked, rejected or thought of negatively by others.
- Making a fool of themselves or being embarrassed, ridiculed or humiliated.
- Doing or saying anything that might be negatively construed.
- Talking to others, particularly strangers, or in a group situation.

DOI: 10.4324/9781003433231-6

- Offending others by their interactions.
- Making mistakes or failing.

Those with social anxiety often perceive themselves negatively, have low self-esteem and seek to be approved of and considered perfect by others, due to an intense fear of rejection (see rejection sensitivity p.114). They will often spend excessive amounts of time preparing what to say in advance of conversations, over-analysing interactions afterwards and criticising themselves for things they should have said and done differently. They often reflect on and repeatedly replay key aspects of conversations, concluding that people must dislike them because of what they said, how they looked, their body language or generally how they came across.

Some pupils with social anxiety may struggle to recognise the difference between *laughing with* them and *laughing at* them, regularly interpreting laughter as *laughing at* them, which further compounds the anxiety. Havranek et al. (2017) draw attention to the similarities between Gelotophobia (the fear of being laughed at) and Social Anxiety Disorder and suggest it as a symptom characteristic for diagnosis.

People with social anxiety often develop avoidance strategies as a coping mechanism for anxiety. They often lack resilience and 'are more likely to think that they won't be able to cope with a situation and therefore to come up with solutions that allow them to escape the situation as quickly as possible' (Willetts & Creswell, 2007, p.136).

Most people have experienced some form of social anxiety at some point in their lives (starting a new school, performing in assembly or presenting in front of a group). Tolerable levels of anxiety can be positive in supporting people to step outside their comfort zone, with the adrenaline almost providing a *superpower* (to perform on stage or present in front of a large group, for example) which becomes liberating and empowering, encouraging repeat performances, rather than future avoidance. However, when the anxiety starts impacting negatively, they may need more comprehensive support.

'Social anxiety becomes a problem when it becomes quite distressing and starts getting in the way of your ability to function and enjoy life' (AnxietyCanada, undated). If children are not given appropriate and effective support, social anxiety can impact negatively on attainment in school, mental wellbeing, behaviour, relationships and day-to-day engagement in social activities such as avoidance of social activities, clubs, events and participation in lessons, 'for example, not being able to put their hand up in class or talk in a large group of peers' (Creswell & Willetts, 2019, p.15). 'Humans are hard-wired to connect with each other . . . But social anxiety gets in the way of people living the lives they want to live' (Goodman in Consiglio, 2023).

Diagnosis

In severe cases, where social anxiety is having a prolonged negative impact on wellbeing, relationships, attainment and daily life, a diagnosis of Social Anxiety Disorder (SAD), previously known as Social Phobia, may be given. The *DSM-5* (American Psychiatric Association, 2013) criteria for Social Anxiety Disorder include:

- Persistent, intense fear of, or anxiety about, one or more specific social situations (expecting to be judged negatively, embarrassed or humiliated).
- Avoidance of, or intense fear around, participating in anxiety-producing social situations.
- Excessive anxiety (seemingly out of proportion to the situation).
- Anxiety or distress that interferes with daily living and is not better explained by a medical condition or other factors.
- The symptoms are long term and severe (they must persist for six months or more).

Research has shown that Social Anxiety Disorder is the third most common mental health condition in the world (National Collaborating Centre for Mental Health (UK), 2013) and is the most common type of anxiety disorder in teenagers (Bailey, 2022). Social anxiety can occur at any time, particularly during childhood, however, the onset is most likely during adolescence.

Comorbidity

Social anxiety has high comorbidity with and can co-exist with other conditions, such as Attention Deficit Hyperactivity Disorder (ADHD), Autism, Obsessive-Compulsive Disorder (OCD), eating disorders, substance disorders, Oppositional Defiant Disorder (ODD) and depression. It is particularly prevalent alongside other anxiety disorders, such as Separation Anxiety (see p.221), school-based anxiety (see p.175) and Generalised Anxiety Disorder (GAD) (see p.7).

Social anxiety and rejection sensitivity

Rejection sensitivity and Rejection Sensitive Dysphoria (RSD) present as overwhelming emotional pain and intense emotional responses (usually anger or anxiety), which are difficult to regulate, in response to (perceived or real) criticism, failure and rejection. It often leads to social withdrawal from situations where the person anticipates they may meet with scrutiny, failure, criticism or rejection. In the classroom, pupils may seemingly overreact to (even constructive) criticism or feedback or making a small mistake in their learning and thus experience heightened emotions, pain and shame. 'If you've got Rejection Sensitive Dysphoria, you're receiving that criticism more like a hammer blow than a piece of friendly advice' (Currigan & Shackleton, 2023).

RSD is prevalent in neuro-diverse pupils, particularly those with ADHD and Pathological Demand Avoidance (PDA). The fear of rejection may be at the heart of social anxiety (DiConsiglio, 2023), so people who are socially anxious can have high levels of rejection sensitivity as they anticipate rejection, 'as they anxiously look for signs that someone doesn't want to be with them, they often behave in ways that push other people away. This behavior creates a painful cycle that can be difficult to break' (Morin, 2023). 'People with social anxiety disorder intertwine that rejection with their views of themselves . . . For some people, rejection is so painful, so traumatic, that they systematically avoid social interactions throughout their life' (Goodman in Consiglio, 2023).

Personal case study:

A few years ago, a friend commented on the way I was slicing a pizza. I remember feeling overwhelmingly criticised to the point that I needed to justify myself in how I was cutting it. I felt that he couldn't possibly like me anymore because I didn't cut the pizza in the way he would have done. I then couldn't cut it anymore, making him take over as I would only get it more wrong.

Moreover, I remember his response to my reaction, whereby he seemed quite shocked that I had taken such offence over a seemingly (to him) mild and amusing comment. We later made a joke of it, with me saying I didn't take criticism well and he still teases me about it today.

I think naming my responses to criticism as rejection sensitivity and knowing that I am not alone in these feelings and responses has helped me to be more reflective in the moment. I have been able to label these feelings as they arise, as 'oh that's just my rejection sensitivity' which has enabled me to react more moderately and to understand my emotions around perceived criticism.

However, this was about five years ago, and it still sticks firmly in my mind. Each time I slice a pizza, it re-triggers the (irrational) feelings of rejection. Even now, whilst writing about it my hands are shaking and I feel almost as nauseous and shamed as I did then.

Reflection opportunities:

- Could having an awareness and understanding of rejection sensitivity help in our interactions with pupils?
- How could we use this knowledge to support socially anxious pupils?

Perfectionism

People with social anxiety and rejection sensitivity often feel severe anxiety and emotional pain around (real or perceived) disapproval or criticism. This leads to emotional dysregulation and triggers the threat response. It can present as intense perfectionism, people-pleasing and over-compliance in order to avoid potential disapproval. People with social anxiety tend to seek reassurance and approval from others and aim to be perceived as perfect by those around them. Saline (2023) describes perfectionism as 'an unhealthy obsession with flawlessness that causes people to set unattainable personal standards, compare themselves to others, and never quite feel "good enough." It can make criticism, even constructive, cut like a knife.'

Perfectionism can lead to a downward spiral of avoidance and 'acts as a maladaptive, inefficient coping mechanism for managing anxiety' (Saline 2023). Perfectionists tend to be exceptionally risk-averse, avoiding tasks or activities where there is a risk of failure due to Atelophobia (the intense fear of imperfection and of making mistakes). Perfectionists and those with social anxiety (often inadvertently or unconsciously) aim to avoid unfamiliar situations, potential disappointment, embarrassment, disapproval and any activity where they may possibly not succeed.

Social anxiety in school

Pupils with social anxiety are usually quiet, avoid drawing attention to themselves and try desperately hard to fit in. They often have a low sense of self-esteem and feel socially inadequate. They may aim to avoid school or key elements of school life, such as social interactions (including break times and eating, drinking or speaking in front of their peers), avoid contributing to performance-based activities where they feel observed and potentially judged by others (such as speaking, answering a question or asking for help in front of the class) due to feeling extremely self-conscious and anxious. 'The individual is desperately trying to create an environment that is constant. So, by avoiding certain situations, the child or young person doesn't need to take any steps into the unknown' (Jennings, 2023, p.14). Through such avoidance, they temporarily feel relief and a sense of control, however, the avoidance feeds the anxiety cycle in the longer term as the pupil never gets to test (and therefore disprove) their negative thinking patterns.

School, being a social place, with plenty of opportunities to meet and interact with new people, can be a huge trigger for children who have social anxiety. Many social situations within the school day become terrifying for pupils. Pupils who have social anxiety usually have a negative view of themselves and are very self-critical. They have reduced confidence, not only in social activities at school and interacting in groups and pairs but also in learning tasks and exams or tests as the anxiety inhibits taking risks in learning and exploring. They may avoid or withdraw from unfamiliar situations and groups of people and struggle with changes to routine. Many pupils who are socially anxious 'find it hard to ask for help, and some may have problems concentrating due to their physical symptoms of anxiety' (Willetts & Creswell, 2007, p.18). Social anxiety can, therefore, impact negatively on a pupil's academic achievements.

Presentations of social anxiety

Intervening early to provide support is usually the most impactful way for adults to support pupils. It is important for school staff to understand and recognise how social anxiety may present for a pupil, physically and behaviourally. By understanding the communicative function of the behaviours, they will be better placed to provide support, empathy and compassion, rather than to reprimand for behaviour presentations that are being driven by fear and anxiety. Socially anxious pupils may present in school as 'quiet and withdrawn' or 'freeze when they are anxious. Some will also cry. They may mutter, avoid eye contact or mumble' (Willetts & Creswell, 2007, p.13). When a child is seeming defiant or refusing to engage in a task or activity or becoming verbally or physically aggressive, it is likely to be driven by intense anxiety. Other pupils may 'disguise fear with aggression' (Jennings, 2023 p.63). When staff begin to reframe thinking from *how can I make this child behave appropriately?* towards *how can I help alleviate this child's anxiety?* the behaviour will naturally improve, due to the reduced stress.

As well as some of the more general presentations of anxiety (see pp.9–12) some of the symptoms which may be indicative of social anxiety include:

Physical symptoms	
■ Physical sensations of anxiety such as butterflies in the stomach, nausea, stomach ache, headache, dizziness before and during social times ■ Nail and hangnail biting ■ Choking (Willetts & Creswell, 2007, p.12) ■ Mind going blank while in conversation or stumbling over words ■ Appearing to freeze in social situations	■ Appearing socially 'awkward' ■ Blushing ■ Shaking, trembling or shivering (often aiming to disguise this by holding hands behind their back or sitting on them) ■ Sweating ■ Shaking voice ■ Panic – racing heart rate, shallow breathing
Behavioural symptoms	
■ Social mimicry and becoming a 'social chameleon' (consciously or unconsciously moulding the self to fit in with the social group – changing the way they speak, dress, interact and their mannerisms) ■ Masking (see pp.13–14) ■ Behaviours to draw attention away from themselves (never putting hand up or asking for help, avoiding eye contact, sitting at the back, avoiding being the centre of attention)	■ Hair over face or covering their mouth with their hand whilst talking ■ Making lots of jokes, being the 'class clown', being loud or appearing over-confident ■ Distancing self from others ■ Nervous laughter ■ Providing short, terse answers when directly questioned ■ Hiding, running away or absence at key trigger times ■ Patterns of missing certain lessons or activities (PE, group reading, peer presentations, drama performances, sports, school trips, activity days, sports days, class assemblies, oral tests)

(Continued)

Continued

▪ Pre-occupation with their appearance due to the need to fit in with others – constantly checking that they look presentable (checking their reflection, touching face, smoothing their hair, pulling at clothing) ▪ Agreeing with others, not expressing their own opinions and conforming to all requests ▪ Perfectionism, people-pleasing and extreme compliance ▪ Seeking reassurance and approval from others ▪ Seeking proximity to or being dependent on a friend or trusted adult ▪ Fidgeting ▪ Avoidance of or withdrawal from certain social situations ▪ Refusal or defiance ▪ Physical or verbal aggression ('however, this is relatively rare as the fear of what other people think usually stops them from doing so' Willetts & Creswell, 2007, p.13) ▪ Using predictable scripts ▪ Not listening or losing track of the conversation as they are preoccupied with how they are coming across or how they are going to respond	▪ Or conversely, excelling in performance-based tasks such as acting, presenting or sports but struggling in small groups or 1:1 conversation ▪ Pre-planning and over-analysing interactions ▪ Struggling to regulate emotions – may cry a lot or present as angry ▪ Avoiding eating and drinking in front of others ▪ Avoiding going to the toilet, or asking to go/avoids drinking or eating for fear of needing to go ▪ Hypervigilance – seeking and planning escape ▪ Reluctance to speak on the telephone or on a conference call as well as in face-to-face situations ▪ Intense emotional reactions to criticism, rejection and mistakes (see Rejection sensitivity p.114)
Internal symptoms/feelings	
▪ Feeling self-conscious in front of others ▪ Negative thoughts about self or others and a fear of disappointing others ▪ Increased or excessive worry around social situations – before, during and after ▪ Worry for prolonged periods of time prior to an anxiety-inducing situation	▪ Feeling lonely, alone and misunderstood ▪ 'Predicting the worst about the social situation and viewing it as having gone badly afterwards regardless of the facts' (Collins-Donnelley, 2013, p.30) ▪ Separation anxiety

The fear of displaying some of these anxiety features in social situations can further exacerbate the social anxiety leading to increased patterns of avoidance.

Risk factors, triggers and maintaining factors

It is important that teachers know what to look out for, alongside the possible risk factors and triggers as well as those 'maintaining factors' which may be contributing to sustaining the anxiety. Early detection and intervention can help to interrupt pupils' downward trajectory and prevent the cycle of avoidance.

Possible risk factors

- Negative self-image and low self-esteem.
- Struggling to cope with change.
- Struggling to regulate their emotions.
- Heightened anxiety over transitions, particularly moving to a different class or school and concerns about making and maintaining friendships and not being in the same class as friends.
- Separation Anxiety (see Chapter 10), school-based anxiety (see Chapter 9) and other anxieties or phobias.
- Propensity to worry excessively.
- Sensory sensitivities and feelings of being overwhelmed.
- Rejection sensitivity (see p.114), hypervigilance towards rejection, fear of being reprimanded, criticised or making mistakes.
- Perfectionism.
- Family history of social anxiety.

Possible triggers

- Crowded and busy or noisy environments.
- Going to new places and meeting new people such as moving school or class.
- Unstructured times such as lunch times and break times.
- Performance-based activities: drama, PE, class productions, reading or speaking aloud.
- Returning to school after a prolonged absence.
- Going into a classroom with others, particularly walking in late.
- Putting hand up/asking for help.
- Speaking in front of others.

- Groupwork and team work, including the fear of not being chosen or not finding a partner.
- Negative social experiences such as bullying and friendship difficulties.
- Peer pressure.

The effects of the recent global pandemic have also impacted social anxiety for many individuals and families. Children and adults needed to stay at home as a necessary safety measure, with leaving the house and socialising being dangerous and social isolation becoming the norm. Increased feelings of safety by being in the home helped to feed avoidance for those with social anxiety, as they did not need to interact socially, and many are still struggling to reintegrate.

Possible maintaining factors

Maintaining factors are those which may be sustaining or reinforcing the anxiety for the pupil and may need to be addressed and changed in order to begin to provide support. When a person engages in social avoidance or partial avoidance techniques (consciously or unconsciously) they are reinforcing to themselves the idea that social situations are a threat and therefore feeding the avoidance. For example, a child may have negative thoughts about a social situation, which triggers certain symptoms (see pp.9–12); by avoiding the situation, they feel reassured and less anxious in the short term, however, this feeds the avoidance and anxiety cycle, making a similar situation even more difficult to face in the future. 'When we are anxious, we look out for things that confirm our anxious thoughts and we discount anything we see that is contrary to them. This way of thinking becomes a habit and keeps our anxiety going' (Willetts & Creswell, 2007, p.35).

Possible maintaining factors include:

- Avoidance of certain social situations, events or groups.
- Partial avoidance, engaging in and repeating safety-seeking behaviours: those behaviours which provide temporary relief from the anxiety-provoking situations (sitting at the back of the room to avoid drawing attention to themselves, speaking very quickly or quietly, responding with minimal information when asked a direct question, avoiding eye contact, volunteering and engaging in roles which avoid social interaction (such as tidying up the coats or books, putting out the chairs, becoming stage crew to avoid performing, scribing in a group to avoid talking).

- Bullying or teasing and concerns over friendships.
- Over-protective peers or family members.
- Negative comments and labelling from peers or adults.
- Modelling of anxious behaviours by peers or adults: 'If people around your child show signs of anxiety and avoid situations that make them anxious, your child (who will be on the look out for information that confirms their anxious thoughts) is likely to learn that the particular situation presents a threat and the best way to respond is by avoiding it' (Willetts & Creswell 2007, p.40).
- Low sense of self-esteem and self-worth.
- Patterns of negative thinking (see pp.47–9) and comparison to others.
- A negative view of the world, being judgemental of people around them and having 'a greater proportion of negative feelings about other people than positive ones' (Jennings, 2023, p.60).
- Misinterpreting the behaviours and perceptions of others.
- Lack of understanding and support from others.
- Feeling that everyone else is better and more interesting.
- Masking and social mimicry (see pp.13–14), meaning signs and symptoms can be missed: 'parents and teachers may not notice that anything is wrong, especially since kids are often ashamed to admit how anxious they are about things that other people don't seem to get upset about' (Ehmke, 2023).
- Participating only because the fear of reprimand is greater than the anxiety, for example, being told to perform otherwise they will be given a detention or threatened with calling home.

'If your child does not get the opportunities to experience social situations, despite their shyness and social anxiety, they will not learn that in fact the situation was not as bad as they thought it would be and that they managed to cope' (Willetts & Creswell, 2007, p.40).

Case study:

Tilly is 15 and is experiencing a significant amount of stress about school, going into Y11 and her up-coming exams. She is spending more and more time at home and withdrawing from her friends. She struggles to identify enjoyable moments, focusing on the negative much of the time.

Her anxiety seemed to heighten in Y7, when she moved to a new school. Tilly has told her caregivers that she doesn't like meeting new people, and worries what people will think of her. When she feels embarrassed (when asked to answer a question or talk about herself) she blushes and her hands shake. She thinks people will think she is weird, so she tries to avoid these situations.

Tilly is a great singer and loves drama and is often in the school productions, saying she feels that 'she doesn't have to be herself'. She often comes across as loud and confident in the playground and classroom. Friends describe her as 'funny' and she is often in trouble for messing around in class and distracting others. Teachers describe her as 'defiant' and 'oppositional'. She seldom completes her learning tasks and never asks questions or contributes to class discussions.

Reflection opportunities:

- What are the signs that Tilly may have social anxiety?
- Why may these signs be missed in school?
- What are some of the factors that may be maintaining Tilly's anxiety?

Chapter take-aways

- Someone with social anxiety feels intense worry before, during and after social interactions.
- A person with social anxiety usually has low self-esteem and fears rejection, often striving to feel liked and tends to be a perfectionist.
- Key factors can contribute towards and maintain social anxiety, and early intervention is key in providing support.

Further signposting

Books

Managing Social Anxiety in Children and Young People – Practical Activities for Reducing Stress and Building Self-esteem by Sue Jennings
Overcoming Your Child's Shyness and Social Anxiety by Lucy Willetts & Cathy Creswell

Websites

ADDitude *What is Social Anxiety Disorder?* https://www.additudemag.com/slideshows/social-anxiety-disorder-in-adults-with-adhd

Child Mind Institute *What is Social Anxiety?* https://childmind.org/article/what-is-social-anxiety

Podcasts

Beacon School Support *Rejection Sensitive Dysphoria and ADHD: What Teachers and Parents Need To Know* https://beaconschoolsupport.co.uk/podcast/rejection-sensitive-dysphoria-and-adhd-what-teachers-and-parents-need-to-know

References

American Psychiatric Association (2013) *Diagnostic and Statistical Manual of Mental Disorders: DSM-5* American Psychiatric Publishing

AnxietyCanada (undated) *Self-Help Strategies for Social Anxiety* Available at: https://www.anxietycanada.com/sites/default/files/adult_hmsocial.pdf [Accessed 23.5.23]

Bailey, E. (2022) *You're Not Shy or Stuck Up. You Have Social Anxiety Disorder* Available at: https://www.additudemag.com/slideshows/social-anxiety-disorder-in-adults-with-adhd [Accessed 23.7.23]

Collins-Donnelley, K. (2014) *Starving the Anxiety Gremlin: A Cognitive Behavioural Therapy Workbook on Anxiety Management for Young People* Jessica Kingsley

Creswell, C. & Willetts, L. (2019) *Helping Your Child with Fears and Worries* Robinson

Currigan, S. & Shackleton, E. (2023) *Rejection Sensitive Dysphoria and ADHD: What Teachers and Parents Need to Know* Podcast Available at: https://beaconschoolsupport.co.uk/podcast/rejection-sensitive-dysphoria-and-adhd-what-teachers-and-parents-need-to-know

DiConsiglio, J. 2023, *Fear of Failing: The Secrets Behind Social Anxiety* Available at: https://neurosciencenews.com/rejection-fear-social-anxiety-22824/#:~:text=At%20its%20core%2C%20Goodman%20said,with%20their%20views%20of%20themselves [Accessed 16.7.23]

Ehmke, R. (2023) *What Is Social Anxiety? When Fear of How You Appear Gets in the Way of Functioning* Available at: https://childmind.org/article/what-is-social-anxiety [Accessed 16.7.23]

Havranek, M., Volkart, F., Bolliger, B., Roos, S., Buschner, M., Mansour. R., Chmielewski, T., Gaudlitz, K., Hättenschwiler, J., Seifritz, E. & Ruch, W. (2017) *The Fear of Being Laughed at as Additional Diagnostic Criterion in Social Anxiety Disorder and Avoidant Personality Disorder?* PloS one, 12(11), e0188024 Available at: https://doi.org/10.1371/journal.pone.0188024 [Accessed 5.2.24]

Jennings, S. (2023) *Managing Social Anxiety in Children and Young People – Practical Activities for Reducing Stress and Building Self-Esteem* Routledge

Morin, A. (2023) *Understanding Rejection Sensitivity and How It Can Affect You* Available at: https://www.verywellmind.com/what-is-rejection-sensitivity-4682652 [Accessed 30.6.23]

NHS (2023) *Social Anxiety (Social Phobia)* Available at: https://www.nhs.uk/mental-health/conditions/social-anxiety [Accessed 13.10.23]

National Collaborating Centre for Mental Health (UK) (2013) *Social Anxiety Disorder: Recognition, Assessment and Treatment* British Psychological Society (UK) (NICE Clinical Guidelines, No. 159) Available at: https://www.ncbi.nlm.nih.gov/books/NBK327674

Saline, S. (2023) *When Perfectionism Stems from ADHD: Challenging the Fallacy of "Not Good Enough"* Available at: https://www.additudemag.com/perfectionism-adhd-not-good-enough-anxiety [Accessed 7.7.23]

Willetts, L. & Creswell, C. (2007) *Overcoming Your Child's Shyness and Social Anxiety – A Self-Help Guide Using Cognitive Behavioural Techniques* Robinson

6
Alleviating social anxiety

Relationships and collaboration

Social anxiety is strongly linked to school-based anxiety, since socially anxious pupils 'often have problems attending school because they expect other children or teachers to think badly of them and so understandably try to avoid it' (Willetts & Creswell, 2007, p.209), consequently, the suggestions in Chapter 10 of this book are also relevant.

It is important to meet social anxiety with acceptance and provide support without judgement (see PACE p.26).

- Ensure a small team of key workers take the time to develop a trusting relationship with the pupil, to check in with them regularly and to support them through those times of the day which they have identified as particularly stressful (such as arriving at school, going into a lesson after break time, starting a learning task).
- Work in collaboration with other staff and caregivers: 'The more people around your child who are following the same principles, the easier it will be for your child to overcome their social fears' (Willetts & Creswell, 2007, p.61).
- 'By taking a nurturing approach, we can establish a feeling of nurture and safety within which the social anxiety can be addressed' (Jennings, 2023, p.13). A nurturing approach benefits all pupils, not only those with anxiety. It supports pupils to build positive and trusting relationships with adults, decreases anxiety, boosts self-esteem, can improve behaviour and resilience and supports mental health and wellbeing.

DOI: 10.4324/9781003433231-7

■ Support pupils to make and maintain peer relationships. Children with social anxiety often misinterpret the perspective and intentions of others, being inclined to assume that others are judging them negatively. Using Bombèr's (2011, p.186) 'Hand of Options' or comic strip conversations (Gray, 1994) can help pupils to begin to see things from the perspective of others and learn that there are multifarious ways of looking at a situation. They can also help pupils to recognise and help to explore different explanations for perceived rejections or criticism.

■ Gently teach, but never insist on, eye contact.

Understand and recognise anxiety

■ The first step to overcoming social anxiety is to help the pupil to recognise and understand their social anxiety – what it is, what triggers it and how it presents for the individual (physically, behaviourally and physiologically). Support can then be put in place to help them to cope and manage these feelings. Noticing and naming the anxiety helps build a vocabulary to define, explain and increase understanding – *I wonder if you don't put your hand up because you are worried what people will think if you get the answer wrong? You might feel that people would laugh at you or think negatively of you?*

  AnxietyCanada (undated) recommend that individuals 'know your social anxiety'. Adults can support pupils to step back and reflect on what they find difficult, explore situations which cause them heightened anxiety and help them to understand how this anxiety may present for them personally (see pp.11–12). Pupils will need support to help them to notice their presentations and triggers (see body mapping p.82) 'It is a lot easier to manage your anxiety when you have a better understanding of it!' (AnxietyCanada undated).

■ Avoid promising or reassuring that their anxieties will not arise, as this is not something that can be controlled. Instead, look at the likelihood of their fears coming true and try and rationalise the thoughts. Aim to reframe negative thoughts (see p.47) and begin to introduce more positive scenarios. For example, if a pupil avoids putting their hand up in class for fear of getting the answer wrong and being ridiculed, a response could be, *Well, it is possible that you will be laughed at and ridiculed, but is that really likely? If you said a joke or something funny they may laugh with you, but if you have a go at answering the question and get it wrong, do you think they would laugh at you? Do you laugh when other people have a go and get it wrong? No, I don't either. What happens when someone answers a question and doesn't quite get it right in this class?*

Teaching and learning

- Teach pupils when and how to ask for help – putting a hand up and admitting to needing support can induce or increase anxiety, leading to avoidance or distraction activities. By teaching pupils an alternative means of asking for help, many anxieties are reduced. This could be using a 'help' card or other pre-arranged signal, such as a piece of Lego® on the corner of the desk.
- Plan group and partner work carefully as this can increase anxiety for many pupils. Choose groups and partners in advance or allow students to work in friendship groups for group-based assignments. Avoid pupils having to choose their own groups or partners as it increases social anxiety and fear of social rejection for many. Provide clear expectations and choices around the roles that individuals need to take within groups (e.g. scribe, lead, reporter). Adjust expectations for key pupils and provide support, where necessary. For those who are struggling, decide whether the pupil needs to work in a pair or group or would be better off with a key adult or working more independently initially.
- Avoid increasing anxiety around speaking and let highly anxious pupils know that they will not be 'cold called' upon to answer a question. Build up confidence by 'warm calling'; preparing all pupils by providing advanced warning of questions or try to let students know that they will be asked a question, allowing them time to plan and rehearse a response (and present it non-verbally, if necessary). Provide the opportunity to opt out of sharing verbally in front of the class by allowing them to hold up the whiteboard or designating a 'reporter' to read their ideas or let them 'phone a friend'.

Case study:

Mrs H was aware of the social anxiety of several of her students. She regularly used to ask a student to give a pre-rehearsed answer, although the students didn't realise that was what was happening. Mrs H would have gone around the room, checking understanding. For feedback, she would then ask a student, with whom she had just discussed or checked a point, to answer a question about that point, meaning they had unknowingly just prepared a correct answer, building their self-esteem, increasing the chance that they would offer to contribute next time.

Case study:

Lottie, a quiet pupil in Y7, who was never in trouble at school, was so terrified of the teacher drawing out her 'lollipop stick' (to be plucked out at random for the pupil to then answer a question in front of the whole class) that she crept into the classroom at lunchtime and threw hers into the bin, so she would never be chosen to speak in front of her peers.

- Trusted friends or buddy systems can often be supportive.
- Be aware that presenting or performing to the class can heighten anxiety and be prepared to make adjustments; provide support, frameworks and rehearsals in advance and encourage pupils to participate in a way in which they feel comfortable and able. Implement step-by-step approaches (see p.132) to help pupils to gradually step outside their comfort zone, while feeling safe and supported rather than overwhelmed.
- Boost self-esteem in other (non-social) areas by providing jobs and responsibilities which require minimal social interaction initially, such as turning on the computers, stacking the chairs, setting up the visual timetable.
- Gradually encourage pupils to take opportunities to step out their comfort zone in other areas. Promote interest and participation

in clubs and activities to boost self-esteem. Initially try activities which are less social in nature, such as climbing, running, Yoga, crochet, puzzles, playing an instrument. It might be possible to slowly build up to participating alongside others – having a shared interest may generate natural conversation starters. Build up to paired activities, such as tennis, boxing, chess.

Personal case study:

I have always had social anxiety and struggled in social situations, feeling like I don't fit in and worrying that people won't like me and I am going to say or do something ridiculous. As I have matured, it has got easier, but I still often feel 'socially awkward'. My rejection sensitivity and perfectionism means that making mistakes feels disastrous.

I am not a natural dancer (by any stretch of the imagination). However, I wanted to keep fit. Several years ago, I went to a local Zumba fitness session with a friend. I was terrified and was hugely out of my comfort zone. I stayed at the back with my friend. The friend stopped going after a while, however, I went back regularly and gradually got to know a few more faces. Through the (fabulous) instructor and others making mistakes and smiling and laughing at themselves, I actually learnt to laugh at myself (rather than quietly dying inside) when I made a mistake (which happens often). I am not going to be on the stage any time soon, but I can now smile while I dance and sometimes my arms and legs even do what I ask them. I dance in the second row (same place, every week, let's not go too far out of the comfort zone), but I have, at times, been in the front row (with a friend at my side). (I haven't progressed to 'whooping' yet, but I am working on it – actually, no, that's a lie, I am never going to be a 'whooper', but that is OK.) I go, I enjoy it and I have fun with a great group of people who I am now lucky enough to call my friends.

What helped me?

- Initial courage to step out of my comfort zone.
- Determination and not giving up when I made a mistake or felt awkward.

- An amazing instructor (who is now also a good friend).
- A group of lovely people, who put me at ease and modelled that making mistakes was normal and OK.
- Realising that each time it gets a bit easier to go to the session and it is now fun.

Making mistakes

Fear of failure, making mistakes and perceived criticism can be a huge barrier to learning and engagement for many socially anxious pupils and perfectionists, often leading to task avoidance or withdrawal (see Rejection Sensitivity p.114).

- 'We provide the children with modelling on how to handle mistakes through our choice of response' (Bombèr, 2007, p.73). Adults need to model making and learning from mistakes as well as how to receive feedback constructively and positively. 'Mistakes are precious gifts that should be shared and learned from' (Knightsmith, 2022, p.35). It is helpful for adults to acknowledge when they make a mistake, indicating what they are going to do to repair the situation, such as apologising when they get something wrong and showing how to put it right, being honest when they don't know something but demonstrating the skills needed to move on and find out (rather than avoiding or giving up).
- Aim to build a school culture around the idea of mistakes as gifts, using real examples. It can be interesting (and enlightening) to research and explore inventions which came from mistakes, such as the implantable pacemaker, the slinky and Play Doh. 'While developing his vacuum, [Dyson] went through 5,126 failed prototypes (yes, he counted), exhausting his savings in the process. Like Thomas Edison, who had more than 10,000 failed experiments before he discovered how to get the bulb to glow, Dyson never interpreted his failed experiments as failures. Instead he saw them as yet one more way not to succeed' (Warrell, 2020).
- Occasionally provide some open-ended tasks which do not have correct and incorrect answers.
- For pupils who struggle with learning tasks, find it difficult to make mistakes and put excess pressure on themselves to do well, Hutt (2019, p.92) suggests creating a pie chart to show that grades

are only one part of the whole person and everyone is made up of lots of different parts. The grades in school do not determine who pupils are as a person. A vocational profile can also be useful in helping pupils to hone in on their strengths, interests and the skills needed for them to achieve their goals.

■ Offer visual supports such as phonics or vocabulary mats, story maps and grammar checklists. Help pupils to get started on a task by providing sentence starters, pictures or real objects and events or role play to help generate ideas.

■ Alleviate anxieties over extended writing tasks by offering alternative ways of recording (at times) such as typing, creating posters, taking photographs or writing bullet points or captions, writing in speech bubbles or provide a scribe or talk to text software.

■ Careful and considered use of language by all adults in school is critical. Positive reframing of suggestions, demands, instructions and feedback can decrease anxiety for all pupils. Currigan and Shackleton (2022) recommend 'setting very clear expectations', 'providing accommodations and being flexible . . . doing whatever we can to build self-esteem and self-worth, and really taking the time to think carefully before we speak'. Elley with Morewood (2022, p.90) advise that adults 'check that your words don't judge an attempt that hasn't been successful' by using what they refer to as a 'gentler approach', suggesting phrases such as 'I can see why you tried it that way', 'yes that would have been my first thought too . . .' and 'that was a great idea, can you see why it didn't quite work out?'

■ Provide pencils or erasable pens, spare work sheets, laptops and whiteboards, so it is easy to rectify when a mistake has been made, until pupils are able to tolerate making an error with less anxiety and distress.

■ Give praise for effort, engagement, attitude, perseverance and 'having a go' rather than for correct answers or 'neat handwriting'.

■ If pupils find it difficult to accept feedback or constructive criticism, initially provide anonymised work for them to 'correct' or mark (including common misconceptions and mistakes which the pupil may need to focus on). Model receiving feedback and how this can support further learning.

■ By implementing strategies to alleviate anxiety throughout the whole day, pupils become less anxious in all situations. 'What does help [rejection sensitivity] is reducing how much stress the child experiences in the classroom. Because the more stress chemicals you've got in your body, the more sensitive you are to feeling under attack' (Currigan & 'Shackleton, 2022).

■ Redirect pupils in a private or less public way, such as by having a quiet word or writing on a sticky note.
■ Gradually help pupils to tolerate making mistakes, whilst feeling a huge amount of positivity and success.

Case study:

Millie was hard-working and always strove for perfection. In her ballet exam, she received 86 per cent (a distinction). After Millie received her grade and feedback, she left the room, totally dejected. On seeing her face, her mum assumed that she hadn't passed the exam and gave her a hug. Millie was concentrating on the 14 per cent which she had missed out on. She kept asking what she had done wrong and how she could improve.

Her mum and dad sat down with her and talked about grade boundaries. They explored the grade boundaries for a distinction, telling her that anything in that boundary was the best mark. They looked at firsts and 2:1s at university and grade percentages for levels 7, 8 and 9 at school. Gradually, Millie began to realise that people could do well and succeed but didn't need to be (and couldn't be) perfect.

Reflection opportunities:

■ How could talking about grade boundaries help Millie overcome her need for perfection?
■ How may this lower some of her anxieties?

Step-by-step approaches (see also p.53)

Each pupil is an individual and will need to work at their own pace. 'In order to better manage social anxiety, it is essential for you to not compare yourself to others and to focus on yourself in your own unique and individual journey' (Jolanta, 2023).

'By learning to relax, you can "turn down the volume" on the physical symptoms of anxiety, which can make it a little easier to face social situations' (AnxietyCanada, undated). Pupils need to be helped to begin to face and overcome their fears because 'avoidance keeps social fears going' (Willetts & Creswell, 2007, pp.95 and 134) and to increasingly step out of their comfort zone in a way that is gradual and supported, alongside pre-taught coping strategies. 'To address social anxiety effectively, you must set a goal that's reasonable and within reach — and be willing to experience some discomfort along the way' (Saline, 2022).

■ Work collaboratively to establish the pupil's personal triggers and find out exactly what it is about the social situation that is causing the anxiety (such as break times, clubs, speaking or presenting in front of the class, performing in drama, reading aloud, saying hello to the teacher or a peer, asking someone to play with them).
■ Make plans with the pupil and, where possible, in collaboration with caregivers and other key adults. The pupil needs to feel the plan is being created 'with' them rather than 'for' them. Provide choices and help them feel a sense of control and of being included and heard. Anxiety can spiral if a person feels out of control.
■ Choose one particular social situation to focus on initially. Have a specific, achievable and measurable goal to work towards, then break this down into smaller, more manageable steps, starting where the pupil feels safe and comfortable. Help them to 'rate how scared they would be doing each step' (Willetts & Creswell, 2007, p.121) from least anxiety-inducing to most anxiety-inducing so that those which cause the least anxiety are tackled first. Resist moving onto the next step too quickly and repeat each step until it feels comfortable and natural for the pupil. 'By practicing the things that make you nervous you are actually expanding your ability to handle them' (Ehmke 2023). If a step is overwhelming, break it down even further, until it feels achievable.
■ While coming up with the plan together, help the pupil to identify their thoughts and explore whether they are helpful and positive or unhelpful and negative. They can then be supported to reframe any unhelpful or negative thoughts into more realistic, helpful or positive ones (see p.88).
■ It is possible to become creative when making a plan and taking the pupil's likes and interests into consideration. A plan may simply be broken down into each small step, or it may be presented in an anxiety ladder or even as 'a rocket flying to the moon (stopping off at stars along the way), or a train going along a track (with the different steps marked at platforms on the way to the final destination)' (Willetts & Creswell, 2007, p.116).

- Plan how to measure success and acknowledge any smaller steps towards success. Use immediate rewards and/or praise for this, alongside each step or goal as it is achieved, as appropriate. Notice and praise effort and attitude and tiny steps of progress.
- It is necessary to talk about anxiety and normalise it as a physical response to certain situations. Anxiety is contagious, but so is calm. Acknowledge anxiety and model using coping strategies and changing patterns of negative thinking, for example, *I am feeling a bit anxious because a new member of staff is starting today. I imagine they are feeling even more nervous than me, meeting all of us. I am going to plan a couple of things to say to them, then take some deep breaths and go and say 'hi' and introduce myself.*
- Teach social skills and foster confidence and a sense of self-worth. 'Addressing social anxiety is not about preventing or avoiding rejection. Addressing social anxiety is about fostering social courage. Being socially courageous means pursuing experiences and knowing that your chances of rejection are not zero' (Goodman, 2021). Observing and discussing social interactions on television programmes and films can be helpful. Using sentence starters, scripts, comic strip conversations or Social Stories ™ (Gray, undated) can help pupils to plan for different social scenarios. Role play and drama can be a useful tool for teaching social skills. 'Drama games start very simply, so that no one is set up to fail' (Jennings, 2023, p.13).

Case study:

Mylah was in Y8 and suffered from social anxiety. She could talk to her friends and several teachers in school on a one-to-one basis but struggled to talk in a larger group. She was unable to contribute to class discussions.

In Drama, the teacher provided the class with a variety of props, including masks. From behind a mask, Mylah joined in with the group work and was able to mime and act. After several sessions, she spoke to the group from behind the mask.

Environmental adaptations

- Implement a careful seating plan for socially anxious pupils to increase their feelings of safety. Encourage pupils to communicate where they feel safe within each space. Some pupils may feel safe in proximity to the teacher or a trusted peer to provide reassurance and support.

■ Eating and drinking in public can often increase anxiety for pupils. Provide smaller, quieter places for the pupils to eat their lunch in a smaller group.

■ Break times can increase anxiety and pupils may need buddy systems in place or access to smaller, zoned areas, support with social situations or access to more structured activities at these times.

■ Using public toilets or changing areas can also increase anxiety. Provide access to facilities at quieter times or access to alternative, more private amenities where possible.

Chapter take-aways

■ Social anxiety is often linked to school-based anxiety due to the social nature of the school environment.

■ Trusting, safe relationships are essential when providing support.

■ Understanding and recognising social anxiety is the first step in overcoming it.

■ Step-by-step approaches can help pupils gradually address specific fears or situations.

■ Certain aspects of the school day and environment can trigger the anxiety and pupils will need support and adjustments around these.

Further signposting

Books

Managing Social Anxiety in Children and Young People – Practical Activities for Reducing Stress and Building Self-Esteem by Sue Jennings

Overcoming Your Child's Shyness and Social Anxiety by Lucy Willetts & Cathy Creswell (Chapter 20 – 'Overcoming Your Child's Shyness and Social Anxiety: A Brief Guide for Teachers' pp.243–50)

Social Anxiety Workbook for Teens: 10-Minute Activities and Tools to Reduce Stress, Conquer Fear, and Boost Social Confidence by Sally Stevens

Websites

AnxietyCanada *Social Anxiety Disorder* https://www.anxietycanada.com/anxiety-disorder/social-anxiety-disorder

Carol Gray *Social Stories* https://carolgraysocialstories.com/social-stories

Young Minds *–Resources* https://www.youngminds.org.uk/professional/resources

References

AnxietyCanada (undated) *Self-Help Strategies for Social Anxiety* Available at: https://www.anxietycanada.com/sites/default/files/adult_hmsocial.pdf [Accessed 23.5.23]

Bombèr, L. (2007) *Inside I'm Hurting – Practical Strategies for Supporting Children with Attachment Difficulties in Schools* Worth Publishing

Bombèr, L. (2011) *What About Me? Inclusive Strategies to Support Pupils with Attachment Difficulties Make It Through the School Day* Worth Publishing

Currigan, S. & Shackleton, E. (2022) *Rejection Sensitive Dysphoria and ADHD: What Teachers and Parents Need to Know* Available at: https://beacon schoolsupport.co.uk/podcast/rejection-sensitive-dysphoria-and-adhd-what-teachers-and-parents-need-to-know

Ehmke, R. (2023) *Tips for Managing Social Anxiety: If Worrying about Embarrassing Yourself is Getting in Your Way, Some Strategies for Beating the Fear* Available at: https://childmind.org/article/tips-managing-social-anxiety [Accessed 16.7.23]

Elley, D. with Morewood, G. (2022) *Championing Your Autistic Teen at Secondary School – Getting the Best from Mainstream Schools* Jessica Kingsley

Goodman, F. (2021) *Why You Feel Anxious Socializing (and What to Do about It)* Available at: https://www.ted.com/talks/fallon_goodman_why_you_feel_anxious_socializing_and_what_to_do_about_it?language=en [Accessed 28.8.23]

Gray, C. (1994) *Comic Strip Conversations* Future Horizons

Gray, C. (undated) *Social Stories* Available at: https://carolgraysocialstories.com

Hutt, R. (2019) *Feeling Better: CBT Workbook for Teens: Essential Skills and Activities to Help You Manage Moods, Boost Self-Esteem, and Conquer Anxiety* Althea Press

Jennings, S. (2023) *Managing Social Anxiety in Children and Young People – Practical Activities for Reducing Stress and Building Self-Esteem* Routledge

Jolanta (2023) *How to Manage Social Anxiety at School* Available at: https://www.youngminds.org.uk/young-person/blog/how-to-manage-social-anxiety-at-school [Accessed 31.8.23]

Knightsmith, P. (2022) *Things I Got Wrong So You Don't Have To: 48 Lessons to Banish Burnout and Avoid Anxiety for Those Who Put Others First* Jessica Kingsley

Saline, S. (2022) *Where Does 'Introvert' End and Social Anxiety Begin?* Available at: https://www.additudemag.com/introvert-social-anxiety-adhd-adults [Accessed 31.8.23]

Warrell, M. (2020) *It's Not Failure That Sets You Back – It's Failing to Risk More of It* Available at: https://www.forbes.com/sites/margiewarrell/2020/01/30/its-not-failure-that-sets-you-back-its-failing-to-risk-more-of-it [Accessed 5.2.24]

Willetts, L. & Creswell, C. (2007) *Overcoming Your Child's Shyness and Social Anxiety – A Self-help Guide Using Cognitive Behavioural Techniques* Robinson

Alleviating social anxiety checklist

SUPPORT MATERIAL

STRATEGY	COMMENTS
Please also refer to Chapters 3 and 10	
Relationships and collaboration	
Small team of key workers to take time to build relationship and provide regular check-ins	
Collaboration with staff and caregivers	
Nurturing approaches	
Support pupils to build and maintain peer relationships	
Do not insist on eye contact	
Understand and recognise anxiety	
Help pupils to recognise and understand their social anxiety	
Support to rationalise and reframe negative thoughts	
Teaching and learning	
Teach pupils when and how to ask for help	
Plan group and partner work carefully	
Provide alternatives to speaking and presenting, where appropriate, and gradually build confidence	
Introduce buddy systems	
Boost self-esteem by providing responsibilities with minimal social interaction	
Supported opportunities to gradually step out of comfort zone	

(Continued)

Continued

STRATEGY	COMMENTS
Making mistakes	
Model making and learning from mistakes	
Research inventions which arose from mistakes	
Open-ended tasks with no correct and incorrect answers	
Visual supports	
Offer alternative means of recording occasionally	
Careful use of language	
Provide 'spares', whiteboards, erasers, laptops, etc. so mistakes are easy to rectify	
Praise effort, engagement, attitude and perseverance rather than correct answers	
Provide anonymised work to feedback on	
Reduce stress and reduce anxiety	
Provide feedback in a less public way	
Ensure pupils feel successful	
Step-by-step approaches	
Work collaboratively to establish triggers	
Focus on one social situation, breaking each goal down into tiny steps	
Start within the pupil's comfort zone	

(Continued)

Continued

STRATEGY	COMMENTS
Gently challenge patterns of negative thinking	
Present plans visually and creatively	
Plan small, achievable steps and plan how to measure success	
Model coping with anxiety	
Teach social skills	
Environmental adaptations	
Implement careful seating plan, within comfort zone	
Provide smaller, quieter places for eating	
Provide support at break times	
Ensure access to quieter changing and toilet facilities	

7
Situational mutism

What is situational mutism?

'Situational mutism', commonly referred to as 'selective mutism' (and previously called 'elective mutism') is described as:

> an anxiety disorder where a person is able to speak in certain situations where they feel comfortable and safe but is unable to speak in other social circumstances, such as with classmates at school or to relatives they do not see very often.
>
> (NHS 2023)

In this book the phrase 'situational mutism' (Hipoliti, 2020) rather than 'selective mutism' (unless referring to medical diagnoses or citing others) has been deliberately used as the term selective mutism appears to imply that the person is 'selecting' and has a choice in their actions – they don't! The importance of this language reframing is to reflect that it is a case of *can't* not *won't*.

The key feature of situational mutism is that an individual cannot speak comfortably to all people in all situations. In certain situations, or with certain, safe people, the pupil speaks readily and confidently (usually at home, with their immediate family), whereas in other situations, where there is an expectation to speak, their speech is limited or absent. Individuals are not 'anxious' all of the time, but are highly anxious in certain circumstances. This tends to form a pattern and continues over a period of time. Situational mutism usually becomes apparent in early childhood, although it can appear later, particularly in adolescence.

DOI: 10.4324/9781003433231-8

It is important to emphasise that situational mutism is *not* refusal or defiance. It is not a case of being shy or quiet; 'shy children may be worried about speaking; children who have SM (selective mutism) are terrified' (Johnson & Wintgens, 2016, p.7). People with situational mutism want to speak but are unable to, at that moment, due to heightened anxiety. They can become afraid of speaking and situations which could lead to an expectation to speak. Hannah (in Johnson & Wintgens, 2012, p.19) states, 'I'd love to speak. I just can't get over this fear of talking and I can't get started.' Cat (2021) describes the situation:

> When I am stuck with selective mutism I feel verbally paralysed by what I think of as a "fear wall" that's sprung up around me like a force-field so that I can't speak to people. I hate its existence, but can't shrug it off no matter how much I long to do so.

Sometimes pupils are able to talk to friends in school, or talk in a whisper, but speaking in situations where they are not comfortable renders them literally 'speechless'. 'Children who have SM want to speak but have an irrational fear or dread – a phobia – of speaking aloud in certain situations; when expected to speak, they inwardly panic, become physically frozen and cannot utter a sound' (Johnson & Wintgens, 2016, p.8). The body engages the involuntary threat response of freeze (see p.4):

- a pupil may be unable to move or may present with a blank expression.
- their muscles may go stiff.
- they may experience rapid, shallow breathing.
- their heart rate may increase.
- they may be unable to 'think straight' (because the logical, rational, thinking part of brain goes offline).
- the muscles in the throat tense up and they lose the ability to speak, laugh or cry out.

Viewing situational mutism as a phobia and therefore a reaction of the body's natural response to threat – a form of freeze or shutdown – rather than defiance or refusal will help staff begin to implement supportive strategies with compassion and empathy rather than behavioural strategies, which will exacerbate the situation by increasing the anxiety.

It is important to note that situational mutism differs from being non-verbal, since a pupil who has situational mutism can speak freely in some situations, whereas someone who is non-verbal is usually non-verbal in all situations.

Situational mutism also differs from 'reactive mutism' (mutism which has a sudden onset as a result of an identifiable, significant, stressful and traumatic event or trigger, causing a person who used to talk freely to stop talking and is often accompanied by flashbacks and nightmares). Reactive mutism is linked to Post-Traumatic Stress Disorder (PTSD) and needs a different form of support, for example, input or therapy from mental health professionals such as CAMHS (Child and Adolescent Mental Health Services).

Situational mutism, can, however, develop into 'progressive mutism', meaning that pupils can stop talking in situations where they have previously spoken confidently, to the extent that they stop talking at all due to extreme anxiety.

Collaboration with caregivers will be important in order to establish the child's speaking habits if, for example, the pupil is comfortable to freely speak in certain, safe situations. Johnson and Wintgens (2016, p.67) suggest keeping a 'record of speaking habits' which may be useful when seeking further information in collaboration with caregivers.

If concerned that a pupil may have situational mutism, please refer to key professionals such as a Speech and Language Therapist (SALT) for further advice and support.

Personal case study:

At the age of 16, I went on a French exchange trip. During the week I was there, I stayed with three different families. Apparently, they were so excited to have an English student and the demand was so great, they thought they would share me around.

I tried to communicate, in French and also in English, but I could almost feel my brain shutting down and beginning to freeze. I couldn't get my words out, I couldn't process what anyone was saying to me, as I was too busy panicking about what I could say in reply. I desperately wanted to talk to them, I just couldn't. The more I tried, the less I could say. The less I said, the more of a failure I felt and the more I felt I had let everyone down and must have been such a disappointment to all the families.

Diagnosis

- *The International Classification of Diseases* (ICD-11, 2018) (the global standard for diagnostic health information) classifies selective mutism as an 'anxiety or fear-related disorder' and the *Diagnostic and Statistical Manual of Mental Disorders* (DSM 5-TR, 2022, p.222) (the standard classification of mental disorders used by mental health professionals in the United States) as an anxiety disorder 'characterized by a consistent failure to speak in social situations in which there is an expectation to speak (e.g. school) even though the individual speaks in other situations'.
- The *DSM 5-TR* (2022) describes 'high profile' and 'low profile' selective mutism. High profile being used to describe someone who does not speak at all in certain situations or with certain people. Low profile being used to describe those who may respond minimally, such as providing short answers to closed questions, or are able to respond to predictable routines, such as answering the register, saying 'thank you' or repeating the words someone else has spoken, but will not initiate interactions or offer ideas.

Therefore, pupils may be able to speak in some contexts within the school environment, for example, they may be able to answer an adult's question in school, since the fear of not answering (and being reprimanded or met with disapproval or needing to fit in with their peers) may be more extreme than the fear of talking. Pupils with low profile situational mutism have high levels of anxiety but may often not be recognised or supported appropriately as their difficulties are masked by their compliance.

In order to receive a formal diagnosis of selective mutism:

- A consistent pattern must have been observed for at least a month (or two months after entering new setting).
- The pupils must talk comfortably to at least one other person in a safe setting, stopping talking or becoming noticeably anxious in the presence of other people.
- The inability to speak in certain situations needs to be impacting negatively on or limiting academic and/or social functioning in order for a diagnosis to be given.
- The mutism cannot be explained by other conditions or difficulties such as speech and language difficulties, hearing impairment, cultural differences or learning needs.

Selective mutism affects approximately 1 in 140 children under 8 years and about 1 in 550 older children (Johnson & Wintgens, 2016, p.36), with reluctant talkers increasing this number, as they often fall under the radar being labelled as shy or quiet and therefore do not always receive the support that they need.

Recognising situational mutism – behavioural and physical presentations

A pupil does not need to have a diagnosis of selective mutism for provision to be put in place. If adults observe pupils who display anxiety around speaking, early intervention has been found to be the most impactful. When working with and supporting pupils with situational mutism, it is essential to remember that it is behaviour driven by intense anxiety and is not a personal choice or act of defiance. The behaviour needs to be viewed as a form of communication and anxiety and adults need to understand the key elements to look out for.

The presentations of situational mutism may change over time for individual pupils. Pupils who are anxious around talking may:

Physical symptoms	
■ Have difficulties separating from caregivers and experience separation anxiety (see p.221) ■ Present as nervous or anxious in a variety of social situations, experience social anxiety or have Social Anxiety Disorder (SAD) (see p.7) ■ Present with serious or blank facial expressions, for example looking like 'a rabbit caught in the headlights' ■ Display stiff or awkward body movements ■ Have sensory sensitivities, in particular to noise, touch and crowds ■ Display hypervigilance	■ Show physical presentations of anxiety – headache, stomach ache, nausea ■ 'Speak fluently in some situations but remain consistently silent in others. They may have a blank expression, or appear "frozen" when expected to speak.' (Solihull. gov.uk, undated) ■ Use an alternative voice – baby talk, accent, whisper, gesture, different language ■ Mask and display social mimicry (echoing what others say or phrases from television programmes)

(Continued)

Continued

Behavioural symptoms	
■ Appear shy, withdrawn and quiet in certain situations ■ Appear defiant, oppositional and refuse to comply; 'strong-willed children will resist (and appear to "refuse") anxiety provoking activities, compliant children will "suffer in silence"' (Johnson & Wintgens, 2016, p.32) ■ Be misunderstood as manipulative, controlling, stubborn or aggressive (driven by fear and the activation of the threat response) ■ Reach a crisis point when at home or in a place of safety	■ Chew on non-edible items, twirl hair, fiddle ■ Fear asking to go to the toilet or asking for help ■ Have difficulty regulating emotions ■ Talk to complete strangers ■ Run away, hide ■ Withdraw from social events and clubs ■ Cover face or mouth ■ '[Avert] eye contact, [grow] a long fringe, not [move]' (Johnson & Wintgens, 2016, p.35) ■ Self-harm
Internal symptoms/feelings	
■ Worry excessively ■ Low self-esteem	■ Loneliness and isolation ■ Feel or want to be invisible

By understanding the reasons behind the behaviours, for example, understanding defiance, and refusal or perceived control and manipulation, as stemming from intense fear and anxiety, adults will be able to offer appropriate support with empathy and compassion rather than sanctions and disapproval.

Comorbidity

Situational mutism has high comorbidity with other forms of anxiety, particularly social anxiety (see Chapters 5 and 6), school-based anxiety (see Chapters 9 and 10) and separation anxiety (see Chapters 11 and 12). It may occur alongside other conditions or diagnoses such as autism, Obsessive Compulsive Disorder (OCD), Oppositional Defiant Disorder (ODD), Attention Deficit Hyperactivity Disorder (ADHD), Body-Focused Repetitive Behaviour (BFRB), specific phobias, sensory processing difficulties, speech and language difficulties or depression.

Recognition and early intervention

Early intervention and support are the most impactful factors in improving social and communication skills, developing relationships and increasing self-esteem, reducing social anxiety and increasing attainment. Patterns of behaviours, if displayed over time, can become embedded and therefore become harder to change. Johnson and Wintgens (2016, p.45) found that pupils who were diagnosed later (in their mid to late teens) also presented with school-based anxiety, self-harm, social anxiety, social withdrawal, low mood and progressive mutism and stated that there is 'no doubt that early intervention . . . is essential to protect children's health and wellbeing'.

It is important that school staff recognise how situational mutism may present in a pupil physically and behaviourally and the possible risk factors and triggers as well as those 'maintaining factors' which may be contributing to sustaining the mutism. By understanding situational mutism school staff will be able to put in support at the earliest stage.

Possible risk factors

Risk factors are the factors that one needs to be aware of and pay attention to as they may contribute to the onset of situational mutism and can include:

■ General anxiety, social anxiety and separation anxiety.
■ Emotional dysregulation.
■ Family history of situational mutism, anxiety or mental health difficulties.
■ Speech and language difficulties.
■ English as an additional language (EAL).
■ Fear of making mistakes.
■ Risk aversion.
■ Hypervigilance.
■ Self-consciousness.
■ Low self-esteem.
■ Dislike of change or surprises.
■ Excessive worry.
■ Under-achievement.
■ Difficulties with social relationships and social skills.

Possible triggers

Situations which may trigger the onset of situational mutism for pupils can include:

■ Transitions to new places or people.
■ Frequent school or house moves.

- Changes or breakdowns in family relationships.
- Bereavement, grief and loss.
- Expressive language difficulties or speech which has previously been misunderstood or ridiculed.
- Bullying.
- Teasing.
- Pupil has been or felt pressured to speak, despite feeling extreme discomfort.
- Anxiety from others has been displayed when the pupil has been unable to speak.
- Lack of consistent and predictable routines.
- Stress and anxiety.
- Crowded, busy or noisy environments.

Possible maintaining factors

Maintaining factors are those factors which may be sustaining the situational mutism for the pupil and need to be identified, addressed and eliminated in order to begin to provide support.

- Pressure to speak applied by others, even when they display discomfort. The fear of not speaking is overtaken by the fear of being reprimanded or ridiculed.
- Bribes or rewards have been offered to 'encourage' speaking.
- Sanctions and reprimands for not speaking.
- Disapproval and negativity from others.
- Teasing and bullying.
- Speech is misunderstood or ridiculed.
- Over-protection and avoidance such as someone speaking for them.
- Negative labelling and reinforcement.
- Lack of understanding and support.
- Family members demonstrate social anxieties and the pupil has seen others express anxiety around speaking, for example, 'silence is modelled as a reaction to strangers' (SMIRA, undated).
- Withdrawal of speech has been used as a means of control or 'silence is modelled . . . to express anger' (SMIRA, undated).
- Avoidance of situations out of their comfort zone, rather than support, thus feeding the anxiety cycle.
- Eye contact is insisted upon despite feeling painful or uncomfortable.
- The pupil has been ignored when trying to communicate verbally or non-verbally.
- Excessive attention is given when the child does talk.

- The pupil's efforts to communicate are dismissed, for example, the child tries to communicate by alternate means and is told *I can't help you unless you use your words.*
- Masking.

Personal case study:

I had situational mutism in my late teens. I was classed as *shy* and *quiet*, but it was so much more than that. It was a crippling fear to speak in certain situations (lectures, seminars, interviews, in front of groups of people). I wanted to speak, I would try to form the words in my head, but I just couldn't vocalise them. I would feel hot, start shaking, get palpitations, go red, panic. By the time I had words in my head which I felt I could say, the conversation had moved on. I was terrified of saying the wrong thing, being judged, being wrong, being laughed at, being disliked and being thought of as stupid.

I was called *the mouse, shrinking violet, rude* and *aloof* to my face (I am not sure I even want to know what I was called behind my back), all adding to my sense of blame and shame. I felt flawed, a failure, not good enough and incredibly misunderstood.

I am sure that avoiding and not recognising the problem exacerbated and prolonged it. However, being 'thrown in at the deep end' didn't help either. In my second year of teaching, my (then) boss told me I had to deliver a speech to a group of 200 parents. I told him I couldn't, but I was told I didn't have a choice. I had sleepless nights for the two weeks building up to it. I couldn't remember anything I had to say. On the day, I stood up, I was bright red, shaking uncontrollably, and read with my head down in a hurried, quiet, trembling voice, just trying to finish. The whole experience was horrendous and confirmed to me (and others) that I couldn't speak to a group of adults. (On the plus side, I was never asked again.)

It still seems strange to me, looking back, that I can now stand and present to hundreds of colleagues. I still get anxious, but I can control it, and I usually enjoy the experience.

So, what helped?

- Recognising and naming the feelings for what they were: anxiety.
- Implementing calming strategies when I felt the physical sensations linked to anxiety, (for me – deep breathing,

positive self-talk, hand massage, a cup of tea, some choco-
late, talking to a friend or friendly colleague).
- Gradual exposure and breaking a task down into smaller, achievable steps to success, rather than the final outcome (for example, I started by tackling a five-minute presentation, just to my husband, then to a trusted friend, then a small, trusted group, gradually building up, over time, as my confidence grew).
- Being overly prepared, particularly initially – reading everything I could, knowing the subject inside out.
- Visual prompts.
- Confidence, understanding and support conveyed by friends, colleagues and managers and being told what I was good at.
- Increased self-confidence.
- Focusing on my strengths and positive self-talk *I can do this, I did it before and the feedback was great.*
- Another thing that helped me personally was stepping out of my comfort zone in a totally different area; I was terrified of putting my face in the water and learning to scuba dive helped me to recognise how anxiety presented for me and boosted my confidence, showing me that I could overcome fear. Over time diving became something that I loved.

Chapter take-aways

- A person who is situationally mute is able to speak confidently in some situations but is rendered unable to speak in other situations due to heightened anxiety.
- Situational mutism is a specific form of social anxiety.
- Situational mutism needs to be viewed as an intense fear or a phobia, rather than as refusal, opposition, manipulation or defiance. Misinterpreting the behaviours increases anxiety and prevents pupils from receiving appropriate support.

Further signposting

Books

Helping Your Child with Selective Mutism by Angela McHolm
The Selective Mutism Resource Manual 2nd Edition by Maggie Johnson & Alison Wintgens

Websites

Ispeak.org *Selective Mutism in The Words of People with Selective Mutism* http://www.ispeak.org.uk

Speech and Language UK *Helping Quiet Children* https://speechandlanguage.org.uk/media/3297/supporting-quiet-children-factsheet-november-2016.pdf

Selective Mutism Information and Research Association (SMIRA) *About Selective Mutism* www.selectivemutism.org.uk

Podcasts

Dr Elisa Shipon-Blum *Unspoken Words: A Selective Mutism Podcast* https://selectivemutismcenter.org/unspoken-words-podcast

Maggie Johnson with Dr Christie *Understanding Selective Mutism* www.selectivemutism.org.uk/videos

Outloud The Selective Mutism Podcast *Tips for Teachers* https://podcasts.apple.com/gb/podcast/tips-for-teachers/id1480028041?i=1000489541178

Pooky Ponders *What is Selective Mutism and How Can We Help?* https://pookyh.buzzsprout.com/1183931/5819794-what-is-selective-mutism-and-how-can-we-help-gino-hipolito

References

Cat, S. (2021) *PDA Masking in Detail* Available at: www.sallycatpda.co.uk/2021/10/pda-masking-in-detail.html [Accessed 2.5.23]

DSM 5-TR (2022) *Diagnostic and Statistical Manual of Mental Disorders* Fifth Edition, Text Revision American Psychiatric Association

Hipoliti, G. (2020) *What is Selective Mutism and How Can We Help?* Available at: https://pookyh.buzzsprout.com/1183931/5819794-what-is-selective-mutism-and-how-can-we-help-gino-hipolito [Accessed 14 December 2020]

ICD-11 (2018) *The International Classification of Diseases* Eleventh Revision Available at: https://icd.who.int/en

Johnson, M. & Wintgens, A. (2012) *Can I Tell You About Selective Mutism?: A Guide for Friends, Family and Professionals* Jessica Kingsley

Johnson, M. & Wintgens, A. (2016) *The Selective Mutism Resource Manual* Second Edition Routledge

NHS (2023) *Selective Mutism* Available at: https://www.nhs.uk/mental-health/conditions/selective-mutism/#:~:text=Selective%20mutism%20is%20an%20anxiety,untreated%2C%20can%20persist%20into%20adulthood [Accessed 28.4.23]

SMIRA (Selective Mutism Information and Research Association) (undated) *Information for Professionals* Available at: http://www.selectivemutism.org.uk/information/information-for-professionals [Accessed 24.2.24]

Solihull.gov.uk (undated) https://www.solihull.gov.uk/sites/default/files/2022-10/Situational-Mutism-Information-Pack.pdf [Accessed 18.4.23]

8
Alleviating situational mutism

Intervene early

It is best to intervene as early as possible when providing support for pupils with situational mutism as this prevents the anxiety from increasing and the behaviour becoming embedded. Different suggestions may work for different people at different times. The aim is not to avoid speaking altogether (which increases and intensifies the anxiety in the long run) but to gently and gradually build up the pupil's confidence in interactions. This is achieved through developing trusted relationships and encouraging communication in a variety of ways, taking the pressure off speaking, until the pupil feels comfortable and ready.

The following suggestions can be used to increase confidence for shy children, those who show some reluctance or anxieties around talking or for early intervention, they are not reliant on a diagnosis.

Please also refer to the Chapter 6 as situational mutism can be viewed as a specific form of social anxiety.

Key adults

- Up relational safety cues (see p.22) by greeting the pupil with a smile, being friendly and showing an interest in them, without expecting a verbal response. Ensure open body language, a sing song tone and smiling facial expression as well as carefully choosing the words used. Gently encourage but do not insist on eye contact.

DOI: 10.4324/9781003433231-9

- Ensure all key adults focus on the pupil's strengths and interests and understand that direct attempts to force or bribe a child to speak are harmful and increase anxiety. Pupils need to know that they will not be asked or expected to speak until they are ready and feel comfortable.
- Key adults will need to take time to build connections, relationships, trust and rapport. Use the PACE approach (see p.26) and inject a sense of playfulness by engaging in fun, inclusive activities where the main focus is not on talking. Take time to get to know the pupil in a way that alleviates anxieties, reduces pressure and is safe, reassuring and encouraging. Shared activities (reading a book, drawing, play dough, cooking, playing a game with no pressure to talk, blowing bubbles and popping them on different body parts, playing farms and making animal sounds or vehicles and making transport noises) to focus on can help to take the pressure off verbal interactions, whilst building a trusting relationship. The importance of play cannot be over emphasised. 'This usually takes the form of facilitated noisy play during which confidence is instilled and trust is built; adults make mistakes which children become eager to "correct" and uninhibited laughter is generally encouraged' (SMIRA, undated).
- Consider having a trusted friend or adult alongside initially to reduce pupil anxiety, while key adults foster positive relationships.

Peer relationships

- A buddy system may help pupils to begin to build positive relationships in school.
- Foster peer relationships by engaging in activities based on shared interests, such as cooking, gardening, playing games or craft activities. Provide similar structured activities at break times to make them easier for the pupil to manage, for example, teach playground games and introduce the pupil to clubs such as cooking, den building, chess, computing, badminton and Lego® to build rapport with others with shared interests. Encourage pupils to play with peers using role-play (dressing up and wearing masks can reduce anxiety), talking through puppets, using toy telephones and walkie talkies. 'Art and music activities can foster comfort and peer relationships by pairing the child with other children who love art or music. Having shared interests is a wonderful way to build social comfort and relationships with peers' (Shipon-Blum, 2021).

Case study:

Ramon and Mr Lynx had a trusting relationship and Mr Lynx noticed that Ramon often played alongside Pedro and showed an interest in Pedro's Lego® activities. Mr Lynx played alongside Ramon and Pedro, using The Triangle Tactic (Johnson and Wintgens, 2016, pp.155–6).

Mr Lynx: Pedro, your Lego® model looks amazing.
Pedro: Thanks, it's a Minecraft world.
Mr Lynx: Wow! I've never played Minecraft, have you Ramon?

Ramon looks at Mr Lynx and nods.

Mr Lynx: Ah, Ramon is a Minecraft expert too. Do you two both play it on the computer?

Pedro answers verbally and Ramon nods.

Mr Lynx: I wonder if Pedro could do with a bit of help building his Minecraft world with Lego®, Ramon?
Pedro: Yeah, he could find some more green bricks and make the side wall.
Mr Lynx: Ah that would be helpful wouldn't it, Ramon? Do you think you could find some green bricks for the side wall?

Ramon nods.

Pedro: Ramon, you can use any colour of green and a bit of brown if you like, so that the house is camouflaged in the forest.

Ramon nods and whispers OK.

Pedro smiles and says 'Thanks'. They look for bricks together and build and Mr Lynx moves away briefly and then returns.

Mr Lynx: Wow, this Mine world is looking fabulous.
Ramon: Minecraft.

Pedro laughs at Mr Lynx's mistake and Ramon smiles.

Reflection opportunities:

- How did Mr Lynx support the relationship between the two children?
- How could he move on to provide more opportunities for the two to interact together?

■ Informing peers about situational mutism (with the pupil's permission) can help avoid negative or surprised reactions when the pupil does speak (which can be detrimental to the pupil speaking again in the future). Johnson & Wintgens (2012, pp.33–5) include suggestions for sharing how peers may be supportive. Pupils may like to highlight strategies that are supportive for them and add their own ideas. Alternatively, the pupil may like help to record a presentation to show the class or find appropriate YouTube videos to share which tell people about situational mutism.

Collaborative approaches

■ Work closely with the pupil and caregivers and with any external agencies who are involved, such as a Speech and Language Therapist (SALT or Educational Psychologist (EP). It will also be important to ensure that all adults who come into contact with the pupil are informed about situational mutism, what works for the pupil and their strengths and ensure that no pressure is put on them to speak.
■ It can be helpful for a trusted adult to act as a 'talking bridge' (Johnson & Wintgens, 2016, p.183) to support the pupil to begin to speak in other situations or with another person, to begin to bridge the gap and provide emotional safety when building new relationships.
■ Talking through puppets, toys, small world characters, the school pet or using role-play props (masks and dressing up clothes) can take the pressure off as it is non-threatening and adds a playful element to interactions. The toys can also act as a 'bridge', with the pupil either talking through or to a toy. They then may, gradually, be able to speak to or through the toy in front of the adult.

Strength-based approaches

■ Find creative ways for pupils to convey their strengths, successes, likes and interests without needing to speak, such as sharing sports trophies or certificates, showing artwork and construction models, using a communication passport or pre-recording a presentation, video or booklet to share or using pictures and other visual cues. Invite them to become an 'expert' in an area of specific interest and they can share written instructions, presentations, photographs or leaflets that they have created.

■ Smile and praise everything that the pupil does well and focus on their non-verbal achievements. Use their strengths and interests as a starting point. Focus and start on what they can do. Build confidence and self-esteem and show that you value them as a whole person rather than making them feel like the speaking element defines them.

■ Boost self-esteem by providing roles and responsibilities that do not involve talking such as tidying the book corner, watering the plants, turning on the computers or jobs that can support pupils to begin to foster relationships such as helping in the canteen, taking the register to the office, helping the site manager sweep the leaves, tidying the library with the librarian, supporting in the ICT suite. Ensure all adults know about situational mutism and how to support and build relationships without pressurising the pupil to talk.

■ Reframe language into positives, for example, use *can't at the moment* rather than *won't*. Avoid negative labels or drawing negative attention to the pupil and draw attention to positives instead. Rather than *defiant* or *oppositional* view the pupil as *highly anxious* or *has activated their threat response*. Brown (2013) provides language reframes for certain situations: '*A child has been ignoring my verbal cues for weeks, and I am beginning to feel disrespected*' becomes '*This child continues to be quite anxious and I may want to explore a new way to engage this child*' '*I feel as if this child is trying to control me*' becomes '*I wonder what the meaning of this behavior is? (clue . . . ANXIETY, FEAR, FIGHT OR FLIGHT RESPONSE).*'

■ Adults need to reflect on their own behaviours and responses. They need to understand the behaviour and the emotions which are driving the anxiety. 'When a child with SM [selective mutism] begins to make you question yourself, question yourself! Do not be afraid to acknowledge that you are offended or uncomfortable. Allow this feeling to act as an alarm that you need to reframe your thoughts and beliefs about this behavior. (Brown, 2013).

Communication

■ Encourage alternative forms of communication to talking initially, particularly when beginning to build relationships (and as a 'stepping stone', alongside or instead of talking at times of stress and anxiety), for example, communicate by text, email, a voice recording, puppets, walkie talkies, Google translate, talking tins (a small device to allow pupils to record and play back their own voice messages) or talking apps.

■ Engage in activities which make noises by playing musical instruments, small world play, such as playing trains and making 'choo-choo' or chugging noises, reading books or playing games which make sounds by pressing the buttons, playing *Operation*. You may be able to build up to taking turns to play and copy drum beats or clapping rhythms. Talking through toys or puppets may also act as a bridge in certain situations.

■ Focus on a shared activity so interactions feel more natural.

■ Talk to the pupil often, even if they don't respond, by noticing aloud and providing commentaries and wondering aloud, such as *I wonder if you would prefer the thick or thin pencil, I think you would like the thick one*, or *I'm enjoying playing farms with you, my favourite animal is the pig, I wonder which one you like*. Use playfulness, have fun or make deliberate mistakes, for example, *I bet your favourite is this chicken (and hold up the cow)*.

■ As the pupil gains confidence and can provide single word answers, begin to introduce positive choices such as, *Would you like the blue pen or the black one?* Ensure the pupil is totally comfortable responding to a positive choice before asking more open-ended questions (such as *Which colour pen would you like?*), which can be overwhelming.

■ Allow processing time before expecting a response. If the pupil does not respond or appears in any way distressed, calmly move on. If the child gives a non-verbal response, acknowledge it as an important communicative step, such as, *Thank you for showing me you needed the black pen*.

Teaching and learning

■ It is important to establish a consistent, positive and genuinely inclusive environment. Ensure that the pupil feels included in all activities and is provided with alternatives to verbal communication (rather than ignored or excluded). For example, pre-warn, plan and rehearse contributions to group or pair discussions to ensure the pupil feels confident to contribute. Alongside verbal responses, offer the opportunity for non-verbal, written responses on whiteboards or sticky notes,, for the whole class (rather than singling out the individual, which will draw attention to them, heightening anxiety rather than lessening it).

- It can be useful to introduce whole class activities which have a focus alongside verbal interaction, such as joining in with actions, movements, gestures, noises, repeating words and phrases, counting, reciting days of the week, playing *Stand up if it is true, sit down if it is false, Simon Says*, etc.
- Much anxiety stems from the fear of being negatively judged. Convey an ethos that it is OK to make mistakes, everyone makes mistakes and that they can be learned from. Displaying inspirational quotes from celebrities who learned from mistakes and researching inventions which arose from mistakes can be helpful (see 'Making mistakes' p.130).
- Pupils may feel comfortable recording their voices, such as reading from a book or sharing some information and playing it back to the adult or class. Allow recorded and video presentations as a bridge when presenting or reading aloud to ease anxieties (never share videos without the pupil's permission as this will break trust).
- Avoid pupils getting themselves into groups by choosing groups and pairs. Pupils with situational mutism or anxiety will usually not initiate interactions and waiting to be chosen can create high anxiety and being among the last to be picked can damage self-esteem.

Case study:

Mylie displays high levels of anxiety and can, at times, totally freeze. She can become worried and emotional and is unable to voice her concerns. Anything out of the ordinary and any sort of change are tricky for her to manage and she needs pre-warning and preparing. For example, before going on a school trip, her parents help her to look on Google maps and on the venue website to help familiarise her with the place in advance. On a Children in Need 'wear something spotty' day, she became very anxious about whether she was wearing enough or too many spots and ended up not being able to attend.

On a recent school trip, the class were told to get into pairs ready to get on the bus. Mylie sat on the carpet and didn't move as the class lined up. She looked around her and the adult repeated that she had to line up. Mylie shook her head and remained rooted to the spot

Reflection opportunity:

- How could this situation have been made less stressful for Mylie?

■ Avoid pressuring children to talk (including 'find a partner' or 'get into groups' scenarios), as this heightens the anxiety. Explain to pupils that they do not need to talk until they are ready and demonstrate all the different ways that the pupil can join in. Encourage the class to hold up the answer on their fingers or a number fan or write it on a whiteboard alongside or instead of putting hands up and speaking the answer as a stepping stone towards talking. Encourage non-verbal as well as verbal means of communication (play instruments, take turns clapping rhythms, communicate through music, song, drama or art, take photos, use puppets, use gesture, nodding, pointing, pictures, symbols, writing, drawing, typing and so on). If pupils understand that all forms of communication are accepted and valued, they are more likely to participate and gain confidence at their own pace.

Case study:

The pupils all answer the register and Jerrie stares at the table. The teacher looks up, sees that Jerrie is there and moves on. Jerrie has a fleece blanket around him and plays with some play dough.

During partner work, he rolls the play dough on the table and pushes his pencil into it. The person sitting next to him moves away to talk to someone else. Jerrie looks around the room and holds his blanket closer around himself. He throws a rubber at the person who has moved away and looks back at his table. The teacher tells him off for throwing the rubber.

Reflection opportunities:

■ What could Jerrie's behaviour be communicating?
■ How could this experience increase Jerrie's anxiety?
■ When is speaking usually expected during the school day and what adjustments could be put in place to support anxious pupils to participate?

■ Teach pupils about a variety of different phobias and that phobias can be overcome. Learning the names for phobias can be fun, for example sharks (Galeophobia), chocolate (Xocolataphobia), tomato ketchup (Mortuusequusphobia), public speaking

(Glossophobia) etc. and why phobias may arise (a phobia may arise as a result of having a negative experience related to that object or situation and the brain's response to threat (anxiety) or there may be a link between a child's phobia and anxieties displayed by caregivers).

Alleviating anxieties

■ The first thing adults need to ask themselves is, *How can I reduce this pupil's stress?* Spot the symptoms (physical, environmental and social, see pp.145–6) and provide support in a pro-active rather than reactive way.

■ Build relationships and confidence initially. Have fun building up to simple games which require increasing levels of verbal interaction:

1. Begin by playing alongside each other using small world play, craft and puzzles.
2. Encourage activities which make a sound such as playing a bongo, driving a train on the track and saying 'chug-chug, choo-choo' or playing with a farm and making animal noises.
3. Teach and play a range of turn-taking games which do not require a verbal response (and teach other children in the class to play these) such as *Draughts*, *Jenga*, *Connect 4*, *Snakes and ladders*, throwing a beanbag or ball to each other, copying music or clapping patterns.
4. It might then be possible to introduce some interactive movement games such as *Simon says* and *Follow the leader* and signing action rhymes.
5. When the child is ready, move onto games which require a single word response, teaching a non-verbal gesture alongside the verbal (such as hand on top of the pile in snap, knocking to signify last card in *Uno* or checkmate in chess) so the pressure can be taken off a verbal response as the child develops confidence.
6. If the pupil feels comfortable, group games such as *What's the time Mr Wolf?* can give pupils the opportunity to recite phrases in a group.
7. Ensure the child is completely comfortable before moving on to more verbally demanding (and socially stressful) games, such as *Guess who* or *What am I?*

■ Encourage pair work with a trusted buddy. Rehearse answers with a trusted peer or adult. Use whiteboards to encourage participation in group work. Allow written and video presentations. Think about how to break tasks down into smaller steps.

Case study:

Kaitlin was in Y9. Her class all needed to deliver a presentation and Kaitlin was very anxious about this. On the day of the presentation, Kaitlin stood at the front, started speaking in a quiet voice and was visibly shaking. She started crying in front of her peers and needed to stop. The teacher told her that she could have another go the next day.

That evening, Kaitlin was physically sick with anxiety, she couldn't sleep or think of anything other than the presentation. She told the teacher in the morning, who tutted and told her she won't be able to give up so easily next year and Kaitlin was given a behaviour point for defiance.

Reflection opportunities:

■ How could Kaitlin's fears have been alleviated?
■ How will Kaitlin feel about the next presentation?
■ How could staff have helped her to feel successful?

Suggestions:

■ The teacher needed to understand the drivers behind Kaitlin's behaviours and understand her extreme anxiety, offering support rather than disapproval.
■ Kaitlin could have been praised for her initial efforts and the focus put on what she has done well – stood up and overcome some of her fears in speaking to the class.
■ The task could have been broken down into small, achievable steps, such as just reading the title and key points initially.
■ Kaitlin could have done her presentation in front of a trusted adult and small group of trusted peers.
■ Kaitlin could have been given the opportunity to record her presentation and play the video/audio recording.
■ It was necessary to start where Kaitlin felt comfortable and provide support and encouragement to take the next brave steps.

- Let the pupil know that you will not *cold-call* on them, but you will only ask them a question in front of the group if they put their hand up (or use a different pre-arranged signal). Allow alternative, unspoken responses alongside. 'If reassured that they won't be chosen to answer questions in class, children will relax and enjoy their lessons; otherwise they will be in a constant state of apprehension' (Johnson & Wintgens, 2016, p.32). When the pupil is feeling more confident, *warm-calling* may be used, where the pupil is told the question and can rehearse the answers, using a pre-agreed signal if they feel able to contribute within the group, or check their response on a whiteboard or quietly first.
- Find alternatives to use alongside speaking for times when a verbal response is expected, such as answering the register (nod, wave, clap, etc.) for everyone, to avoid one pupil feeling singled out. As the pupil gains confidence, they may feel able to add a verbal response alongside the agreed alternative.
- During shared reading sessions, ask closed questions which can be responded to verbally, ask the pupil to point to key words or match words to pictures. Ask a caregiver to provide a video of them reading at home (only with the pupil's permission). Include pauses in shared reading sessions for children to fill in gaps if they are able.
- Non-verbal supports alongside verbal interaction are useful to reduce the pressure to speak, such as using photographs, pictures, the written word or gestures. For example, asking for help can induce anxiety and providing a visual 'help card' or establishing another pre-agreed signal, such as a piece of Lego® on the corner of the desk, can help. Provide a visual system for the pupil to indicate that they need to leave the classroom (card, pegs, sign language, signal, etc.).
- Offer positive choices and options, with the option of a non-verbal response alongside verbal replies.
- Pre-warn of, and prepare for, any changes to routine, such as timetable changes or change of adult and ensure all adults know how to respond and support appropriately. A one-page student profile can be useful to show strengths, how to support consistently and strategies that help (and those that don't).
- Set up a worry box or similar means for all pupils to communicate their worries without the need to talk.
- It can be helpful if staff develop an awareness of 'low risk' and 'high risk' activities (Johnson & Wintgens, 2016, p.178).'Low risk' activities are those that usually cause the least anxiety, such as a familiar activity with a trusted peer, speaking along with

a large group, continuing repeated or rote sentences, reading aloud (for competent, confident readers), structured, planned and rehearsed activities, closed questions with single word answers, providing factual content (rather than opinions). 'High risk' activities include speaking in front of an audience or under time pressure, unfamiliar subject matter, reading aloud (beginning or unconfident reader), unplanned conversations, questions requiring personal opinions or talking about themselves, reasoning, longer explanations or justifications and child-initiated conversations. Staff can then support pupils to engage in the lower risk activities initially.

■ 'All pressure to speak must be removed by all those with contact with the child' (SMIRA, undated) and it is essential to ensure all adults (particularly less familiar staff) are aware not to pressure the pupil to talk and, instead, to engage in commentaries and narratives, allowing the pupil to respond with alternative methods to talking (for example, when answering the register).

■ Some useful phrases for adults to use to reassure pupils who struggle to talk in certain situations (adapted from Johnson, 2018) are:

  ■ *Talking to new people can feel scary and your words don't come out. It's OK, you don't need to talk to play these games.*
  ■ *There are lots of ways to join in and have fun like singing, clapping, laughing or making train noises while you are playing.*
  ■ *It's OK, there's no need to talk unless you feel comfortable, I just want you to enjoy your time here.*
  ■ *You're not the only one who finds it hard to talk sometimes.*
  ■ *Don't worry, I'm not going to ask you to answer any questions unless you show me that you want to.*
  ■ *Not everyone can talk straightaway in new places. Just like not everyone knows their four times table or all their phonic sounds. You can join in by listening and thinking and can start talking when it feels right.*

■ Literal thinkers may need certain scenarios reframed, such as 'stranger danger', and pupils may need teaching that they can talk to 'safe' strangers, such as supply teachers, new children in school, new members of school staff, canteen and library staff.

Step-by-step approaches

The aim is, not to avoid speaking altogether, but to gently build up the pupil's confidence, develop relationships, gradually scaffold and encourage communication in a variety of different ways. Each pupil will be different and it is important to start where the pupil feels comfortable and confident, gradually building up the steps in a way that they feel supported and ready. A useful starting point for one pupil may be playing alongside one key adult in order to build a relationship, whereas another pupil may need to become comfortable with initiating interactions and work on saying 'hello' to a key adult.

- It is essential to include the pupil in creating each step of a plan. They need to feel a sense of ownership and control and be able to indicate where they feel comfortable. Find ways to help them to communicate their priorities and barriers to speaking. Establish the pupil's concerns or what is causing distress by drawing and writing or sorting pictures or sentences of situations to explore what they feel comfortable with and use this as a starting point.
- It will be important to look carefully for any signs of discomfort and anxiety. 'Communication should never be an unpleasant or anxiety-producing experience' (Johnson & Wintgens, 2016, p.56). For each step reassure the pupil that they do not need to do anything they do not want to, they will not be pressured into speaking and that they will be going at their own pace. Break each step down into smaller chunks or go back a step or part step if necessary.
- Anxiety rating scales to score each step as it is completed can be useful to record progress and encourage reflection. Pupils can also be taught coping strategies to support them to manage their anxiety.
- Face fears in small steps, focusing on what they can do and already feel comfortable with (things which do not cause stress or anxiety) and using this as a starting point. Plan tiny, graduated steps to make activities more manageable, rather than avoid them completely. Do not move onto the next step until the pupil is completely comfortable with the current one.
- It might be useful to make step-by-step plans to overcome other (real or imaginary) phobias, for example, making a step-by-step plan to help someone to overcome their fear of spiders (see example on pp.53–4) as a starting point.

- It may be useful to present the pupil with one small step at a time to avoid them feeling overwhelmed rather than working on a whole plan at once.
- For each step, aim to change only one small thing at a time, to minimise feeling overwhelmed, for example, if a new person is introduced, ensure a familiar, trusted adult is alongside, engage in a familiar activity, in the same safe space each time. Similarly, if the target is to say 'hello' to the teacher, or answer the register, do this in the same place each day and plan a predictable response.
- Ensure that all step-by-step plans are shared with all key adults and that the focus is on one small step at a time to ensure that it is successful and that trust is not broken.
- As a team, with the pupil, decide what success will look like and how to measure this.
- Alongside the plan, the pupil should be taught a range of regulating techniques to help reduce and manage anxiety. Model, teach, verbalise and practise the chosen regulation strategies regularly, when the pupil is calm so that the strategies become embedded and natural (see Chapter 3). Provide extra support at key times of stress such as around changes to routine and transition times. Positive self-talk can be a useful coping and calming strategy, for example, teach and rehearse phrases such as 'it's OK to let the teacher hear my voice' (Johnson & Wintgens, 2016, p.171) and positive visualisation, such as visualising themselves answering the register positively and successfully.

Environmental adaptations

- Provide an exit strategy such as access to a safe space and calming activities for the pupils to reset if they are feeling overwhelmed. Rehearse using this regularly, while they are calm. Provide a visual cue, such as a card for them to use, so they do not need to verbalise where they are going when they need to leave the classroom.
- Engaging with a safe, trusted adult in a quiet, non-threatening area, with some fun games and activities is usually a good starting point, before introducing and building up peer or group relationships.
- Use a considered seating plan to ensure the pupil feels safe, comfortable and able to learn.

Recognition and consequences

- Avoid rewards for talking as these are ineffective, increase pressure and heighten anxiety. Explore ways to provide recognition for other (non-verbal) achievements and efforts.
- Never sanction for not talking or interacting as this heightens anxiety. Remember that behaviour is a means of communication. Situational mutism is an involuntary activation of the threat response and conveys extreme anxiety or panic rather than defiance, opposition or refusal. The pupil 'cannot' respond in that moment, rather than 'will not' respond and needs support to alleviate those anxieties. 'Gentle encouragement, pleading, cajoling, insistence, threats, bribes, rewards and punishments all make the child more afraid of speaking. SM (Situational Mutism) is the result of a subconsciously learned fear. The only way to overcome it is to *unlearn* this fear' (Johnson & Wintgens, 2016, p.8).

Chapter take-aways

- Pupils who are situationally mute need key, trusted adults in schools to build up positive, trusting relationships.
- Pupils need to feel reassured that they will not feel pressured to speak when they are not comfortable to do so.
- Never reward or sanction for speaking and not speaking.
- Situational mutism is extreme anxiety and fear rather than defiance.

Further signposting

Books for adults

Supporting Quiet Children: Exciting Ideas & Activities to Help 'Reluctant Talkers' Become 'Confident Talkers' by Maggie Johnson & Michael Jones

The Selective Mutism Resource Manual Second Edition by Maggie Johnson & Alison Wintgens

When the Words Don't Come Out by Maggie Johnson & Alison Wintgens Available at: www.selectivemutism.org.uk/wp-content/uploads/2017/09/When-the-words-wont-come-out.pdf

Resources to share with children

Can I Tell You About Selective Mutism? by Maggie Johnson & Alison Wintgens
I am Lenny Brown by Dan Freedman
My Friend Daniel Doesn't Talk by Sharon Longo
The Cat Did Not Eat My Tongue by Artur Raushen

Websites

Hamish and Milo *Amazing Me – Helping Children with Their Self-Esteem and Self-Worth* https://hamishandmilo.org/wellbeing-emotion-themes/amazing-me-helping-children-with-self-esteem
Selective Mutism Information and Research Association (SMIRA) *Information for Professionals* www.selectivemutism.org.uk/information/information-for-professionals
Striving to Speak *Brave Voices* https://strivingtospeak.com

Podcasts

Pooky Ponders *What is Selective Mutism and How Can We Help?* https://www.buzzsprout.com/1183931/5819794-what-is-selective-mutism-and-how-can-we-help-gino-hipolito

References

Brown, S. (2013) *How Your Perception Influences Someone with Selective Mutism* Available at: https://www.syracusenycounseling.com/blog/2013/8/5/how-your-perception-influences-someone-with-selective-mutism [Accessed 2.5.23]
Johnson, M. (2018) *Shyness? Reluctance to Speak? ASD? Or Selective Mutism? People Who Can Speak . . . but Don't* Available at: https://www.bournemouth.ac.uk/sites/default/files/asset/document/selective-mutism-handout.pdf [Accessed 3.5.23]
Johnson, M. & Wintgens, A. (2012) *Can I Tell You About Selective Mutism?: A Guide for Friends, Family and Professionals* Jessica Kingsley
Johnson, M. & Wintgens, A. (2016) *The Selective Mutism Resource Manuel* Second Edition Speechmark
Shipon-Blum, E. (2021) *7 Reasons Why You Should Encourage Art & Musical Expression in Your Child/Teen or Student with Selective Mutism* Available at: https://selectivemutismcenter.org/7-reasons-why-you-should-encourage-art-musical-expression-in-your-child-teen-or-student-with-

selective-mutism/#:~:text=It's%20endless%20why%20encouraging%20
creativity,relaxed%20in%20a%20tense%20situation.

Selective Mutism Information and Research Association (SMIRA) (undated)
Info: Suggestions for Intervention Available at: https://www.selectivemut
ism.org.uk/info-suggestions-for-intervention [Accessed 24.5.24]

Alleviating situational mutism checklist

STRATEGY	COMMENTS		
Please also refer to Chapter 6			
Intervene early			
Early intervention is most impactful			
Key adults			
Up safety cues – smile, open body language, sing song tone – without expecting a verbal response			
Focus on strengths and interests. Ensure pupils know they will not be expected to speak until ready and comfortable			
Build positive relationships based on the PACE approach			
Consider having a trusted friend or adult alongside, while building relationships			
Peer relationships			
Consider buddy systems			
Foster relationships based on shared interests			
Teach peers about situational mutism, if appropriate			
Collaborative approaches			
Work closely with pupil, caregivers and external agencies			
Consider a trusted adult as a 'talking bridge'			
Try talking through different toys			

(Continued)

Continued

STRATEGY	COMMENTS	
Strength-based approaches		
Be creative in supporting pupils to share their strengths and interests and focus on non-verbal achievements		
Provide roles and responsibilities that do not involve talking		
Reframe language into positives		
Communication		
Encourage alternative forms of communication alongside verbal communication		
Focus on an activity to take the pressure off talking		
Notice and comment aloud		
Careful use of questioning		
Allow processing time		
Teaching and learning		
Ensure all tasks are genuinely inclusive		
Introduce a focus alongside verbal interactions		
Consider paired speaking activities		
Ensure school ethos conveys that it is OK to make mistakes		
Option of non-verbal or recorded presentations		
Carefully plan for group and paired working		

(Continued)

Continued

STRATEGY	COMMENTS
Encourage many different means of participating	
Teach about different phobias and how they can be overcome	
Alleviating anxieties	
Reduce stress, spot triggers and provide support	
Play games which require increasing levels of verbal interaction	
Encourage pair work with a trusted buddy	
Avoid cold-calling	
Use non-verbal alternatives alongside spoken responses	
Encourage pointing to words, matching pictures to words and filling in gaps as alternatives to reading aloud	
Offer positive choices	
Pre-warn and prepare for changes and use one-page profiles	
Set up a worry box	
Awareness of low and high-risk activities	
Use key phrases to reassure	
Step-by-step approaches	
Include the pupil in creating each step	
Be aware of anxiety and be prepared to go back a step if necessary	

(Continued)

Continued

STRATEGY	COMMENTS
Use anxiety rating scales to score each step	
Start with what pupils can achieve and face fears in tiny steps	
Consider presenting one step at a time to avoid feeling overwhelmed or make a plan for a different phobia first	
Work collaboratively	
Teach pupil coping strategies alongside the plan	
Environmental adaptations	
Provide an exit strategy	
Provide quieter spaces with key adults to build relationships	
Carefully considered seating plan	
Recognition and consequences	
Avoid rewards for talking and explore ways to provide recognition for non-verbal achievements and efforts	
Never sanction for not talking	

9
School-based anxiety

What is school-based anxiety?

School-based anxiety describes emotional stress or feelings of over-whelm stemming from aspects of the school environment, often resulting in an inability to attend school or engage in certain aspects of school life. Certain elements of school induce heightened anxiety, leading to the perception that school is frightening. Consequently, individuals may feel that they do not have effective strategies to cope or supports in place, and therefore begin to avoid the situation.

There are on-going discussions around the terminology used to describe school avoidance, with Emotionally-Based School Avoidance (EBSA) often used, in order to highlight the emotions which may lead to disengagement and avoidance. Anxiety is not always the driver behind non-attendance or persistent absence; there is a difference between school-based anxiety and truancy. Truancy tends to refer to non-anxiety-based, unauthorised absences which are often without parental knowledge and can be related to anti-social activities, academic difficulties or a disengagement from education (Kearney, 2008, p.452) and often needs a different approach to support.

The term school refusal 'generally refers to anxiety-based absenteeism, often from separation, generalized, or social anxiety' (Kearney, 2008, p.452). However, the phrase 'school refuser' 'appears to connote wilful behaviour' (Pelligrini, 2007) suggesting that the pupil is making a conscious choice not to attend and has some control over the behaviour. Morgan with Costello (2023, p.1) suggest reframing 'school refusal' 'in terms of barriers to attendance'.

The term 'school phobia' highlights the emotional- or anxiety-based aspects of non-attendance, however this label suggests 'within-child' explanations for the behaviour, thus deflecting 'attention from the school

DOI: 10.4324/9781003433231-10

environment as an important element in understanding and addressing it' 'the crucial issue is to understand the functions of this behaviour, and the needs it serves' (Pelligrini, 2007). In other words, adults need to understand the emotions and drivers behind the behaviour and the environmental barriers in order to begin to provide support.

As the focus of this book is on 'understanding anxiety', the term 'school-based anxiety' has been used as the relevant chapters refer to those pupils whose avoidance is being driven by high levels of anxiety around school or elements of school life. The importance of the language reframe away from the term *school refusal* or *absconding* has, therefore, been deliberate, to convey the emotions and anxieties which are driving the avoidance. It is to communicate the fundamental understanding that it is not that the pupil *won't* attend school, often they would desperately like to, they just *can't* at that time, due to an overriding emotional or anxiety-driven response. Adults therefore need to think about support and adjustments which could be provided so that the pupils *can* attend. 'Understanding non-attendance as an act of self-preservation not defiance is an important place to start' (Vodden, in Fricker, 2023, p.149).

The term 'non-attendance' has been avoided within the broad description, because early indicators of avoidance usually manifest while the pupil is physically attending school regularly, for instance anxiety around key aspects of school life, such as relationships, certain lessons, particular times within the school day or concerns about factors outside of school, which are heightening anxiety. As Morgan with Costello (2023, p.232) affirm, 'no child can absorb information if they are in distress and bums on seats does not mean that children are engaged and learning'.

Reframing the language used around school avoidance reframes the way in which adults think about and address the difficulties. Staff can be empathic and compassionate in their reactions and interactions, shifting the focus from being a 'problem' within the child towards looking at environmental, relational and other barriers to attendance.

A pupil experiencing school-based anxiety usually feels a huge amount of distress when attending, or talking and thinking about attending, school. This may be accompanied by high levels of shame around their inability to attend and feelings that they are letting others, and themselves, down.

School attendance has been, and continues to be, an on-going important issue for school staff.

> It is thought that between 1% and 5% of the school population are experiencing EBSA (Emotional Based School

Avoidance) at any one time and that it affects between 5% and 28% of children at some point in their academic journey (note the wide range is due to the measures that researchers take from conservative estimates focused on chronic non-attendance to those where EBSA is only just beginning to be documented by a school).

(Feeney et al., 2023)

Post-pandemic, many pupils struggled to return to, or engage fully, in school. Home was regarded as a place of safety. Social and physical distancing and isolation became the norm during periods of lockdown. Many pupils discovered that they felt calmer and safer at home. They learnt that they could access learning from the safety of their own home with no need to mix with the outside world. There was a lack of socialisation, interaction and play with peers, which, for many, led to higher social anxiety than ever before and schools are continuing to report increased levels of school anxiety and avoidance.

Hadi (2021) states,

the figures for school refusers are shocking, and there are many more who are no longer refusers who have been off-rolled and are home schooled because they cannot cope with the culture of stress in many schools. These children often experience mental health conditions including high anxiety.

Schools need to be genuinely inclusive and support all pupils with the many challenges which face them in school. 'Poorer attendance may be a symptom of a child struggling in the school environment' (Johnson, 2024, p.17). Neurodivergent pupils and those with additional needs often find the demands of school life and the school environment overwhelming which further increases anxiety about school. Sensory sensitivities can make school feel unpredictable and unsafe.

Now, more than ever, adults need to get all aspects of school right for everyone.

Possible barriers to attendance, protective factors and supports

There are usually several factors, for each individual pupil, that contribute to school-based anxiety. School-based needs, such as academic support, sensory sensitivities, bullying or support with social relationships (West Sussex County Council, undated) will need to be effectively addressed. Only by recognising, reducing and adjusting the school factors which are driving the behaviour, anxiety and avoidance, whilst supporting the pupil to recognise and manage these and providing effective support, can the anxiety be alleviated. There is usually a combination of two or more of the barriers below (although this list is far from exhaustive) that contributes to school anxiety, reduced engagement, avoidance and non-attendance. Every pupil is unique and it is important to establish where the barriers and triggers lie for each individual.

Alongside identifying possible barriers to attendance or engagement and establishing exactly what the pupil is finding difficult, it is important to recognise and develop areas of strength or resilience which may help to 'protect' them and promote school attendance.

Factors within school

Possible barriers to school attendance and engagement within school	Possible protective factors and support
Sensory overwhelm – crowds, noise (school bell or fire alarm), smells, clothing, flickering lights, crowds, unpredictability of other children, etc.	Environmental adaptations and reasonable adjustments Reduce distractions Safe spaces and access to quieter areas Planned sensory and movement breaks Sensory supports if required (e.g. ear defenders, fidget tools, caps)
Transitions within the school day – into and out of school, movement to a different classroom or area of the school or a change of adult or activity	Minimise and plan for transitions (see p.58) Warnings and countdowns Transitional objects in school (see p.232) Visual supports
Changes to routine/ unpredictable and inconsistent routines and adults	Consistent, predictable routines and structures in place Visual timetables and 'oops' cards Prepare and pre-warn the pupils as much as possible of up-coming changes One-page profile so all staff are clear about needs
Transitions to a new school or a change of class and teacher	Careful management of transitions (see p.58) Enhanced transition plans (see p.65)

Possible barriers to school attendance and engagement within school	Possible protective factors and support
Key times of stress – exams, groupwork, oral presentations, key lessons	Teach pupils to recognise symptoms of anxiety and teach coping strategies (see Chapter 4) Alleviate anxieties, e.g. provide support, pre-warn, familiarise using walk throughs, practise with any adaptations or adjustments Support and check-ins from key adults
Key areas of stress – playgrounds, corridors, canteens, toilets, changing rooms	Allow access to corridors, lockers and toilets at quieter times of the school day Quieter zones at break and lunch times Safe spaces and key adults Support and check-ins
Difficult relationships with key members of staff	Focus on positive pupil-adult relationships (see Chapter 2) PACE approach (see p.26) Regular check-ins from key adults Safe spaces Up safety cues – tone, body language, language used Positive language reframes (see p.24) Restorative approaches (see p.36) Staff reflection
Difficulties (or perceived difficulties) accessing the work/ unmet learning needs	Temporarily reduce demands Reframe language and increase choices Scaffolding and adaptive teaching Visual supports Adult or buddy support to get started Alleviate anxieties (see pp.207–8) Pre-teaching
Friendship difficulties or bullying	Robust and effective anti-bullying policy Focus on supporting peer relationships and teaching social skills Peer mentoring and buddy systems Active listening to understand Restorative conversations Continued monitoring and intervention
Returning to school after a prolonged absence	Reintegration plan drawn up with pupil, caregiver and key adults Maintain relationships during periods of absence/establish relationships prior to return

(Continued)

Continued

Possible barriers to school attendance and engagement within school	Possible protective factors and support
Previous or on-going negative experiences in school/history of suspensions and exclusions/fear of being reprimanded	Language reframes and focusing on strengths Understanding behaviour as a form of communication, understanding of the diversity of needs Agree and focus on priorities Reasonable and effective adjustments and 'Differentiated Discipline' (Bombèr, 2020) Review behaviour policies to incorporate relational approaches (see p.240)
Lacks a sense of belonging or connectedness to the school/ does not feel welcome or valued in the school setting	Welcoming smiles and routines Strength-based approaches Value diversity and difference through displays, curriculum content, books, staffing and resources as well as language used and ethos Build a sense of belonging and connectedness and be genuinely inclusive Offer a range of different extra-curricular activities Value all successes, inside and outside school
School environment and ethos	Increase feelings of positivity around school Ensure each individual feels welcome and valued Review curriculum and resources to reflect and celebrate diversity and promote genuine inclusion
Lack of robust attendance procedure and policy within the school	Review and improve whole school policies and practices, e.g. key adult calling home and maintaining contact during periods of absence Whole staff training on school avoidance and welcoming approaches
Social and communication misunderstandings or difficulties	Clear, direct language Visual supports Social Stories™ or comic strip conversations (Carol Gray) Restorative conversations

Possible barriers to school attendance and engagement within school	Possible protective factors and support
Certain topics and celebration days – Mother's/Father's Day, religious festivals, birthdays, topics and stories involving death, loss, evacuation, war, non-uniform days, off-timetable days, etc.	Collaborate with caregivers (and pupils if appropriate) to gain awareness of possible triggers Sensitive handling of sensitive topics Pre-warn and prepare pupils Safe spaces and key adults for times of overwhelm and to reflect and talk

Factors within home

Possible barriers to school attendance and engagement arising from within the home or family	Possible protective factors and support
Caregiver anxiety and concerns/ family history of anxiety and school avoidance	Welcoming approaches which alleviate anxieties Providing and signposting towards support for caregivers Listen carefully to concerns and work collaboratively to provide support and address any issues arising
Changes to or difficulties in family circumstances	Providing and signposting towards support for caregivers Trusted adults for pupil to share concerns with Creative activities to reflect and express emotions
Other members of the family being at home	Ensure school is welcoming, the pupil feels valued and sense of belonging Trusted adults and relational approaches Engaging curriculum Extra-curricular clubs Collaboration with caregivers to balance 'push' and 'pull' factors
Concerns about the health or safety of loved ones	Phone calls home Trusted adults for pupil to talk to Creative activities to reflect and express emotions Transitional objects (p.231)

(Continued)

Continued

Possible barriers to school attendance and engagement arising from within the home or family	Possible protective factors and support
Being a young carer	Identify and provide support for young carers Build relationship Listen Provide support and signpost pupils and families towards further support
A high number of family/school transitions	Communication and collaboration with family/previous schools Routine, structure, predictability, safety Increase sense of belonging and ensure pupils feel welcome and valued Key adults in school Enhanced transition plans Plan for beginnings and goodbyes Ensure a sense of belonging

Individual factors

Possible barriers to attendance and engagement which could arise within the individual pupil	Possible protective factors and support
Low self-esteem/does not feel successful	Boost self-esteem and success rate – roles and responsibilities based on their interests Strength-based approaches and language reframes (see p.24) Build resilience
Lacks interest/motivation in learning tasks /ambition/sense of direction	Hands-on, multisensory learning Broad, balanced, diverse and inclusive curriculum Play-based learning Hook their interest and use passions and interests as a starting point Explore and develop ambitions, aspirations, strengths and successes *I can* attitude

Possible barriers to attendance and engagement which could arise within the individual pupil	Possible protective factors and support
Anxiety/separation anxiety	Key adults and relational approaches Transitional objects Step-by-step approaches (see p.208) Reassurance Support separation anxiety (see p.227)
Difficulty recognising and regulating emotions	See Chapter 4 Providing opportunities to explore and express emotions and ensuring the pupil feels heard and understood Key adults to support and co-regulate
Shame, rejection sensitivity fear of failure/making mistakes	Feedback on anonymous work rather than their own Avoid calling out or public displays of test scores Relational approaches and logical consequences which do not induce shame (see p.245) Recognition for effort rather than output
Loss, bereavement, separation and change/adversity/trauma	Provide support, key adults, listen Ensure school is a safe base Positive relationships with trusted staff Seek professional support and advice and signpost caregivers to further support
Neurodivergence	Celebrate diversity and value difference through whole school ethos Strength-based approaches – 'difference' not 'deficit' Whole school training and understanding of individual needs Environmental adaptations Reasonable adjustments Ensure policy and practice promotes genuine inclusion Key adults Visual cues for all pupils, as needed Sensory supports and movement breaks Safe spaces

(Continued)

Continued

Possible barriers to attendance and engagement which could arise within the individual pupil	Possible protective factors and support
Social, Emotional and Mental Health (SEMH) needs	Promote positive discussions around mental health and wellbeing, removing stigma Key adults, relational approaches Safe spaces Collaboration with caregivers and outside agencies Pastoral care School counsellors Reasonable adjustments Scaffolding and adaptive teaching Emotional support and co-regulation Strength-based approaches Genuine inclusion
Special Educational Needs and Disabilities (SEND)	Collaboration with caregivers and outside agencies Reasonable adjustments Scaffolding and adaptive teaching Chunking work Visual supports Strength-based approaches Genuine inclusion

Early indicators

School-based anxiety and avoidance tend to occur when 'stress exceeds support, when risks are greater than resilience and when "pull" factors that promote school non-attendance overcome the "push" factors that encourage attendance' (Thambirajah et al., 2008, p.33). The 'pull' factors being the possible barriers to attendance and the 'push' factors being the protective factors and supports. It is therefore the role of adults in school to reduce stress and possible barriers and increase the protective in-school supports.

Case study:

Ash is 12. On arrival at the school gate they are told by a member of the Senior Leadership Team that they are late and Ash needs to attend break time detention, they are then sent into school.

Reflection opportunities:

- What effect could this experience have on Ash's attendance?
- How could the very start of the school day be made into a positive experience for all pupils?
- How does it feel when you walk in late to a staff meeting or training session? How would you like to be greeted?

Suggestions:

- Staff greet all pupils with a smile and welcoming remark to support pupils to feel valued and positive – leave any reflective conversations for key adults to have later.
- If punctuality needs addressing, have a key, trusted adult have a supportive conversation later, to establish if the pupil needs support.
- Be curious about why the pupil was late, and treat all pupils with empathy and compassion. Make reasonable adjustments or provide support, as necessary.

Case study continued:

Following a supportive conversation with a trusted member of staff, who stepped in, seeing that Ash seemed upset, it was discovered that Ash was a young carer. Having been up caring for their mum since 5am, they then went to the shop to get breakfast for their two younger siblings, got both siblings up, fed and dressed and delivered to two different schools before arriving at their own school ten minutes late. When asked why they hadn't told anyone before, they replied 'no-one asked'.

(In my opinion Ash deserved a medal for arriving ten minutes late, not a detention.)

Intervening early can prevent non-attendance from becoming embedded and results in much improved outcomes for the pupil. Listening to concerns of caregivers is paramount, as early warning signs are usually more noticeable in the home. 'Fear is often at its height either just before leaving home or on the journey to school' (Bowlby, 1998, p.301). When early warning signs are observed, it is important to work in collaboration with the pupil and caregivers to gather further information about what is impacting on the pupil's attendance, in order to put strategies in place to support them as soon as possible.

Adults need to remain curious about what is driving the behaviour and be aware of the early warning signs that a pupil is experiencing heightened anxieties around school, which may affect engagement and attendance. Early indicators include:

- Missing certain lessons or school activities.
- A marked change in behaviour, engagement and attainment.
- Task avoidance.
- Lack of or reduced motivation.
- Increased requests or need to access the toilet.
- Fear of making mistakes, perfectionism, extreme conformity.
- Accessing lessons or engaging in tasks with a high level of adult support.
- Being on a reduced or highly bespoke timetable.
- Attending school but often not in class or not engaging in learning tasks.
- Increased lateness/absence and missing school regularly due to 'minor' ailments.
- A change or reduction in friendships.
- Withdrawal from social situations and activities.
- Difficulty expressing and regulating emotions and extreme reactions to seemingly small stressors.
- Physical presentations or displays of anger, anxiety, stress or increased threat response reactions (fight, flight and shutdown).
- Physical presentations of anxiety such as nausea, stomach pain, headaches or physical sickness are more apparent in response to key school-based activities or on Sunday evenings and weekday mornings and disappear during school holidays.
- Negative talk about school or staff.
- Reports from home of difficulties accessing morning routines (getting dressed in school uniform, leaving the house, getting out of the car, etc.).
- Reports from home that the pupil is leaving their house or bedroom less frequently.
- Increased anxiety across a range of areas.
- Separation anxiety (see Chapters 11 and 12).

The process of getting ready for school represents a difficult transition. Younger children are more likely to experience the distress of this transition in the form of physical feelings. The physical feelings are genuine and tell the child that she cannot cope. The child may adhere to a rigid morning routine in order to feel more secure.

(Eisen & Engler, 2006, p.117)

Once some of these early warning signs of anxiety and school avoidance have been identified, supportive strategies to alleviate the anxieties will need to be implemented.

Maintaining factors

It is important to understand the drivers behind school avoidance in order to provide effective support. Staff will need to consider the possible key barriers to attendance and establish the factors which are maintaining and reinforcing the cycle of avoidance for the pupil. Once these factors have been identified, it will then be possible to explore the support that could be provided. Maintaining and reinforcing factors could include:

- Friendship or relational difficulties.
- Pupil is 'made' to attend school, with little or no support given and key barriers to attendance not addressed appropriately or effectively.
- Increasing gaps in learning due to missed lessons.
- Avoidance feeds the anxiety further.
- The pupil engages in enjoyable activities while at home and fears missing out.
- The pupil is concerned about the safety of those in the home.

Collaboration with caregivers and actively listening to their concerns is essential in early intervention. Bodycote's research (in Morgan with Costello, 2023, p.42) found that when 'parents tried to share their concerns with the school . . . staff dismissed those concerns, insisting that their children were "fine in school"' and she states, 'it was crucial for parents and schools to work in partnership to identify and overcome the barriers that were stopping each child from attending' (Morgan with Costello, 2023, p.46).

The Children's Commissioner for England (2023, p.10) found that those most at risk of persistent absence were:

- Pupils with Special Educational Needs and/or Disability (SEND).
- Pupils with mental health conditions (including anxiety).

- Young carers.
- Children with a history of exclusion and absence.

Further reporting:

- Having an Education, Health and Care Plan (EHCP) was associated with four additional days of absence per term, relative to not having any SEND support.
- Low attendance was often the result of the school being unable to deliver required reasonable adjustments or provide a suitable learning environment, respectful of the child's additional needs.

The Behaviour and Mental Health in Schools report (Rainer et al., 2023) found that the experience of certain behaviour management techniques at school (isolation, exclusion, suspensions, sanctions for lateness or non-attendance and whole class sanctions) impacted on the mental health of young people including 'feeling negatively about themselves, feeling worthless, invisible, and disappointed in themselves'. Young people described how experiencing such behaviour management techniques led to them disliking school and increased feelings of anxiety, particularly in relation to school attendance. In the same report, caregivers conveyed that when their children with existing mental health difficulties experienced those same behaviour management techniques, their difficulties heightened, in some cases these 'experiences led their child to self-harm and to experience suicidal thoughts'. By moving away from traditional behavioural approaches to focus on the individual needs of every pupil, schools become safe, enjoyable places which work for everyone, thereby reducing anxiety and increasing attendance.

'Punitive measures [fines, prosecutions and referrals to social services] don't deal with students' distress or feelings of being unsafe or anxious in school. In fact, they often add to the child's feelings of guilt and distress. . . . Rather than relying on the 'stick' of punishment and stigma, we need to look to the 'carrot' of a student-centred, trauma-informed approach that meets the needs of all the young people in our care' (Caress, 2023). Schools need to find ways to support pupils and caregivers rather than punish them.

Chapter take-aways

- School-based anxiety is emotional stress, stemming from aspects of the school environment, resulting in the inability to attend school or engage in certain aspects of school life.

- Adults need to understand the barriers to attendance, recognise the early warning signs, increase protective factors and make effective reasonable adjustments to support pupils.
- Punitive methods are ineffective for school avoidance that stems from anxiety, and pupils and caregivers need support rather than punishment in order to break the cycle.

Further signposting

Books

Can't Not Won't – A Story of a Child Who Couldn't Go to School by Eliza Fricker

Square Pegs: Inclusivity, Compassion and Fitting In – A Guide for Schools by Fran Morgan & Ellie Costello

Websites

Anna Freud *Addressing Emotionally Based School Avoidance* https://www.annafreud.org/schools-and-colleges/resources/addressing-emotionally-based-school-avoidance

Autistic Girls Network *Reasonable Adjustments Possible at School* https://autisticgirlsnetwork.org/reasonable-adjustments-possible-at-school

Carers.org *Supporting Young Carers in School* https://carers.org/resources/all-resources/15-supporting-young-carers-in-schools-a-step-by-step-guide-for-leaders-teachers-and-non-teaching-staff

Dr Pooky Knightsmith *School Anxiety/EBSA – Starting the Day Well* https://www.youtube.com/watch?v=-FO46lUI7Mk West Sussex County Council *Emotionally Based School Avoidance* https://schools.westsussex.gov.uk/Page/10483

Hertfordshire County Council *Emotionally Based School Avoidance Guidance for Parents* https://www.hertfordshire.gov.uk/microsites/Local-Offer/Media-library/Documents/Emotionally-Based-School-Avoidance-Parent-guidance-PDF-642kb.pdf

Podcasts

Association for Child and Adolescent Mental Health (ACAMH) *Emotionally Based School Avoidance* https://www.acamh.org/freeview/emotionally-based-school-avoidance-recording

Beacon School Support *Support Strategies for Pupils with Emotionally Based School Avoidance* https://beaconschoolsupport.co.uk/podcast/76

Pooky Ponders *School Anxiety* https://www.pookyknightsmith.com/podcast-school-anxiety-starting-the-school-day-right

References

Bombèr, L. (2020) *Know Me to Teach Me – Differentiated Discipline for Those Recovering from Adverse Childhood Experiences* Worth Publishing

Bowlby, J. (1998) *Attachment and Loss: Separation, Anger and Anxiety* Pimlico

Brukner, L. (2014) *The Kids' Guide to Staying Awesome and in Control – Simple Stuff to Help Children Regulate Their Emotions and Senses* Jessica Kingsley

Caress, A. (2023) *A Whole-School Approach to Emotionally-based School Avoidance* Available at: https://www.ocr.org.uk/blog/a-whole-school-approach-to-emotionally-based-school-avoidance/#:~:text=Taking%20a%20whole%2Dschool%20approach&text=Taking%20time%20to%20think%20about,the%20needs%20of%20the%20child [Accessed 6.9.23]

Children's Commissioner for England (2023) *Attendance is Everyone's Business – Children's Commissioner's Submission to the Persistent Absence Inquiry* Available at: https://www.childrenscommissioner.gov.uk/resource/attendance-is-everyones-business/ [Accessed 8.9.23]

Eisen, A. & Engler, L. (2006) *Helping Your Child Overcome Separation Anxiety or School Refusal: A Step by Step Guide for Parents* New Harbinger Publications

Feeney J., Dosi, R., Morgan H. & Stenning, A. (2023) *Emotionally Based School Avoidance (EBSA) Toolkit for Schools* Buckinghamshire Council

Fricker, E. (2023) *Can't Not Won't – A Story of a Child Who Couldn't Go to School* Jessica Kingsley

Hadi, F. (2021) *Return of 14 Year Old Exams Despite Rise in School Refusal and Mental Health Issues for Teens* https://www.disabilityrightsuk.org/news/2021/october/return-14-year-old-exams-despite-rise-school-refusal-and-mental-health-issues [Accessed 16.3.23]

Johnson, S. (2024) *All About SEMH; A Practical Guide for Secondary Teachers* Routledge

Kearney, C. (2008) School Absenteeism and School Refusal Behaviour in Youth: A Contemporary Review *Clinical Psychology Review 28*(3): 451–471 Available at: https://www.sciencedirect.com/science/article/abs/pii/S027273580700133X [Accessed 18.2.24]

Knightsmith, P. (2023) *KEYNOTE | Emotionally Based School Avoidance (EBSA) 1 – Prevention* Available at: https://www.pookyknightsmith.com/keynote-ebsa-school-anxiety-prevention [Accessed 17.1.23]

Morgan, F. with Costello, E. (2023) *Square Pegs: Inclusivity, Compassion and Fitting In – A Guide for Schools* Independent Thinking Press

Pelligrini, D. (2007) School Non-Attendance: Definitions, Meanings, Responses, Interventions *Educational Psychology in Practice* 1: 63–77.

Rainer, C., Le, H. & Abdinasir, K. (2023) *Behaviour and Mental Health in Schools* Children and Young People's Mental Health Coalition

Thambirajah M., Grandison K. & De-Hayes L. (2008) *Understanding School Refusal: A Handbook for Professionals in Education, Health, and Social Care* Jessica Kingsley

West Sussex County Council (undated) *Emotionally Based School Avoidance (EBSA) and Autism Information for Parents and Carers* West Sussex Educational Psychology Service

10

Alleviating school-based anxiety

Relational approaches

Pupils need to feel safe and secure in school and building positive relationships is crucial (see Chapter 2).

- Each pupil is individual and taking time to foster a trusting, positive relationship with them (and their caregivers) is essential. Adults need to work collaboratively and genuinely understand what is driving the avoidant behaviour in order to be best placed to provide support. It is important to be curious about what the behaviour is communicating in a way that is compassionate, accepting and empathic rather than one which induces blame or shame. Knightsmith (2023) suggests that adults who support pupils who are struggling to attend school need to be 'consistent', to 'care' and 'communicate' to form a 'connection' and to remain 'curious' and 'calm'.
- When under stress, the brain automatically seeks proximity and comfort from those who are trusted and feel safe. Find out from the pupil which adults in school help them to feel safe. Try to establish what it is about these adults that helps them and see how this can be replicated when building relationships with a wider circle of staff. Use this as a starting point to create a small team of key adults to build a positive, genuine relationship with the pupil and become their champion, checking in regularly with them during the day, particularly at the beginning and end of the school day, at key trigger times or times of high anxiety,

DOI: 10.4324/9781003433231-11

being there to listen to concerns and to support them to feel safe, happy and valued in school. Staff and caregivers need to become the pupil's 'stress regulator' (Bombèr, 2020) to help them navigate stressful times. Pupils need to be familiar with where and how they can access these safe faces when they are becoming stressed and distressed.

■ There needs to be a whole school approach and training on school-based anxiety for all staff, including breakfast and after-school club staff, lunchtime supervisors, site managers and all 'front-facing' staff – those first faces seen by pupils (staff on the gates and in the front office). Not only are they the key people who can pick up on early indicators, such as arriving at school in distress, separation anxiety, dips in punctuality or arriving 'just in time', they are also the first people to greet the pupil and can set the (negative or positive) tone for the rest of the day.

Case study:

Codie is 13. Her school attendance has taken a steady decline over the past year and she hasn't been to school at all for the last three weeks. Her tutor and her dad have been collaborating to try and encourage her into school to work in a small group, for a reduced part of the morning. Codie arrived in school at the beginning of the fourth week. As she arrived in the front office, she was told that she couldn't go into school wearing her hoodie (as per the school uniform policy). Codie said she would take it off when she got into the Nurture room. The office staff re-stated that they wouldn't let her in until she removed the hoodie. Codie sat down shouting, *"What is the point? My dad said just try and get in and now I have to deal with all this.*

Reflection opportunities:

■ How could this have been made a more positive experience for Codie?

Suggestions:

■ All staff greet Codie with a smile and welcoming remark to support her and make her feel valued and positive.
■ Key adult whom she has a relationship with meets and greets Codie.

- Tactical ignoring/reasonable adjustments made around uniform/trusted adult to address uniform once she is settled, if necessary or appropriate.
- Whole staff Emotionally Based School Avoidance (EBSA) training.
- Agree priorities and approaches for Codie and share these with the whole staff.

- Positive first encounters are essential in reducing anxiety and supporting all pupils into school. Conversely, negative initial encounters can contribute to a downward spiral of shame and avoidance. Welcome all pupils in with a smile and a positive comment. Any difficulties or issues can be addressed later alongside a trusted member of staff with whom the pupil has a positive relationship with curiosity, empathic listening and compassion.

Case study:

Ruby is 6. She arrives at her class late. The teacher stops talking to the class, gives her a beaming smile and says, *Oh Ruby, I am so glad you are here. I was just starting to worry that we might not see you today. We were all hoping you would come in. Get yourself settled and join us on the carpet when you are ready.*

Reflection opportunities:

- How might this interaction make Ruby (and other children) feel?
- What impact can a welcoming, positive approach have on attendance?

- A positive relationship between the pupil and a trusted adult is absolutely essential. If a pupil is not attending, staff will need to find alternative ways of building and maintaining relationships, connections and a sense of belonging through periods of prolonged absence, such as by telephone, email, postcards home or engaging in activities remotely. Key staff may arrange to meet with the caregiver and pupil in a more neutral or relaxed environment.

It would be useful to embrace and extend those approaches which were implemented during periods of lockdown to provide adjustments, find alternative means of learning and build relationships for pupils who are currently unable to attend in order to build connections and avoid increasing gaps in learning.

Case study:

Bella was 13. Her attendance had been declining at the end of primary school and she did not return to school after lockdowns. She did not attend her new secondary school at all for the first 18 months.

Bella's mum and key school staff met. Bella did not feel able to attend but her voice was shared through her mum and collaboratively they made a plan to support Bella begin to engage. It was very clear that Bella never had had the opportunity to build a positive relationship with any member of school staff and going into school was terrifying for her. Staff needed to work hard to build up a trusting relationship to help her to feel safe just talking about school.

One of the pastoral teaching assistants (TAs) began to work with Bella and her mum. They agreed to meet online each morning at a set time. Bella didn't have to put her camera on. The TA engaged in some playful remote activities to begin to build a relationship. Initially, Bella was very nervous and the TA just chatted for a few minutes. On the days Bella was unable to engage remotely, the TA would phone home and check in (via her mum, if necessary). Over a period of time, Bella began to engage and the TA and Bella built up a positive relationship. The TA gave Bella a remote tour of key areas of the school and they laughed together about her bad videoing skills.

After a few weeks of continued relationship-building and some online learning tasks, Bella felt able to visit school at a time of day when the pupils were in their lessons, so it wouldn't be busy and they met face-to-face whenever Bella felt able to. During this time, teachers sent projects or learning packs home and Bella gradually began to engage in some of this, discovering that she had a real flair for art, and the art teacher sent her a positive email praising her art project.

Over time, Bella began to feel slightly more confident. She began to access a small Nurture provision, within the school, for an hour every day, with her trusted TA, a teacher and four other pupils. She is currently attending school for key lessons. The TA checks in on her regularly and Bella can go and see her when necessary. It has been a very gradual, step-by-step plan, with Bella being completely comfortable with each step before moving forward. She has a way to go but she has made those terrifying first steps and things are moving in the right direction. The absolute commitment from the (incredible) TA, Bella's mum, Bella and school has been key to Bella's success.

- Aim to problem solve and devise plans with the pupil to ensure that they feel included and that decisions are made *with* them rather than *for* them.
- Actively listen with compassion and empathy, encouraging pupils to share what helps them (and what doesn't) and ensure all staff are mindful and respectful of this information. 'If we do not show ourselves as willing to listen, we leave children, especially younger children, with two main routes for expressing their emotions; they act out or they shut down' (Morgan with Costello, 2023, p.17).
- Make time for *'if . . . then'* conversations, so pupils are encouraged to voice their worries with a trusted adult and collaboratively problem solve to find solutions. Present these solutions visually, as necessary, as a reminder, for example, *'if this happens . . . I can do . . . or go to . . .'.*
- Create a safety plan together, when the pupil is calm, so they know where and who to go to when their threat response is activated. If a pupil's flight response is regularly activated, chasing and following will increase their sense of threat, so when they feel the need to run they need pre-planned safe spaces and safe faces to go to. If a pupil's fight response is often triggered plan how to release these feelings safely (see p.97). Rehearse the plan regularly, so it becomes natural and embedded.
- Pupils need safe spaces and key adults to go to if they are feeling overwhelmed and to help them navigate relationship difficulties. A positive whole school ethos and a robust, clear anti-bullying policy is essential. 'Experiencing bullying should be explored when a child is identified as at risk of being persistently absent from school and action taken to reduce the bullying' (Anti-Bullying Alliance, 2023). Pupils need to feel listened to and trust that

issues will be taken seriously and resolved in order to feel safe moving forward.

■ Some pupils will need support to foster positive relationships and make and maintain friendships. Introduce buddy or mentor systems and support small group play by teaching structured games and setting up activities for those with similar interests, provide smaller areas or zones at break times and lunchtimes. Support pupils with the expectations of social interactions and teach and rehearse conversation starters if necessary.

■ Adults need to remain self-reflective and to ensure that their reactions, responses and language is positive, encouraging and non-judgemental. 'When a child is struggling, adults must recognise that their reactions can help or make things a whole lot worse' (Not Fine in School, 2019).

Collaboration with caregivers

■ A positive relationship between school staff and home is essential. 'It is through working together and developing joint understanding that schools and families can break the cycle of anxiety avoidance and help children and young people to develop resilience in the face of their individual needs' (Feeney et al., 2023).

■ When working with caregivers, staff need to be aware of, and sensitive to, caregiver stress and anxiety. Having a consistent, trusted person (or small key team) of contact can help lessen some caregiver anxieties and helps build trusting relationships to support collaboration. Caregivers may have had anxiety around school themselves or have other children who struggle to attend. The stress of the morning routine will likely be incredibly high for many and they could be in a negative cycle, with families highly distressed and dysregulated before the school day has begun. Caregivers may also have felt dismissed and unheard by professionals in the past and may have felt blamed and judged. Be open to listen, empathise, care and support.

■ Be aware of the environment and the message being conveyed when arranging meetings to put pupils and caregivers at ease, make them feel valued and welcome and encourage them to talk in a safe way, without judgement or blame. Little things make a huge difference, such as sitting at a round table rather than 'interview style' and offering a drink and biscuits.

Case study:

Tom is 5. His pre-school and early years were largely during the pandemic lockdowns. Some of his family members were vulnerable so he spent a large proportion of time in the family home. Tom struggled to attend in Reception and for the first few weeks of Y1, he was unable to leave the house for school in the mornings. Seeing his uniform set out for him caused huge amounts of distress.

School wanted to support Tom and his mum but they were unable to meet in school as his distress levels were so high. Therefore, school suggested that they meet in the family home.

On the day of the visit, mum got up at 4.30am and spent the morning rushing around, tidying the house, and trying to get Tom dressed, to eat his breakfast and to get her older two children safely to school.

The head teacher and another senior member of staff (both professionally dressed in their suits and ties, with their lanyards on) arrived at the house at the agreed time and were welcomed in. As they said 'hello' to Tom, he ran screaming to his mum and hid under the table, crying and did not come out while the two members of school staff were there.

Reflection opportunities:

■ How could the meeting have been made into a more positive experience for Tom?
■ How could staff help Tom and his mum to feel safe?
■ How might they have begun to build a relationship with Tom?

Suggestions:

■ Adults need to reduce anxieties and begin to build a relationship so they could take toys/activities to begin to try and 'hook his interest' (having had a conversation with Tom's mum in advance to find out his interests and likes).
■ Get down on the floor and play – getting down to the child's level increases feelings of safety.
■ Consider meeting on neutral ground (in the park, library, etc) to take the pressure off mum and keep home as Tom's safe place.

- Caregivers need to feel that their child is safe and cared for at school and that their needs are being met. Establish positive relationships, acknowledging that caregivers know their child and are the best people to support their child to come into school. Start by sharing the pupil's strengths, what they love and what they do to relax and regulate at home. Actively listen to concerns and collaborate in a way that is genuinely accepting and non-judgemental. Provide support and encouragement and help caregivers and pupils to begin to take small and gradual steps forward, while feeling supported, empowered and valued. 'Where there is a lack of triangulation between the child, their school and the carers involved, there is going to be confusion and inconsistency. Connection – genuine, open, honest and empathetic – is key' (Bootman in Morgan with Costello, 2023, p.64).

- A team approach is the most effective and gives a consistent message of collaboration and high expectations for success, with appropriate support. Ensure that the pupil knows that all adults are working together to ensure that the school feels safe and to make it a positive environment for them. Decide as a team, what successful first steps may look like and what each member of the team can do to support the pupil.

- Aim to explore, with the family, the reasons for the pupil not attending school. For example:

  - Are they concerned about the safety, welfare or health of key family members and feel reassured by being at home and close to them?
  - Are other family members at home, so they fear missing out if they go to school?
  - Are they able to spend much of the day doing things that they enjoy, such as getting out of bed later, playing video games, outings with family members, playing with favourite toys or engaging in other interests, watching television. etc? (see 'Barriers to attendance', p.177).

Collaboratively, explore how these issues can be addressed to increase the 'push' factors towards school and reduce the 'pull' factors towards home (see p.184). School needs to feel appealing to the pupil, so work together to try to reduce the more motivating and rewarding activities at home during school hours and try to introduce engaging and interesting school-based tasks if the pupil is at home.

- It is important that the learning gap doesn't widen while the pupil cannot attend, as this will increase anxiety. Set interesting school-based projects and remote or online learning activities to be completed during the periods of time that the pupil is struggling to attend (see p.207).
- Use the pupil's interests and strengths to try to engage them in tasks or encourage them to attend lessons that they particularly enjoy as a starting point. Identify any support the caregivers may need to help the pupil to be successful (see 'Suggestions for caregivers', below).
- It often takes a long time to recover after the threat response has been activated, so if a caregiver reports a difficult start to the day the pupil will probably need more time with key adults and more sensory and movement breaks throughout the day in order to remain calm and able to engage.
- Collaboration with outside agencies, such as Child and Adolescent Mental Health Services (CAMHS), local authority reintegration officers and attendance workers, educational psychologists and outreach teachers, can be effective in creating reintegration and provision plans.
- Staff can help caregivers to feel supported by signposting and helping them to find out more about anxiety and school avoidance.

Suggestions for caregivers (see also Chapter 12)

- Rae (2021) suggests developing a visual plan to establish calming evening and morning routines. By encouraging the child to contribute to the plan, they will have a sense of control and ownership. To facilitate calmer mornings, Rae advises preparing as many things as possible the night before. This might include laying out uniform, preparing lunch boxes and snacks and ensuring PE kits and school bags are packed and ready and that both shoes are by the front door.
- Try to establish a calm bedtime routine, such as a shared story, hot chocolate, lavender scented bath or listening to relaxing music together while watching a bubble lamp.
- Acknowledge how difficult the situation is and be aware that just talking about school can heighten anxieties. Listen, validate and acknowledge your child's feelings offering empathy, understanding and reassurance that you support them. *I can hear that you're feeling worried about school, that must feel really hard for you, I am here to help you and X will meet you in the morning to play with*

the Lego®, as we planned. Having actively listened and validated their feelings, try to move the conversation on to more positive aspects of the day, such as pastoral time, PE, computing, seeing friends, break times or something that you plan to do together after school, such as going to the park, going for an ice cream or watching a film together.

■ When everyone is calm, explore and rehearse coping strategies, such as breathing or grounding techniques, listening to music, using a stress toy, blowing bubbles, watching a funny video clip together, playing with playdough, colouring, etc. Dr Karen Treisman provides suggestions for setting up a regulating box (see further Chapter 4, 'Signposting' p.102). Having rehearsed calming strategies together, in anxious moments model using them (for example, if you see your child becoming stressed, start playing with playdough or blowing bubbles with the aim of them mirroring).

■ Be aware of how your own emotions can influence your child and aim to model positivity and calm. Learn healthy and appropriate ways to calm your own reactions. Learning regulating techniques together can help you both to calm. Adults can then begin to model and manage their own emotions in front of the child. A child soon picks up on adult anxiety and this will feed into their own.

■ Increase your child's sense of ownership and control, by asking them what would be most helpful for them and how they would like you to support them. Explore all suggestions (yours and theirs, however far-fetched – the humorous ones will add a sense of playfulness and can help reduce defensiveness) and write them down in a mind map, then highlight the ones they prefer and cross off any that will not work.

■ Avoid avoiding! Aim not to completely avoid situations that induce anxiety (such as leaving the house or meeting new people) as, although avoidance provides temporary relief, it then feeds the anxiety cycle, making it more difficult to engage in the activity next time. Avoidance gives the message that the distressing feelings are too hard to cope with. Instead, start with what is manageable and gradually build up, step-by-step, ensuring that the child feels supported and safe each step of the way.

■ It is essential, as a caregiver, to be positive about school, as children quickly pick up on (and adopt) similar negative thoughts. Avoid speaking negatively about school, staff, policy or systems or attributing blame. Focus on, and draw attention to, all the positive aspects of school, such as preferred activities, friends, favourite lessons and the best snacks in the canteen rather than the negatives. Each day, encourage your child to identify things that have gone well, recording this visually in a jar or book, on a paperchain or on a sticky note to be referred to in the future.

■ Discuss long- and short-term goals and ambitions such as friendships, career aspirations, personal strengths and interests and link these to aspects of school life.

■ If your child struggles to get out of bed and ready for school in the mornings, plan and establish a predictable morning routine and present this visually. Alternatively, add a playful element and make games out of getting ready, such as having a dressing race, in order to reduce the stress.

Case study:

Edwin (age 10) was finding it difficult to get ready for school in the mornings. He would struggle to get out of bed, then shout and scream that he didn't have time to shower, gel his hair and get ready and was going to be late. By the time he was ready to leave the house, both mum and Edwin were stressed and exhausted.

When Edwin was calm, he and his mum sat down and came up with suggestions of things that might help in the mornings. All ideas were written down, and the tension was lifted by some wild and whacky ones being included, which made them both laugh.

By chatting through what he was finding difficult, his mum was able to offer support and Edwin was able to reflect calmly. They established that if he didn't get up at 7am, he panicked, got cross and everything spiralled because he didn't think he would have time to play with his Lego® (which he felt calmed him for the day). They wrote down a plan and Edwin stuck this on his wall. Mornings became much calmer.

6.50 – alarm (press snooze)
6.55 – mum will bring me a cup of warm milk
7.00 – get up (my alarm will go off again and mum will come in and remind me)
7.05 – shower, do hair, get dressed
7.30 – play Lego®
8.00 – eat breakfast
8.30 – walk to school

■ If your child is not attending school, aim to keep clear and predictable routines in place while they are at home. Avoid getting in the habit of waking up late, watching television or playing computer games during school time as this can inadvertently reinforce their desire to avoid school. Maintaining boundaries, clear structures and routines will help to reduce anxiety. Aim to focus on learning or school-based activities during the school day and give lots of positive attention and praise when they engage in these. A visual timetable, similar to those used at school, will help to provide structure and will make reintegrating into school a little easier. Encourage your child to get dressed into their school uniform (even if they do not go in to school). During the day, support them to complete the work set by school, engage in online learning, read a book together and complete topic work linked to those subjects being taught at school. Try to plan regular movement breaks outside throughout the day at break and lunchtimes. Aim to limit screen time to work-related tasks, research and remote learning and save games and social media for out of school hours.

For some children, screen time helps manage their anxiety and engage in a world where they feel safe and in control. Asking them to stop using screens can sometimes trigger stress responses, resulting in distress and dysregulation and it can take time for families to get the balance right. Aim to provide clear and consistent routines and boundaries and provide warnings that screen time is coming to an end. It can be useful to give an element of choice about when to finish, such as *Do you need two minutes or five minutes more before you stop?* or you could consider playing an online game together for the last few minutes. Transitioning away from screen time can be easier if followed by another, highly motivational activity (based on their interests, such as cooking or playing football together). Ensure children know when they can access screens. Having time limits and locks on devices can also be useful. A gradual reduction of screen time may be necessary, if the behaviour has become entrenched.

Case study:

Ryder was 6 and was finding it increasingly difficult to get into school in the mornings. When he was in school, his behaviours escalated, becoming unsafe and he was sent home. He ended up being in school for an hour a day. When he was at home, he spent the time with an older sibling, who was not attending school, and with his dad, who had recently returned to the family home. Ryder's dad was working hard to rebuild relationships, so when the boys were at home, the three of them played together on the X-Box, went to the park and went swimming. The pull to be at home was great, and Ryder preferred to be at home than at school.

Ryder's dad worked very closely with school and realised that being at home was just too much fun for Ryder and he had no incentive to go to school. Ryder and his dad built in some time after school where they could have some 1:1 relationship building time. His dad worked with the boys to establish a culture of 'work' and learning during the school day and the X-Box and the park were saved for before and after school. Dad enrolled in a college course and undertook DIY and gardening around the home and Ryder's sibling (and Ryder, when he struggled to attend) were encouraged to engage in learning tasks and helping with the jobs during school hours. Gradually, Ryder was able to increase the time he spent in school, without the fear of missing out on more enjoyable activities at home, and the relationship between he and his dad remained strong.

■ Seek medical advice and support, particularly if your child's anxiety is impacting their engagement and attendance at school, their relationships with others or if it is accompanied by self-harm, depression, suicidal ideation, eating disorders or other concerns.

Communication

■ How adults communicate with and in front of pupils can impact how safe they feel. Using a prosodic, sing song tone of voice, open body language and gestures, getting down on their level and smiling as well as using positive, calm language all increase feelings of safety (see Chapter 2). Aim to up these safety cues from the moment the pupil is greeted by school staff.
■ The difficulties pupils have in articulating their anxieties and the problems adults have in understanding pupil stress and emotional experience of school are often key barriers to identifying and thus providing support for pupils experiencing school-based anxiety (Thambirajah et al., 2008). By noticing aloud and using Emotion Coaching (see p.32), staff can support pupils to begin to make sense of their feelings. Naming emotions can help pupils to understand them and begin to manage them more appropriately. Aim to 'step into the pupil's shoes' to develop a shared

understanding and provide compassion and empathy. For example, *I can see that you are feeling anxious about coming into school this morning, I am here to help and support you. We could take the school dog for a walk together around the playground or go and play a game in the Hub and see how we can make this easier for you.*

■ If a pupil displays catastrophic or negative thinking patterns (see p.47) about school or elements of school life, try to help them name them and label them as *a negative thought, not a fact* and gently help them to challenge or reframe these unhelpful thought patterns using empathy scripts.

Negative thought	Empathic response
Everyone hates me	I am so sorry you feel that everyone hates you at the moment, it is hard when those negative thoughts pop into your head. Can you think about some times when everyone doesn't hate you? I saw you playing Uno with George yesterday, I know he really enjoyed that and I think you did too, didn't you?
I'm so stupid, I get everything wrong	I am so sorry you feel that you get everything wrong at the moment, it is hard when those negative thoughts pop into your head. Can you think about some evidence to prove that negative thought wrong?
I hate school	I am so sorry that you hate school at the moment, it must feel hard to think that way and still come in every day. Are there any times when you don't feel like you hate school? I remember when we were playing basketball together last week and we couldn't stop laughing. I enjoyed doing that activity with you.

■ Reframing the language used when thinking and talking about behaviours and anxiety helps adults to respond more positively and with empathy and understanding. For example, use the phrases *highly anxious* or *scared to come to school* rather than *refusing to attend*. It is a question of *can't attend* rather than *won't attend*.

Sense of belonging and connectedness (see also 'Belonging and connectedness', p.237)

An important contributing factor to school anxiety and feelings of negative self-worth is the lack of a sense of belonging and connectedness within the school or class. Schools need to ensure that all pupils feel included, welcome and valued.

- Explore where in school individual pupils feel a sense of belonging and connectedness. 'Whilst an individual my feel "settled" and that they "belong" in one space, it doesn't mean they will feel the same in a different area within the school space or with different individuals they find there' (Johnson, in Morgan with Costello, 2023, p.170). Where there are feelings of disconnect, staff will need to support pupils to begin to build relationships and find ways to ensure the environment feels safe and inclusive.
- Provide opportunities for pupils to engage with peers in activities that they enjoy (such as creative and craft activities, cooking, gardening, looking after school pets, sports and music) to increase self-esteem and a sense of belonging. Hill (2023) reports on a school in West Sussex at which the 'persistent absence rate has improved from 29 per cent last academic year to 17.9 per cent this year, bucking national trends' by introducing a range of clubs such as Kin-ball, Dungeons and Dragons and Street Dancing. These activities hooked the pupils' interest and gave them a reason to attend in the mornings.

Teaching and learning

- Schools need to evaluate whether the curriculum is somehow contributing to or maintaining school avoidance by increasing anxiety. It is necessary to reflect on pupil engagement with the curriculum and any barriers to learning and provide adaptive teaching, appropriate scaffolding and support.
- Consider how those pupils who currently cannot attend, due to high levels of anxiety, can access learning. It is important to ensure that the learning gap doesn't widen as this will increase anxiety further, making it even more difficult for the pupil to return to school. Learning activities such as online tasks, home learning packs, research projects and key reading texts should be sent home (all carefully pitched so that the pupil can achieve them and feel high levels of success). Ensure that staff feedback positively on any small steps towards engagement. 'Not supplying learning opportunities during absence means a student gets further behind, adding to anxieties returning to school. A school's duty to educate does not stop because a student is absent due to illness, SEND (diagnosed or not) or bullying' (Not Fine in School, 2019).

- If a child who has not been attending manages to access a lesson, or part of a lesson, aim to avoid excluding them further by inadvertently drawing attention to their missed sessions. For example, avoid discussing or marking home learning which they have not completed or focusing on the previous day's learning without some pre-teaching first. Try to focus on the new skills and learning for the lesson so they feel included and successful.
- It will be important to help pupils to catch up following periods of absence or disengagement. Pre-teaching key skills and concepts to increase confidence can help. Providing checklists, visual prompts and breaking work down into achievable chunks can also be supportive.
- Consider small group work, nurture or mentor sessions, where appropriate, for those pupils who are in school but struggling to access the classroom.

Case study:

Ben was 10 and described as 'a real concern' because he had been out of school for so long. Staff eventually encouraged him to attend a Hamish & Milo group wellbeing intervention programme (see 'Signposting' below). He came into the group late but he attended weekly in school. He made a sock puppet which he loved. He took great care in making it and he was immensely proud of it. He responded positively to the activities without feeling pressured.

Step-by-step approaches

Avoidance of certain activities, lessons, places or aspects of the school day, although providing short-term relief for the pupil, can maintain and increase anxiety and feelings of being unable to cope with the situation, thus leading to further withdrawal. Before making any plan, address any contributing factors from school such as environmental, curricular and relational barriers to attendance. A successful plan can only be put in place once these issues have been effectively addressed, reduced and adjusted to meet the pupil's need and the pupil feels heard and reassured that school is a safe place to be.

Scaffolding and step-by-step approaches to support pupils who are experiencing school-based anxiety need to start with what the pupil can do and already feels comfortable with. A plan can then be made to gradually build on this, with small increments to support pupils to feel safer and increase their engagement in school. This approach increases the pupil's sense of control over the situation so that they are gradually able to feel comfortable with those aspects that are causing anxiety. Alongside this, the pupil will need to be taught and rehearse a range of coping strategies (see Chapter 4).

- Explore the underlying reasons behind any changes in behaviour, disengagement or non-attendance in order to provide support and establish exactly what it is about school that the pupil is finding difficult. McMillan (2023) in her research with a group of secondary aged pupils found that the most common reasons pupils gave for school avoidance were:

  - The fear of adults shouting at them or their friends.
  - Uniform discomfort.
  - Bullying.
  - Environmental overwhelm.

  Once the barriers have been established, adults can make adaptations and provide support.

- Establish where exactly the anxiety lies for individuals, in terms of key times or places, social times or transition times to establish trigger points and safe areas. Suggestions for exploring this information with the pupil include:

  - RAG rate (Red, Amber, Green) the timetable to establish lessons, activities or places where the pupil feels most comfortable. Encourage a relaxed conversation about what feels safer about those that they have rated green (such as environment, friends, relationships with staff, a subject they enjoy/feel a sense of achievement, multi-sensory learning) to establish if there are particular relationships, lessons or activities within lessons (e.g. writing, working as part of a group, reading aloud, verbally answering a question) which they find easier or more difficult. Consider how those 'green' activities could be replicated. Choose, with the pupil, one or two amber lessons and aim to put strategies in place to help these become green for the pupil.
  - Sort photos of different places in the school or map the Landscape of Fear (Ripley, 2015) to establish safe areas and trigger points within the physical environment (such as toilets, corridors, assembly hall, changing rooms, canteen) and plan solutions and make adjustments.
  - Rate statements or pictures related to coming into school or aspects of the school day out of ten to establish those times

that they find the most difficult. Ideas for home may include ranking the following statements or pictures in order of easiest to most difficult:

- Putting uniform on.
- Getting out of bed.
- Showering.
- Eating breakfast.
- Getting shoes on.
- Cleaning teeth.
- Coming away from technology.
- Leaving the house.
- Getting in the car or walking to school.
- Leaving caregiver at the school gate.

Ideas for school may include ranking the following statements or pictures in order of easiest to most difficult:

- Going into the classroom with children in it.
- Leaving caregiver.
- Specific lessons/aspects of learning.
- Sitting next to (or not sitting next to) a particular pupil.
- Being in an empty classroom.
- Being in the Nurture room.
- Playtime outside.
- Wet play.
- Answering a question.
- Talking to adults.
- Accessing the canteen.

- Sort *Risk and Resilience* cards (see 'Further signposting', p.213) to establish where pupils feel confident and safe, and where extra support or adaptations may need to be provided.
- It can be helpful to explore with pupils what a 'good' day and a 'bad' day in school looks like for them. Williams (2020) draws on the work of Moran (2001) encouraging pupils to draw their 'ideal safe school', which can be easily adapted to support pupils experiencing school-based anxiety, to establish how school feels for the pupil. Give the pupil two pieces of paper with a very simple outline of a school building on them, label one 'my safe' school and one 'my unsafe' school. Ask the pupil to think of things that would contribute to a school that they would not like to attend (their 'unsafe' school), repeat with a school they would like to attend (their 'safe' school) (reiterate

that these are not real schools). Pupils can write and draw or adults can scribe for them. Guide the pupils to talk about key aspects of the school such as the classrooms, relationships, outdoor areas, etc. This idea helps pupils and adults discuss what they value within the school setting and enables pupils to express fears or areas of concern. Alternatively, Morgan-Rose (2015) recommends using Lego® with pupils to create models of their 'ideal' classroom in order to explore those aspects of school which are important or anxiety-inducing.

■ Engage in conversations, collaborate and problem solve together with caregivers and pupils to establish what pupils feel comfortable with to establish a starting place, when they are calm and in a safe, nurturing, relaxed environment. Increase the pupil's feelings of control by offering positive choices and ensuring that they are involved in creating each step so that everything is planned *with them* rather than *done to them*.

■ Starting points for a pupil who is not attending school, depending on where the pupil is comfortable in that moment, could include:

  ■ Looking at pictures on the school website.
  ■ Wearing uniform at home.
  ■ Accessing a learning task at home.
  ■ Walking past school.
  ■ Visiting school and walking around the outside/when it is quiet.
  ■ Building relationships with key adults (virtually or in person).
  ■ Accessing a safe space in school with a trusted adult and engaging in an enjoyable task.
  ■ Accessing lunchtime with trusted friends.
  ■ Attending a favourite lesson or club.

■ Each step of the plan needs to feel very achievable and realistic for the pupil. They need to quickly see and feel success, so it is important to start with steps that feel the least overwhelming. Prioritise and focus on key targets and temporarily remove things that could cause additional stress, where possible. Discuss as a team, what success looks like and how it will be measured and celebrated. It may be necessary to return to previous steps at times, particularly after periods of absence and following periods of transition and change.

■ Look at 'safety needs' (Eisen & Engler, 2006, p.139) and establish those safe faces and safe places in school and any transitional objects (p.231) that could bridge the gap and support a pupil to make those initial steps into school.

Recognition and consequences (see also Chapter 13)

- Avoid sanctions for, or drawing attention to, punctuality. 'Some schools give an after-school detention to children who are persistently late. For a young carer, this creates a strong disincentive to attend school, as they cannot help being late and can't afford to stay after school as they are required to provide care, so they make the decision to not attend school at all' (Children's Commissioner for England, 2023).
- As a staff, agree priorities (and communicate these to all involved) for pupils who are vulnerable, anxious or struggling to attend and greet them in a way that is positive. Focus on those current priorities (supporting the pupil to attend and feel safe), implement reasonable adjustments and agree to address non-priority issues in a different way. Avoid reprimands or sanctions for uniform, punctuality, lack of homework, difficulties engaging in, focusing on or starting a task, missed learning or missing equipment. Instead, provide support and praise the small steps towards engagement and attendance. The priority, at this point, is to break the cycle of avoidance by forming positive relationships, ensuring that the pupil feels safe and a valued part of the school community and to boost self-esteem and feelings of success.
- Avoid judgement and increasing anxiety and pressure (such as telling pupils that their parents will go to prison/have to pay fines if they don't attend). This increases distress and anxiety and is detrimental to reducing school-based anxiety. 'Until we understand that, for a significant group of children, non-attendance is not a wilful act, we will continue to get drawn into a battle of wills where alternative approaches are not seen to be required' (Vodden in Fricker, 2023, p.149). 'We believe we should be tough on the causes of persistent absence rather than tough on parents and children to ensure we can get them back into school' (Anti-Bullying Alliance, 2023). Schools need to provide support for pupils to reduce their anxiety and increase their sense of safety.

Chapter take-aways

- Building positive relationships is crucial to ensure that pupils feel safe and secure in school.
- Collaboration with pupils and caregivers is essential in breaking cycles of avoidance and implementing effective support and adjustments.

- School-based anxiety is a case of *can't* rather than *won't* so bribes, threats and sanctions serve to increase stress rather than improve attendance.

Further signposting

Books

Can't Not Won't – A Story of a Child Who Couldn't Go to School by Eliza Fricker

Square Pegs: Inclusivity, Compassion and Fitting In – A Guide for Schools by Fran Morgan & Ellie Costello

Understanding & Supporting Children & Young People with Emotionally Based School Avoidance (EBSA) by Tina Rae

Resources

School Wellbeing Risk and Resilience Card Set by Jerricah Holder

Websites

Creative Education Training *Simple Strategies to Support Children with EBSA* https://www.creativeeducation.co.uk/available-courses/?_keyword=EBSA#course_results

Dr Pooky Knightsmith *Emotionally Based School Avoidance – Prevention* https://www.pookyknightsmith.com/keynote-ebsa-school-anxiety-prevention

Dr Pooky Knightsmith *School Access Plan* https://www.pookyknightsmith.com/download-ebsa-school-access-plan

Elemental Health *Reducing Teenage Anxiety* https://www.ehe.org.uk

Hertfordshire County Council *Emotionally Based School Avoidance – Guidance for Schools* https://dacorumdspl.org.uk/wp-content/uploads/2021/03/EBSA-School-Guidance-March-2021.pdf

Not Fine in School *Experiencing School Attendance Problems & Barriers?* https://notfineinschool.co.uk

Podcasts

Pooky Ponders *Using Transition Activities to Move Between Activities, Places or People* and *School Anxiety/EBSA* https://www.creativeeducation.co.uk/explore-our-podcast-pooky-ponders

SENDcast: *I Can't Go to School*– https://www.thesendcast.com/i-cant-go-to-school

References

Anti-Bullying Alliance (2023) *Written Evidence Submitted by the Anti-Bullying Alliance (National Children's Bureau)* Available at: https://committees.parliament.uk/writtenevidence/118262/pdf [Accessed 7.9.23]

Bombèr, L. (2020) *Know Me to Teach Me – Differentiated Discipline for Those Recovering from Adverse Childhood Experiences* Worth Publishing

Children's Commissioner for England (2023) *Attendance is Everyone's Business – Children's Commissioner's Submission to the Persistent Absence Inquiry* Available at: https://www.childrenscommissioner.gov.uk/resource/attendance-is-everyones-business [Accessed 14.10.23]

Eisen, A. & Engler, L. (2006) *Helping Your Child Overcome Separation Anxiety or School Refusal: A Step-by-Step Guide for Parents* New Harbinger Publications

Feeney J., Dosi R., Morgan H. & Stenning, A. (2023) *Emotionally Based School Avoidance (EBSA) Toolkit for Schools* Buckinghamshire Council

Fricker, E. (2023) *Can't Not Won't – A Story About a Child Who Couldn't Go to School* Jessica Kingsley

Hill, J. (2023) *How a School's New Clubs are Lifting Attendance and Wellbeing: Inspiring the Kids Who Don't Normally Engage in Clubs* Available at: https://schoolsweek.co.uk/how-a-schools-new-clubs-are-lifting-attendance-and-wellbeing/ [Accessed 17.7.23]

Knightsmith, P. (2023) *Using Transition Activities to Move Between Activities, Places or People* Available at: Using Transition Activities to Move Between Activities, Places or People (buzzsprout.com) [Accessed 29 June 2023]

McMillan, A. (2023) *Ange McMillan's Profile Page* (LinkedIn) [Accessed 29.6.23]

Moran. H. (2001). Who Do You Think You Are? Drawing the Ideal Self: A Technique to Explore a Child's Sense of Self *Clinical Psychology and Psychiatry* 6(4): 599–604.

Morgan, F. with Costello, E. (2023) *Square Pegs: Inclusivity, Compassion and Fitting In – A Guide for Schools* Independent Thinking Press

Morgan-Rose, F. (2015) *The Ideal Classroom with Lego Prompt Sheet* Available at: https://theidealclassroomcouk.files.wordpress.com/2017/04/building-the-ideal-classroom-with-lego-prompt-sheet-june-2014-updated-2015.pdf [Accessed 10.3.21]

Not Fine in School (2019) *A Child is Struggling to Attend School – What Can We Do* Available at: https://notfineinschool.co.uk/professionals [Accessed 29.3.23]

Rae, T. (2021) *Sunday Evening and Monday Morning Plans* https://www.youtube.com/watch?v=Z8JmRgjCics [Accessed 17.3.23]

Ripley, K. (2015) *Autism from Diagnostic Pathway to Intervention: Checklists to Support Diagnosis, Analysis for Target-Setting and Effective Intervention Strategies* Jessica Kingsley

Thambirajah M., Grandison K. & De-Hayes L. (2008) *Understanding School Refusal: A Handbook for Professionals in Education, Health, and Social Care* Jessica Kingsley

Williams, J. (2020) *Drawing the Ideal Safe School – A Tool for Children Who Are Anxious About Returning to School to Use with Parents/Carers* Dudley Educational Psychology Service Available at: https://drive.google.com/file/d/1DF9ie2Zr8rG_OXxt9pCKKDhqoE2EAmHZ/view

Alleviating school-based anxiety checklist

STRATEGY	COMMENTS
Please also refer to Chapter 12	
Relational approaches	
Build positive relationships with caregivers and pupils	
Establish safe spaces and safe faces in school	
Whole school welcoming approach and positive first encounters each day	
Find ways to build and maintain relationships, connection and belonging for those not currently attending	
Problem solve collaboratively and actively listen to pupils	
Encourage pupils to voice their worries	
Meet and greets and predictable morning routines	
Effectively support with relationship difficulties and ensure a robust anti-bullying policy is in place	
Ensure adult responses are positive, encouraging and non-judgemental	
Collaboration with caregivers	
Relationship between school and home is essential. Aim for a key point of contact to build relationships	
Be aware of, and sensitive to, caregiver stress and anxieties	

(Continued)

Continued

STRATEGY	COMMENTS
Aim for an environment for meetings where caregivers and pupils are put at ease	
Share positives, listen and alleviate caregiver fears	
Team approach	
Establish 'push' and 'pull' factors and barriers to attendance	
Ensure the learning gap does not widen further	
Support regulation	
Collaboration with other agencies and signposting towards support	
Suggestions for caregivers	
Predictable routines (morning and evening) and visual plans	
Listen and validate feelings with empathy	
Explore and rehearse coping strategies together	
Avoid feeding the anxiety cycle but gradually face fears, step by step	
Be positive about school	
Discuss goals and ambitions	
Engage in playfulness and problem solve together	

(Continued)

Continued

STRATEGY	COMMENTS
Aim for predictable routines that mimic the school day, on days when children are unable to attend school	
Seek further support and advice	
Communication	
Communicate signs of safety, verbally and non-verbally	
Emotion Coaching and empathy scripts	
Language reframes	
Sense of belonging and connectedness	
Explore where pupils feel a sense of belonging	
Encourage group activities based around their interests	
Teaching and learning	
Identify any curriculum barriers	
Consider how those not currently attending can access learning, providing positive feedback towards small steps of engagement	
Support 'catch-up' following absences	
Consider smaller groups for those struggling	
Step-by-step approaches	
Establish barriers to engagement or attendance	

(Continued)

Continued

STRATEGY	COMMENTS
Problem solve collaboratively	
Start within the pupil's comfort zone	
Plan small, achievable steps and plan how to measure success	
Look at 'safety needs'	
Recognition and consequences	
Avoid sanctions for punctuality, for those currently struggling to attend	
Agree current priorities and make reasonable adjustments to break the cycle of avoidance	

11
Separation anxiety

What is separation anxiety?

Separation anxiety is intense fear of and distress at being separated from a significant other. Infants often struggle to separate from their caregivers, feeling threatened and unsafe with unfamiliar people or places. This natural stage of development is usually outgrown by the age of three. When older children experience extreme and prolonged anxiety when separating from key caregivers, they may need further support to manage this, particularly if it impacts their participation, wellbeing, relationships or school attendance.

Separation anxiety may relate to fear of not seeing each other again, due to anxiety that 'some harm will come to the child if their carer is not present (such as they will get taken or injured), or that harm will come to their carer in the child's absence' (Creswell & Willetts, 2019, p.18–19). Separation distress can be triggered by life experiences and traumatic events, such as change, bereavement or loss, or witnessing domestic violence. Genetics and personality can also play a role. Often it is not a single cause which leads to the anxiety, but a combination of factors.

Separation anxiety is adaptive and involves an activation of the threat response which has evolved in order to keep the individual safe.

> Because being alone carries an increased risk of danger, especially for young individuals and others who are weak, the fear response to inaccessibility of mother can usefully be regarded as a basic adaptive response, namely a response that during the course of evolution has become an intrinsic part of man's behavioural repertoire because of its contribution to species survival.
>
> (Bowlby, 1998, p.211)

DOI: 10.4324/9781003433231-12

Separation anxiety is the most common anxiety disorder in children younger than 12 (NHS, 2023) and 'has many consequences, particularly for school-age children, including excessive worry, sleep problems, distress in social and academic settings, and a variety of physical symptoms that, left untreated, can cause social and academic decline' (Vaughan et al., 2016).

Comorbidity

Separation anxiety may occur alongside other conditions or diagnoses such as depression, Obsessive Compulsive Disorder (OCD) and other anxiety disorders, such as Generalised Anxiety Disorder (GAD), panic attacks, phobias and social anxiety. Furthermore, 'as many as 75 percent of children with separation anxiety experience some form of school refusal behavior' (Eisen & Engler, 2006, p.114).

Recognising separation anxiety

Alongside more general presentations of anxiety (see pp.11–12), symptoms of separation anxiety may include:

- On-going and extreme distress when separating, or thinking about separating, from their caregiver that appears excessive for their developmental age.
- Struggling to be out of sight of caregivers in the home, such as fear or refusal to be in rooms of the house alone, go to the bathroom alone, sleep alone, go upstairs alone, and fear of being home alone (for older pupils).
- Extreme worry about something bad happening to a loved one when they are not there.
- Difficulty sleeping, nightmares or repeated negative thoughts that something bad will happen causing separation from loved ones, such as around themes of death or becoming separated or lost.
- 'Constantly checking on your family members when they are away from you (such as texting or phoning family members a lot)' (Collins-Donnelly, 2013, p.31).
- Showing physical presentations of anxiety – muscle aches and tension, headache, stomach ache, nausea, sickness, etc. when separation is anticipated or discussed.
- Anxiety presentations of behaviour or 'survival tactics' (Eisen & Engler, 2006, p.40), such as opposition, refusal, aggression or

defiance, upon separation or when separation is anticipated. 'What may look like manipulation . . . [is] often a child's desperate attempt to avoid feeling anxious . . . The attention-getting behaviour (like whining, crying, or throwing tantrums) shows you that he is overwhelmed and cannot cope' (Eisen & Engler, 2006, p.40). Behaviours which seem oppositional or manipulative are conveying that the child is scared and needs support.

■ Clinging to a caregiver and panic attacks upon separation or when thinking about separation.
■ Struggling to get out of bed, get ready in the morning or leave the car or house.
■ Bringing comfort items from home into school and displaying distress when being separated from such objects.
■ Seeking reassurance and connection.
■ Finding it difficult to go to social events or to someone else's house without their caregiver.

Case study:

Sid is 8 years old. His parents have recently separated and Sid spends the majority of time at his mum's and sees his dad every other weekend. There is some animosity between the parents. Since the change to living arrangements, Sid has found it very difficult to access school. He clings to his mum and shouts, hits and spits. When he does come into school, he clings to several toy cars from home and goes and hides in the book corner.

Reflection opportunity:

■ How could Sid be supported to have a smoother transition into school and separate from his mum more successfully?

If you have concerns that a pupil may have separation anxiety or it affects their participation in relationships, school, social activities and everyday life, seek further professional support.

Triggers and risk factors

Separation anxiety usually begins in childhood but can sometimes continue or be triggered later, in adolescence or adulthood.

Risk factors may include:

- Bereavement, trauma or loss which caused separation, for example, illness requiring the child and caregiver to be apart (such as hospitalisation of the caregiver, child or sibling), death of a loved one, loss of a pet, parental divorce, moving out of the family home (such as going to boarding school, into foster care or due to evacuation), incarceration of a caregiver, domestic abuse within the home (current or previous).
- Intense worry about the safety of a loved one while the pupil is not there, such as concerns about the presence of an abusive person in the home, aggressive neighbour disputes, war, mental or physical ill health of a loved one, being a young carer.
- Lived traumatic experiences such as being in a car accident, a house fire, war, divorce or death.
- Transitions such as moving house, school or class, caregiver starting work or pupil starting school.
- Presenting as generally anxious and worrying excessively.
- Family history of anxiety.
- School avoidance and school-based anxiety.
- Environmental overwhelm and sensory sensitivities.
- Extended periods of absence (illness or holidays).
- Intense fear of being alone or getting lost or separated from loved ones.

Maintaining factors

Maintaining factors are those factors which may be sustaining or reinforcing the separation anxiety for the pupil and need to be identified, addressed and eliminated in order to begin to provide support. Maintaining factors include:

- Continued anxiety and patterns of negative thinking around separation that have not been explored and the pupil has not been supported and taught coping strategies by a trusted adult.
- Feeding the cycle of avoidance by avoiding separation or not being supported to confront their fears in a gradual and safe manner. 'Most children's separation anxiety is sustained by avoiding situations that are perceived as potentially dangerous to them or others ... every time a child avoids a separation-related situation, he believes that disaster was prevented. Thus, avoidance only leads to more avoidance' (Eisen & Engler, 2006, p.17). Caregivers often

inadvertently feed the anxiety cycle, leading to further avoidance, because seeing children in such high levels of distress often leads to feelings of guilt and thus increased avoidance of future separation.

■ Lack of opportunities for age-appropriate independence, over-protection and reassurance, such as being 'protected' and 'shielded' from 'potential anxiety-provoking scenarios' (Eisen & Engler, 2006, p.36).

■ Being forced or misled into separation rather than supported through it, which breaks down trust and increases anxiety about future situations. (Situations include where caregivers sneak away from the child when they are not looking, having previously reassured them that they will remain there.)

■ Significant events and potential threats to the safety of self or caregiver.

■ Criticism, disappointment, disapproval and frustration are conveyed by others, intensifying and fuelling the pupil's feelings of failure.

■ Negative labelling (such as *shy, clingy, attention-seeking, quiet, manipulative, controlling*). These are counteractive, dismissive and potentially reaffirming as the pupil then believes them to be fact and they impact the child's self-image, becoming difficult to change and move on from.

■ Anxious behaviours are modelled by others. 'You have to reveal through your body language and facial expressions that you're confident that he can cope with the separation-related confrontations' (Eisen & Engler, 2006, p.45).

■ Environmental issues, bullying or relational difficulties that are not being appropriately addressed or needs that are not being effectively or appropriately met in school.

Chapter take-aways

■ Separation anxiety is the fear and distress caused by thinking about or being separated from a significant other (usually the primary caregiver).

■ Separation anxiety can stem from a fear that harm may come to the caregiver or the pupil while they are separated, or from the fear that they will be permanently separated.

■ Staff need to recognise the signs, risk factors and maintaining factors in order to provide support.

Further signposting

Books

Helping Your Child Overcome Separation Anxiety or School Refusal: A Step-by-Step Guide for Parents by Andrew Eisen & Linda Engler

Podcasts

Aware Parenting *Separation Anxiety* https://podcasts.apple.com/au/podcast/episode-18-separation-anxiety/id1455772681?i=100044 6243960

References

Bowlby, J. (1998) *Attachment and Loss: Separation, Anger and Anxiety* Pimlico

Collins-Donnelly, K. (2013) *Starving the Anxiety Gremlin* Jessica Kingsley Publishers

Creswell, C. & Willetts, L. (2019) *Helping Your Child with Fears and Worries* Robinson

Eisen, A. & Engler, L. (2006) *Helping Your Child Overcome Separation Anxiety or School Refusal: A Step by Step Guide for Parents* New Harbinger Publications

NHS (2023) *Anxiety Disorders in Children* Available at: https://www.nhsinform.scot/illnesses-and-conditions/mental-health/anxiety-disorders-in-children#:~:text=Nearly%20300%2C000%20young%20people%20in,in%20children%20younger%20than%2012 [Accessed 29.6.23]

Vaughan, J., Coddington, J., Ahmed, A. & Ertel, M. (2016) Separation Anxiety Disorder in School-Age Children: What Health Care Providers Should Know *Journal of Pediatric Health Care* Available at: https://www.jpedhc.org/article/S0891-5245(16)30363-7/fulltext [Accessed 4.5.23]

12
Alleviating separation anxiety

Relational approaches

Early intervention is most impactful when supporting children with separation anxiety and lessens the likelihood of it worsening or becoming embedded.

- Building up a positive relationship with the pupil is key in helping them overcome separation anxiety and fostering a sense of emotional and physical safety within school (see Chapter 2). The family will need a small team of key adults to support the separation and check in with the pupil regularly to provide reassurance and support.
- Planning for beginnings and endings is important. Establish safe and predictable routines (particularly for the start and end of each day) in familiar places, with consistent, trusted adults. Try to implement a 'soft landing' into a preferred activity and the opportunity to calm and reset on arrival at school. Consider daily *meet and greets* with a trusted, familiar adult in a safe space for the pupil to offload, reset and prepare for the day. Have a predictable routine, for example, meet in the same place, engage in some regulating, fun, non-pressured settling-in activities (a special job, sensory play, eat breakfast together, play a game) and respond to any questions or worries before going through the visual timetable for the morning, ensuring the pupils is clear of expectations. The trusted adult may need to support the pupil to settle in the classroom and check in with them regularly throughout the day. (Aim for the same structure each day, even if the pupil arrives late.)

DOI: 10.4324/9781003433231-13

Planning for the end of the school day and ending on a calm, positive note is also important in supporting pupils to feel confident about returning the next day. The morning routine could be replicated at the end of the day, to provide time to reset and decompress before going home. Allow the pupil to talk through and offload any worries, but also ensure that all of the positives are highlighted so that the pupil is leaving each day feeling positive, with as little anxiety as possible.

Case study:

James is 7. He found it very difficult to leave his mum in the mornings. A trusted adult was available to meet him at the gate each morning. James and his mum established a fun goodbye routine and James brought a train from home with him. James and his key adult used to then pretend to shrink and climb aboard the train and 'chug chug' into school. They would 'disembark' the train at the same station each morning (the sensory room) and James, the trusted adult and the train would read a book together before going through the visual timetable and going into the classroom. His trusted adult would help him say goodbye to his train and put it on the shelf where he could see it and settle him into his learning task. She would meet him at the end of the day and they would take the train, go to the sensory room and engage in a similar activity to the morning, before going to meet his mum at the gate (in the same space each day).

Reflection opportunities:

- How could having a safe adult and predictable routine support pupils into school?
- How can playfulness help children to be successful?

- Establish safe places and faces within school where the pupil can go if they are feeling overwhelmed. Rehearse visiting these regularly, when the pupil is calm. Take a photograph of the faces/ places to use as a visual reminder.
- Teach the pupil how the brain works so that they know that their emotions and reactions are due to their threat response being activated, and even though the situation is frightening, they are not in real danger (see p.5). Once they begin to recognise that their threat response has been activated, they can begin to be

taught to calm it, using regulating and coping strategies (see Chapter 4).

■ Plan extra support for key trigger times and transitions (see p.58).

Collaboration with caregivers

■ Effective collaboration and communication between caregivers and a small team of key adults in school is essential in order to plan a way forward, ensure that expectations are shared and that everybody is working towards the same goals in a consistent way.

■ Work collaboratively to establish whether the pupil struggles to leave the caregiver in a variety of situations or only when entering school. Knightsmith (2023) discusses the importance of ensuring that the child feels safe within the setting and that the anxiety is about saying goodbye to the caregiver, rather than distress or anxiety about something within the school environment. Open discussions with the pupil, caregiver and trusted member of staff should be effective in establishing this, as well as careful observation and monitoring of the pupil within the school setting to rule out any sensory, environmental, curricular or relational barriers.

■ Staff need to be aware of and empathic towards parental anxieties and distress and provide support and reassurance. Caregivers may have anxieties around separation themselves as well as being concerned for their distressed child. They may also have been through a very stressful time during the morning in the build up to arriving at school.

■ If a pupil arrives at school distressed, phone or email home as soon as the pupil has settled to reassure the caregivers that they are OK, otherwise they will probably assume that their child has been upset all day increasing parental anxiety.

■ Aim to share and send home a positive message at the end of each day. Encourage the caregiver to share something positive each morning as well (unrelated to separation or attachment, it can be about something helpful that the child has done, something they did well at volleyball club, etc.).

■ If the separation anxiety is stemming from fearing for an adult's safety whilst they are out of sight, it can be useful to collaborate with caregivers and pre-arrange a convenient time for the pupil to make a phone call or send a text home (ensure the caregiver is able to answer if this is planned) in order to provide some reassurance that they are safe and well.

Suggestions for caregivers to support their child with separation anxiety

- ■ Have a set, predictable (but allow for some flexibility) routine for getting ready in the morning. Rae (2021) suggests a Sunday evening and Monday morning plan to support your child (see p.201).
- ■ 'Encourage parents to be positive and decisive when saying good-bye to their children. It's important for parents to tell children that they are leaving, and to do so confidently and in an upbeat way. This will boost children's confidence (even if not at first) that it is safe to be left, and that their parent will return' (AnnaFreud.org, undated).
- ■ Establish a set, predictable (but allow for some flexibility) routine for drop off times to help ensure predictability and an element of playfulness, which reduces stress. Create a fun, short and sweet 'goodbye ritual' such as a kiss on the cheek and both turn around and high five, a silly wave or funny phrase and a clear goodbye before heading off. Practise this at home at a calm time and try to have fun and laugh coming up with ideas (because laughing reduces stress). Leave quickly without drawn out goodbyes. Avoid creeping off as this will diminish trust.
- ■ Try using transitional objects to reassure your child that you will think of each other during the day (see p.231).
- ■ Validate your child's feelings with empathy, for example, *I can see how difficult you are finding this today, you are being really brave, I miss you too when we don't see each other. I am going to squeeze our matching owl toy and I will know we are thinking about each other and I look forward to seeing you after school.*
- ■ Reassure your child that you will see them later, including being explicit about when that will be and what you will do together after school. Be sure to keep to these arrangements in order to develop trust. Make certain you are always on time (early) to collect them and always wait in the same place so anxiety does not rise while they try to find you.
- ■ Give the message that you believe your child can cope and model using coping strategies. Staff and caregivers should use and model the use of these regulation strategies so that they can be (or seem) the embodiment of calm, in the moment, to reduce heightening the situation or the child's anxiety.
- ■ Providing a split timetable can be useful, so alongside the pupils' visual timetable, adults add 'a Social Story™ (Gray) of what family members will be doing while they are away from them . . . You

could add reunions to their timetables so that they can see when you will be coming back together' (SparkleAppeal.org, undated).

■ Show your child kindness, reassurance and support, while gradually encouraging developmentally and age-appropriate independence. Help them to increasingly tolerate being apart from you in very small steps.

■ Try to find patterns and identify triggers and situations which induce anxiety for your child. Knowing what increases stress for your child and being proactive and planning ahead can help you implement supportive strategies, and gradually help them to face their fears (rather than avoiding them) so that they become more confident.

■ Try playing games which promote separation, such as *Hide and Seek* to help your child begin to tolerate being apart from you, in a safe, fun and playful way, starting with very obvious hiding places, where they will find you quickly and very gradually building up to more tricky hiding places. 'You are normalizing your absence and pushing the bounds of your child's ability to cope each time you hide. When the child hides, they are telling themselves that they are going to be OK even if they can't see [their trusted adult]' (Milligan, 2023).

Transitional objects

Separation anxiety may return at times of stress and during periods of transition such as in new or unfamiliar situations and pupils will need increased adult support at these times. A transitional object is something which is used to remind a child that they are thought about and can remain connected to key people while they are apart.

■ Discuss, as a team, some suitable transitional objects which could be used to bridge the gap between home and school. It can be useful for the child and caregiver to each have the same or similar transitional objects to maintain connection so that the pupil feels 'kept in mind' (Bombèr, 2007, p.94) while they are apart. When they look at their transitional object, they will be reminded that the caregiver will be looking at the matching object and thinking of them. This is especially useful for pupils who have insecure attachments. Ideas include:

■ Each having matching mini soft toys or squishies.
■ Each having matching little stone gems or shells.

- ■ Matching hearts drawn on the hand.
- ■ Photos or key rings with pictures of each other.
- ■ Laminated kisses (Knightsmith, 2023).
- ■ Friendship bracelets – choose a colour of thread for each appropriate family member (SparkleAppeal.org, undated).
- ■ 'Invisible string' (Karst, 2018).
- ■ Matching buttons sewn into clothing.
- ■ A note in a pencil case or lunchbox.
- ■ A sensory tool.
- ■ A piece of fabric with caregiver's perfume or aftershave on or sprayed some onto child's jumper.
- ■ Caregiver and child both have the same snack.

- ■ A transitional object from school to take home (such as a class mascot, the teacher's 'special' pen, a plant to look after or a small set of Lego® to build to show the next day, etc.), which the pupil brings back into school each day, can also help bridge the gap between home and school and give the pupil a reason to return the next day.
- ■ A transitional object within school, when pupils need to be parted from a key adult, for example, if the teacher is out of the class they may ask the pupil to look after a special pen, scarf, pencil case, etc. This helps to reassure the pupil that the adult will return to them.

Case study:

Polly struggled to go to Phonics, in a different classroom, with a different teacher. The teacher gave Polly her scarf to look after until she came back. This was sufficient to make Polly feel secure enough to leave the classroom and trust the teacher would be there when she returned.

Step-by-step approaches

Before implementing a step-by-step plan to begin to overcome separation anxiety, address any factors in school which are making the pupil feel unsafe and teach and model healthy coping strategies (see Chapter 4).

- Establish where exactly the anxiety lies for the individual. Rate statements related to leaving the caregiver or create lists of 'separation fears' to establish what it is about the situation that is causing the anxiety. At the same time, establish supportive factors and things that the pupil feels will help them to feel safe.
- Work collaboratively to gradually increase the time the pupil can tolerate being away from their caregiver, 'children will only be able to conquer separation anxiety if they confront and feel the fear' (Eisen & Engler, 2006, p.17). This, however, needs to be carried out in a safe, gradual and supported way. 'It's important to understand that children have to confront their fears at their own pace. If you push too hard, your child may shut down and refuse' (Eisen & Engler, 2006, p.38). It is important to start where the child feels comfortable and build up from there.
- Agree as a team (school staff, caregivers and the pupil) what small steps towards success may look like and find ways to measure and celebrate each small success.

Chapter take-aways

- Intervention is most impactful in supporting pupils when provided early.
- Positive, trusting relationships built between school staff, caregivers and pupils are essential.
- Predictable routines support a child's sense of safety.
- Transitional objects can bridge the gap between home and school.
- Step-by-step approaches can support pupils to begin to overcome their fears in a way that is gradual, safe and supported.

Further signposting

Resources to share with pupils

Help Your Dragon Overcome Separation Anxiety by Steve Herman
Owl Babies by Martin Waddell
See You Soon: A Children's Book for Mothers and Toddlers Dealing with Separation Anxiety by Ms Dilraz Kunnummal
Starving the Anxiety Gremlin by Kate Collins-Donnelly
The Colour Monster Goes to School by Anna Llenas
The Invisible String (1–6) by Patrice Karst & Joanne Lew-Vriethoff

Websites

Autism Little Learners *Separation Anxiety Social Story for School* https://autismlittlelearners.com/separation-anxiety-social-story-for

Dr Tina Rae *Sunday Evening and Monday Morning Plans* https://www.youtube.com/watch?v=Z8JmRgjCics

Raisingchildren.net.au *Anxiety: The Stepladder Approach for Children and Teenagers* https://raisingchildren.net.au/toddlers/health-daily-care/mental-health/anxiety-stepladder-approach

Podcasts

Pooky Ponders *How Can We Support Children with Separation Anxiety?* https://www.creativeeducation.co.uk/explore-our-podcast-pooky-ponders

References

AnnaFreud.org (undated) *Separation Anxiety* Available at: https://www.annafreud.org/early-years/early-years-in-mind/common-difficulties/separation-anxiety [Accessed 12.7.23]

Bombèr, L. (2007) *Inside I'm Hurting* Worth Publishing

Eisen, A. & Engler, L. (2006) *Helping Your Child Overcome Separation Anxiety or School Refusal: A Step-by-Step Guide for Parents* New Harbinger Publications

Gray, C. (2023) *What is a Social Story?* Available at: https://carolgraysocialstories.com/social-stories/what-is-it [Accessed 2.6.24]

Karst, P. (2018) *The Invisible String* Little, Brown Book Group

Knightsmith, P. (2023) *How Can We Support Children with Separation Anxiety?* Available at: https://pookyh.buzzsprout.com/1183931/12887775-how-can-we-support-children-with-separation-anxiety [Accessed 29.6.23]

Milligan, T. (2023) *Hide and Seek for Separation Anxiety* Available at: https://www.pathwaystopeacecounseling.com/post/hide-and-seek-for-separation-anxiety [Accessed 22.2.24]

Rae, T. (2021) *Sunday Evening and Monday Morning Plans* Available at: https://www.youtube.com/watch?v=Z8JmRgjCics [Accessed 17.3.23]

SparkleAppeal.org (undated) *Supporting Children and Young People with Anxiety and Worry: A Toolkit to Help Support Children with a Disability or Developmental Difficulty with Their Anxiety and Worry* Available at: https://www.sparkleappeal.org/ckfinder/userfiles/files/sparkle%20anxiety%20toolkit.pdf [Accessed 22.7.23]

Alleviating separation anxiety checklist

STRATEGY	COMMENTS
Please also refer to Chapter 10	
Relational approaches	
Small team of key adults to build relationships	
Safe, predictable routines at the start and end of each day	
Establish safe spaces and faces	
Teach the pupil how the brain works	
Plan for key trigger times and transitions	
Collaboration with caregivers	
Collaboration with caregivers to plan and share strengths and expectations	
Be empathic of parental anxieties	
Contact caregivers when the pupil is settled	
Share positives	
Reassure pupil of caregiver safety, where possible and appropriate	
Suggestions for caregivers	
Predictable routines (but allow for some flexibility)	
Positive, predictable and fun goodbyes	
Transitional objects	
Validate emotions	

(Continued)

Continued

STRATEGY	COMMENTS
Reassure that you will return and share after-school plans	
Model coping strategies	
Split timetables and Social Stories™	
Gradually increase developmentally appropriate independence	
Be proactive and plan for trigger times	
Games which promote separation in a safe, fun way	
Transitional objects	
Use transitional objects to bridge the gap between home and school	
Consider transitional objects from school to home	
Use transitional objects with key adults in school	
Step-by-step approaches	
Establish exactly what is causing the anxiety	
Start from where the pupil feels comfortable. Provide support, scaffold and intervene early to plan small steps	
Collaborate and decide what success may look like	

13
Whole school approaches to reducing anxiety

Belonging and connectedness

Approximately 25 per cent of adolescents feel a sense of 'disconnect' (Allen & Kern, 2019) and that they do not fit in or belong in school. This figure could continue to increase, without intervention.

- Schools need to foster a sense of belonging and connectedness for all pupils. Brown (2021) states 'the opposite to belonging is fitting in' and often, pupils look like they are belonging, but are actually masking (see p.13) and do not feel genuinely accepted. Schools need to embrace uniqueness, difference, diversity and genuine inclusivity. To foster a sense of belonging, schools must adapt to the needs of the pupils, rather than pupils needing to 'fit in' in order to 'belong'.
- Pupils need to be greeted positively by each individual staff member at the school gate, as they enter the building and each classroom, because relationships are paramount. Smile and welcome all pupils in, addressing any issues later, once they are settled. 'When a child feels they are valued, wanted and belong in a school setting, they become less hypervigilant and more resilient when things inevitably become difficult' (Bagley, in Morgan with Costello, 2023, p.134).
- Daily rituals in the classroom, such as acknowledging and welcoming each pupil in, help every individual to feel valued. Starting the day with a question or riddle and ending the day with the answer, or having a silly handshake or dance can set the mood

DOI: 10.4324/9781003433231-14

and provide a sense of playfulness, increasing the sense of group connectedness and belonging. 'Encourage all adults . . . to focus on making students feel important, valued and like they belong. Introduce the idea of daily acts of botheredness that build into strong bonds of trust' (Dix, 2017, p.52).

■ Joining school clubs and extra-curricular activities can be helpful in developing connections in groups with shared interests.

Whole school ethos, culture and policy

With continuing concerns around the high levels of school-based anxiety post pandemic in the UK, particularly among pupils with Special Educational Needs and Disabilities (SEND), schools must develop a positive culture and ethos for each individual. Pupil and staff physical and mental wellbeing needs to be at the heart. If a pupil does not feel happy and safe within the school environment it is unsettling, traumatising and setting them up to fail. The first step is ensuring a genuinely inclusive and supportive ethos and environment, which underpins the values within all school policies and practice. Once schools get this right for anxious and vulnerable pupils, they will get it right for all pupils.

While implementing strategies to support individuals, it is important to scrutinise the culture and ethos of the whole school. In order to reduce anxiety and improve attendance, staff and leaders need 'to explore what can be done to prevent children becoming persistently absent in the first place. Not to keep asking the question; how do we get them in? But having the courage to ask the question: what needs to change to prevent the issue in the first place' (Vodden, in Fricker, 2023, p.151).

Reflection opportunity – how welcoming is your school?

Spend ten minutes in the school reception area or at the school gate at the beginning of the school day. Imagine it is your first day, that you are an anxious pupil or one struggling to engage in school (see also case studies (p.185 and 194).

■ What do you see, hear, smell?
■ What happens that is calm and welcoming?
■ Does anything happen that is not calm and welcoming?
■ Is it the same (predictable) every day?

- Is school a welcoming and positive experience for everyone, from the moment they enter the gate?
- What helps pupils to reduce anxiety from the moment they enter school?
- Is there anything in place which could heighten anxiety?
- What could be improved?
                    (Adapted from a training activity, McMillan, 2023)

There are adaptations that schools can make to ensure that each and every pupil feels physically and emotionally safe, secure, heard and understood in school. Fricker (2023, p.12) states 'I honestly think that if we had more flexibility, if we had safety, connections and strong relationships alongside learning, we would need fewer *supports*'. Schools need to understand individual needs to make reasonable, appropriate and effective adjustments. Ultimately, if the system doesn't fit the child, it is the system that needs to adapt, not the child.

- Schools need to be flexible, inclusive and nurturing for each individual pupil. 'Inflexible cultures can produce anxiety in those unable to meet expectations' (Minahan, 2013). 'If you believe in equality, then you have to embrace flexibility. If you think school should be fair to all, then it needs to adapt to all' (Carter, in Morgan with Costello, 2023, p.69).
- Review policies to ensure that mental health and wellbeing are at the core and confirm that policies encourage flexibility and appropriate reasonable adjustments for individual needs. For example, ensure uniform policies take into account a range of sensory needs. Anna Freud recommend 'a whole school or college approach to mental health and wellbeing is best served by a separate mental health and wellbeing policy' and offer guidance on writing this (see 'Further signposting', p.252).
- Ensure a robust, inclusive attendance and welfare policy is in place. All staff need to understand school-based anxiety and how to support pupils and families effectively. Review attendance policies and ensure that they reflect understanding of anxiety-based school avoidance and are openly inclusive in supporting pupils who struggle to attend due to heightened anxiety.
- Ensure a flexible and nurturing approach taking account of personal needs and circumstances (see 'Case study', p.185). For

example, if pupils are late or absent, staff follow up with curiosity and caring, compassionate discussions, providing offers of support rather than blanket sanctions. 'Some schools give an after-school detention to children who are persistently late. For a young carer, this creates a strong disincentive to attend school, as they cannot help being late and can't afford to stay after school as they are required to provide care, so they make the decision to not attend school at all' (Children's Commissioner for England, 2023, p.13).

■ All children (and adults) need to feel safe in school. Anti-Bullying Alliance (2023) clearly defines bullying and how to report it (in child-friendly language). Pupils need to know that bullying is always taken seriously and to feel heard. Policy needs to address preventative measures to combat bullying, as well as reactive measures, and to do so quickly, ensuring those involved know that it will be addressed effectively and the steps that will be undertaken to plan to prevent reoccurrence. 'There is evidence that schools with a robust and effective whole-school approach and training relating to anti-bullying helps to reduce persistent absence' (Anti-Bullying Alliance, 2023).

■ Implement a Relational Policy and guidance in place of, or alongside, the Behaviour Policy to implement trauma-infused approaches (Treisman, in Barnados, undated) with the pupil's emotional needs at the heart. Bombèr (2020, Chapter 11) includes a relationship policy which schools can adapt and make their own. This should be underpinned with the understanding that all behaviour is communication and a means of meeting a need. The focus needs to be on developing executive function and teaching emotional understanding and regulation skills. Ensure that the policy details where and who pupils can go to when they need to regulate or calm and that the emphasis is on teaching the skills of regulation, reflection and restoration, rather than instilling sweeping sanctions. The ability to express ourselves verbally reduces when under increased stress so it is important to consider how all pupils can communicate their needs and feelings, particularly those with Speech, Language and Communication Needs (SLCN).

■ Ensure regular, on-going, up-to-date, high-quality, whole staff training on Neurodivergence, Anxiety, behaviour regulation, Special Educational Needs and Disabilities (SEND), Social, Emotional and Mental Health (SEMH), Adverse Childhood Experiences (ACES), trauma and attachment and wellbeing.

Relational approaches

- Value and promote the importance of relationships. Staff need to take time to build positive, trusting relationships with pupils and their caregivers. They need to engage in collaborative approaches in order to develop shared understanding and to meet the needs of all pupils. Collaboration and communication with pupils and caregivers ensures individual needs are met and concerns are addressed early to prevent escalation and ensure that each pupil feels listened to and valued.

  Young Minds (undated) found that 'in general, teachers were not viewed as trusted adults, perhaps because the structures and expectations of education impact on their ability to build these types of relationships with students'. Schools need to find ways to address this issue, as relationships in school are paramount, not only to a pupil's emotional safety and wellbeing, but also to their academic success. Pupils feel safer when they are in proximity of trusted adults. 'Schools need to recognise that relationships are the anchor on which children learn, flourish, and make behavioural changes, and therefore a relational approach is integral' (Treisman, 2017, p.152). Adoption of a PACE approach can help adults build trusting relationships (see p.26).

- Vulnerable pupils need a small team of key trusted adults to provide regular wellbeing check-ins and become their champion, add to their sense of value and belonging and help ensure that each pupil is looked out for and feels genuinely cared for. Relational and flexible approaches are essential when understanding and responding to behaviour. 'The emphasis needs to be on "reading" the student and reacting accordingly by prompting and teaching the student coping strategies with a focus on skill building and managing anxiety-provoking activities' (Minahan, 2018, p.77).

- 'After decades of punitive behaviour policies, exclusion has not reduced – rather it has increased significantly' (Bagley, in Morgan with Costello, 2023, p.131). Such 'one-size fits all' approaches (Rainer et al., 2023) and sanctions are often unfair, break down trust, increase feelings of shame and rejection and instil fear and stress. Instead, pupils need relational intervention and to be taught the necessary skills and regulation strategies within a supportive, understanding setting.

Focus on mental health and wellbeing

Treisman (2021, p.160) reflects on the mantra shared by the Wellness Project in Kenya 'wellbeing leads to well-doing'. The European Education Area (undated) defines wellbeing as 'a state in which pupils are able to develop their potential, learn and play creatively' stating that wellbeing at school means:

- Feeling safe, valued and respected.
- Being actively and meaningfully engaged in academic and social activities.
- Having positive self-esteem, self-efficacy and a sense of autonomy.
- Having positive and supportive relationships with teachers and peers.
- Feeling a sense of belonging to their classroom and school.
- Feeling happy and satisfied with their lives at school.

Statistics around current mental health and wellbeing are hugely concerning:

- 'Around 1 in 16 children (6 per cent) aged 10 to 15 in the UK are unhappy with their lives, and almost 1 in 8 (12 per cent), an estimated 562,000 of 10–15-year olds, are unhappy with school' (The Children's Society, 2022).
- Anxiety is the most prevalent mental health disability affecting students across the United States (Minahan, 2019).
- Suicide is the leading cause of death for 5–19-year-olds (MHFA England).
- Children with SEND were found to have poorer wellbeing than children without SEND, 37 per cent of children with SEND were found to have possible depression compared to 7 per cent of children without SEND (Children's Commissioner for England, 2023, p.10).

Schools need to urgently address and respond to these issues.

- Priority needs to be given to the provision of up-to-date training on positive mental health and wellbeing and engagement with specialist services to provide support.
- Focus on positive mental health and wellbeing, ensuring pupils feel listened to, understood, supported and able to seek help. They need to know where and who they can go to, as and when necessary. Relationships are at the heart of ensuring that pupils

feel listened to and heard. 'At a base level, young people who are struggling with their mental health, and perhaps coping in unhealthy ways, are looking for someone to stop and to listen to them' therefore 'one of the most important things we can do is just sit, and listen' (MacDonald, 2019, pp.123 and124).

■ Staff wellbeing is a crucial factor. An 'essential task for all who engage therapeutically is to look to ourselves first. We cannot pour from an empty cup' (Rae, 2023). Staff are more able to support pupils and co-regulate alongside them when they themselves feel valued, appreciated and able to seek advice and support from colleagues and leaders without feeling blamed or judged. 'When the wellbeing of all staff is prioritized as part of a mindful and compassionate trauma-informed approach, they too will feel much more emotionally contained and consequently be better equipped to reflect and respond' (Conkbayir, 2023, p.206).

■ Schools need to promote a healthy work-life balance. Mental health first aid training and supervision need to become the norm. Schools need to model the approaches being used with pupils and introduce safe spaces for school staff to reflect and unburden. As staff begin to model regulation and restorative approaches with pupils, they will increase their own emotional understanding. Schools need to develop strength-based approaches with staff as well as pupils, ensuring each individual feels valued.

■ Staff and senior leaders must be aware of staff burnout and intervene early to provide additional support. Burnout can present as overwhelming exhaustion, feeling ineffective, deskilled and unmotivated, emotional dysregulation and social withdrawal. It can lead to emotional distancing from pupils and on to 'blocked care' (Hughes & Baylin, 2012) – where open, engaged, empathic and reflective care becomes suppressed due to a relationship which seems unreciprocated, despite being continually offered by the adult. Signs of blocked care in school staff could include a lack of empathy and compassion, providing tasks and activities but with no sense of joy or passion, defensiveness, staff distancing themselves from the child, responding to incidents reactively rather than proactively, blaming and judging and enforcing punitive sanctions rather than teaching skills, regulation and providing support.

The ways to begin to overcome blocked care include using strategies such as:

■ Focusing on personal wellbeing.
■ Implementing regulation strategies.

■ Taking time to build (or rebuild) relationships with the pupil.
■ Using empathy and compassion to understand that the behaviours are communicating a need or a response to the environment.
■ Being positive, focusing on the pupil's strengths and positively reframing the narrative around behaviour.

■ Collaborative approaches are essential. Engage in positive interactions, based on the PACE approach, with pupils, staff and caregivers, and ensure all voices are listened to, understood and valued.
■ Teach awareness of anxiety symptoms and be aware of key trigger points, intervening early with support. For example, at exam times focus on wellbeing (sleep, eat, drink water, boost self-esteem, physical exercise), reteach and rehearse regulation strategies, support executive function and provide inclusive revision tips and timetables.

Strength-based approaches

■ When talking to and about pupils (with the pupils themselves, with peers, with caregivers, with colleagues in the staff room), flip the narrative. Reframing language to be more positive improves pupil self-esteem and supports adults to reflect on incidents, provide support and problem solve with increased compassion and kindness. Avoid labels such as *challenging, naughty, misbehaving, kicking off* or *inappropriate* and use language such as *distressed, overwhelmed, anxious* or *dysregulated*. Rather than 'behaviour managers' adults need to become 'stress regulators' (Bombèr 2020). 'Triangulate your botheredness with other colleagues . . . Encourage the notion that students are discussed positively in the staffroom' (Dix, 2017, p.52). Share successes and pass them on.
■ Review policies to ensure such positive framing. 'The language you use in your behaviour plan will become the common language in your school. Gone unchecked it can encourage discrimination, negative assumptions and a presumption of guilt . . . The right language gives everyone a chance to better interpret and process children's behaviour. It encourages a trauma-informed and needs-based conversation which, in turn, promotes strategies that are likely to change behaviour, not punish it' (Dix, 2021, pp.126 and 127).

Teaching and learning (see also p.207)

- A lot of bullying is caused by a lack of understanding – therefore, ensure the school ethos and the curriculum is inclusive and embraces, celebrates and values difference, including cultural, racial and neuro- diversity and disability. Consider whether the curriculum, books, resources and displays are truly inclusive and reflect and celebrate the achievements and successes of a range of different people. Check 'posters around school reflect diversity and inclusion and share positive "can do" stories' (Elley with Morewood (2022, p.29). Ensure all members of the school community feel included and valued. Is difference celebrated across the whole school ethos? Is inclusion truly inclusive?
- Ensure the curriculum incorporates trauma- and attachment-informed practices to increase understanding and includes teaching of emotions, emotional wellbeing, regulation strategies, social skills, resilience, positive relationships, restoration and repair. Implementation needs to be scaffolded according to need and regulation strategies should be regularly taught, rehearsed, modelled and embedded across the school day.
- Celebrate non-academic and academic successes ensuring the focus is not solely on grades and league tables.
- Value play in the curriculum beyond the Early Years. Engaging in pretend, guided and free play could be 'an effective strategy to close achievement gaps' (Dowd & Thomsen, 2021, p.37).

Recognition and consequences

Unfortunately, some traditional behaviour management methods of rewards and sanctions (such as moving pegs up and down, names on the board, isolation and exclusion) can heighten anxiety for many pupils and do not positively change behaviour or 'teach the skills of flexibility and frustration tolerance' (Greene, 2014). They may have a short-term impact on a certain behaviour, gaining compliance through fear and control, but, for the most vulnerable pupils, they are retraumatising, impact negatively on mental health and wellbeing and lead to anxiety and feelings of disconnect and rejection. Furthermore, they do not take account of what is happening within the pupil emotionally or provide pupils with the ability to regulate and make effective changes. 'Children do well if they can' (Greene, 2014) and educators need to show them the way.

- Review policies to eliminate shame-inducing approaches which can cause rejection and induce anxiety in pupils. 'We need to urgently move away from a system where we punish and exclude children and young people for their life experiences and needs, and instead move to a place of compassion and understanding' (Lamb, in Morgan and Costello, 2023, p.i). 'You do not want to unintentionally punish the student for having an elevated level of anxiety and subsequent poor performance . . . Remember, the student *cannot* act appropriately because of anxiety; it's not that he won't' (Minahan, 2018, p.75; emphasis in original).
- Isolation and exclusion do not improve behaviour, they do however increase feelings of shame and rejection. Instead, pupils need quiet, calm reflection, with a trusted, compassionate adult. They need to collaboratively problem solve to find logical consequences, which will support them to begin to make changes without inducing further shame, anxiety or trauma. 'Disaffected children need a trusted adult with whom they can talk through their issues. This requires engagement – not isolation' (Conkbayir, 2023, p.196) 'Look around any isolation room . . ., and I would lay good money that more than 80% of the children in there have additional needs . . . Others will be struggling with hidden needs that are all too obvious to those who work with them every day: trauma, anxiety, attachment, grief or plain old-fashioned neglect' (Dix, 2017, p.114). Use incidents as a teaching opportunity to explore logical consequences together. In this way, pupils are encouraged to become more independent, and are increasingly prepared to find solutions for themselves in the future. 'We want to help our kids build skills, not just control their behaviour in the moment' (Siegel & Payne Bryson, 2020, p.154).
- Consider the appropriateness of imposed sanctions (does forgetting a pencil, being late or having a logo on clothing truly warrant five hours in isolation?) and move towards logical consequences and repair. 'If the purpose of discipline is about teaching someone to change their ways then making pupils feel even worse is not going to change anything; it will only reinforce their sense of shame' (Pickthall, in Morgan with Costello, 2023, p.119). Be reflective and consider alternative, relational methods to respond to incidents, which aim to make long-term improvements by teaching skills, problem-solving, emotional regulation and alternative means of getting their needs met. 'Re-direct behaviour using more child-centred strategies, such as positive modelling, listening, empathizing and talking through alternative ways of responding to challenging situations' (Conkbayir, 2023, p.193).

- Schools should implement 'differentiated discipline' (Bombèr, 2020) in order to understand what is driving the behaviour and supporting pupils to restore, repair and put things right in a way which does not induce shame, but teaches them the skills to try a different approach next time. 'Damaged children need people, not punishment' (Dix, 2017, p.108). If a child struggles with reading, adults sit beside them and teach them to read, if a child struggles with Maths, an adult sits beside them and offers support. Why then, if a child struggles to regulate their behaviour does an adult often reject and punish them? 'For most people, fairness means that everyone is treated exactly the same. Reward and praise for the same things and the same consequences for the same types of behaviour. We would never apply this theory when it comes to learning. Long have we been wise to the fact that children require differing levels of support depending on their individual strengths and challenges. The same applies to behaviour approaches' (Carpenter, 2022). Pupils need equity rather than equality in all aspects of school life.
- Staff need to understand the communicative function of the behaviour. 'Anxiety very often exhibits itself as anger and embarrassment. They are merely displaying the symptoms of their anxiety. It is therefore vital that the child or young person is supported on an emotional level and not punished for displaying such symptoms' (Rae, 2023). Be curious and understand behaviour as a means of communication, unmet needs and response to the environment, so that reasonable adjustments can be made to ensure that each individual need is met. Many behaviour presentations are the activation of the threat response, communicating that the pupil feels unsafe and anxious. Consider what is happening for the pupil and why they are struggling to cope.
- 'Stressed brains cannot learn' (Conkbayir, 2023, p.191), so the emphasis needs to be on reducing pupil stress and anxiety. Be proactive – look for patterns and devise a plan for trigger times and moments of dysregulation by providing support and teaching pupils the skills they need to cope with those situations. Create 'a culture in which triggers are predicted and systems put in place accordingly' so that 'a crisis is far less likely to happen' (Elley with Morewood, 2022, p.121), whereby schools are setting pupils up to succeed rather than to fail.
- In order to feel safe and secure children need clear, consistent structure, boundaries and expectations alongside a powerfully nurturing approach. Golding's (2017) 'Two Hands of Discipline' provides a useful analogy, where Hand One provides connection

with warmth and nurture, Hand Two provides structure, supervision and boundaries.

■ Be self-reflective and aware of how an adult's reactions, responses and words impact on a pupil's behaviour, anxiety and stress – the adult has the ability to escalate or de-escalate a situation, to further distress or de-stress a child. For example, shouting or raised voices (within earshot of a pupil, not necessarily aimed at the pupil) can trigger the threat response (see p00) and pupils will need calm support rather than reprimands. 'When adults change their behaviour in response to a child's intense reactions, it can change the child's behaviour' (Siegel & Payne Bryson, 2020, p.152).

■ Communicate individual needs and reasonable adjustments to all members of staff to ensure a consistent approach. Pupils who are 'overwhelmed with shame' need adults who are 'very sensitive in the way that we challenge them' doing so 'in a way that engages their thinking, so that they can learn from experiences rather than immediately reacting out of fear and panic and remaining stuck' (Bombèr, 2007, p.16). Ensure the start of each day is welcoming and positive and, particularly for anxious or vulnerable pupils, leave redirection until the pupil is settled, calm and with a trusted adult. For example, aim not to address punctuality, homework or uniform as the first interaction of the day. For many vulnerable and anxious pupils, breakfast clubs or personal *meet and greets* can support them reset and regulate before they enter the classroom.

■ Reasonable adjustments are made to meet a need, so should not be used as a reward, for example, a pupil has regular movement and sensory breaks because they need them, not because they have completed their learning. (In fact, if they are not completing their learning, they probably need more breaks rather than fewer.)

■ Where possible, avoid removing break times as sanctions – social time is important and most pupils need regular, large cognitive and movement breaks. Research has shown that access to outdoor spaces, particularly green spaces, can improve behaviour and learning. 'Findings suggest that everyday play settings make a difference in overall symptom severity in children with ADHD. Specifically, children with ADHD who play regularly in green play settings have milder symptoms than children who play in built outdoor and indoor settings' (Faber Taylor et al., 2011).

Case study:

Max is 7. He was very unsettled in the mornings, and struggled to get up, dressed, out of the house and into school on time. Mornings were so difficult that he was usually late and arrived distressed. Two members of staff were needed to coax him away from his mum. Max was generally described as 'OK in school'. However, his attendance was dropping and when he was in, he didn't concentrate on his school work and sometimes left the classroom and wandered around. He didn't get much work done and usually had to miss his break times to complete his learning.

Max's mum shared that Max thought that he didn't have any friends. School reassured her that Max had lots of friends.

Reflection opportunity:

■ How could staff support Max to feel more settled in school?

Case study continued:

Following concerns from Max and from home, school stopped taking away Max's play times as a sanction for missed learning. Max has told his mum that he has his friends back and he no longer struggles to come into school in the mornings. His missed work is caught up at other times in the day, however, with support and scaffolding he is more able to complete his work in lesson time.

■ Aim for immediate praise and recognition. Reward effort, attitude, the use of coping strategies and the implementation of new skills rather than 'appropriate behaviours' and correct answers. Be aware that public praise can increase anxiety for some pupils and they may need quieter, less direct forms of praise, such as a sticky note left on the desk or a quiet word or gesture.
■ Avoid public rewards, praise and displays for attendance such as 100 per cent attendance certificates (which will be overwhelming and impossible to achieve for many, resulting in despondency and pupils giving up trying as well as setting those who struggle or can't attend up to fail). Instead, implement achievable, personalised attendance goals, so that all pupils feel motivated and successful.

■ 'When you are stumped by behaviour, when you don't know what to do next, when nothing seems to work, kindness is always the best response' (Dix, 2017, p.159).

Restorative approaches

■ Restorative approaches allow for collaborative problem-solving (Greene, 2014), giving pupils a sense of responsibility and control to increase impact and make lasting positive change with relationships held at the heart. 'When conflict appears in the classroom, as it inevitably will, the difference between punitive and restorative discipline can be the difference between continuing or ending cycles of trauma' (Pathways to Restorative Communities, 2021). The adult's response is key. Restorative conversations 'enable pupils to explore the effect of their actions on others, resolve conflict, repair, and move on with empathy, understanding and kindness in a way that is non-shaming and helps them to make better choices, should a similar situation arise in the future' (Thynne, 2022, pp.11–12).

■ Don't be afraid to apologise. It is important to model what to do when things go wrong and how to restore relationships, using phrases such as *I'm sorry I got that wrong, what could I do better to help you next time?* This might also be a starting point for collaborative problem-solving with pupils, once everyone is calm.

■ Where possible, resolve difficulties and restore relationships on the same day because leaving issues 'hanging over' until the next day increases anxiety immensely.

Environmental adaptations and unstructured times

We need to be 'creating environments which aim to increase feelings of safety and trust, and to decrease feelings of threat, danger, dysregulation and stress' (Treisman, 2021, p.154).

■ Carry out anonymised pupil safety surveys to obtain honest feedback on how safe and supported pupils feel in school and to explore any areas which increase anxiety. These can be helpful in determining key areas for development and inform any sensory and environmental adaptations and adjustments.

■ When pupils are displaying unexpected behaviours, staff need to think about the environment around them and the needs being met by the behaviour (such as sensory-seeking or sensory-avoiding, escape, anxiety, connection-seeking) and ensure measures are put in so that that these needs are met in more appropriate ways.

■ It's also essential to create a supportive and inclusive environment that accommodates individual differences. Reasonable adjustments are key and schools need to be meeting the needs of all pupils, not the majority of pupils. Anxiety often goes hand in hand with neurodivergence but it doesn't have to if the environment is right and all pupils are taught managing and coping skills. Value diversity; it is brain *difference* not *deficit*.

■ Provide access to sensory supports and quieter, safe spaces and key adults as the norm and for everyone, when necessary, to avoid pupils feeling singled out.

■ Plan break times and unstructured times and explore ways to reduce anxiety, for example, offer safe, quieter spaces to avoid feelings of overwhelm, sensory gardens, access to music, dance and drama. Teach pupils how to play a range of different structured games and provide a range of play equipment to encourage vestibular and proprioceptive input, such as scooter boards, scooters, trikes, tyres, sand and water, balls, bean bags, blocks, boxes, climbing equipment, trim trails and access to green natural spaces.

Chapter take-aways

■ Behaviour is communication, a response to the environment and a means of meeting a need. Schools need to move away from punitive, reactive, 'one-size fits all' approaches to behaviour (Rainer et al., 2023) towards 'differentiated discipline' (Bombèr, 2020).

■ Pupils need to be taught how to recognise and regulate their emotions and anxieties and a range of coping strategies.

■ Positive relationships with adults in school are essential.

■ Mental health and wellbeing need to be at the heart of every policy and practice.

Further signposting

Books

Behaviour Barriers and Beyond by Rachel Thynne

Independent Thinking on Restorative Practice: Building Relationships, Improving Behaviour and Creating Stronger Communities by Mark Finnis

Know Me to Teach Me by Louise Bombèr
Square Pegs by Fran Morgan with Ellie Costello
When the Adults Change Everything Changes by Paul Dix

Websites

Anna Freud *Ensure There is a Robust Mental Health and Wellbeing Policy* https://www.annafreud.org/schools-and-colleges/5-steps-to-mental-health-and-wellbeing/leading-change/ensure-there-is-a-robust-mental-health-and-wellbeing-policy/#:~:text=Although%20schools%20are%20not%20required,behaviour%20amounts%20to%20a%20disability

Anna Freud *School and College Resources* https://www.annafreud.org/schools-and-colleges/resources

Charlie Waller Trust *Practical Advice and Information* https://www.charliewaller.org/resource-library

Mental Health First Aid (MHFA) England *Learn to Support Young People* https://mhfaengland.org/organisations/youth

NHS *Five Steps to Mental Wellbeing* https://www.nhs.uk/mental-health/self-help/guides-tools-and-activities/five-steps-to-mental-wellbeing

OPAL (Outdoor Play and Learning) *Outdoor Play and Learning for Schools* https://outdoorplayandlearning.org.uk/welcome/for-schools

Podcast

Pooky Ponders *How to Promote Belonging in School* https://pookyh.buzzsprout.com/1183931/12191671

References

Allen, K. & Kern, P. (2019) *Boosting School Belonging: Practical Strategies to Help Adolescents Feel Like They Belong at School* Routledge

Anna Freud (undated) *Ensure There is a Robust Mental Health and Wellbeing Policy* Available at: https://www.annafreud.org/schools-and-colleges/5-steps-to-mental-health-and-wellbeing/leading-change/ensure-there-is-a-robust-mental-health-and-wellbeing-policy/#:~:text=Although%20schools%20are%20not%20required,behaviour%20amounts%20to%20a%20disability [Accessed 9.9.23]

Anti-Bullying Alliance (2023) *Written Evidence Submitted by the Anti-Bullying Alliance (National Children's Bureau)* Available at: https://committees.parliament.uk/writtenevidence/118262/pdf/#:~:text=It%20found%20some%20evidence%20that,could%20help%20improve%20school%20attendance [Accessed 7.9.23]

Barnados (undated) *The A-Z of Childhood Adversity Jargon Buster* Available at: https://proceduresonline.com/trixcms1/media/8082/tx330-a-z-of-child hood-adversity-jargon-buster.pdf [Accessed 13.2.21]

Bombèr, L. (2007) *Inside I'm Hurting: Practical Strategies for Supporting Children with Attachment Difficulties in School* Worth Publishing

Bombèr, L. (2020) *Know Me to Teach Me – Differentiated Discipline for Those Recovering from Adverse Childhood Experiences* Worth Publishing

Brown, B. (2021) *The Difference of 'Belonging' and 'Fitting in'* Available at: https://www.youtube.com/watch?v=a_xDRYZ5b7c [Accessed 24.1.24]

Caress, A. (2023) *A Whole-School Approach to Emotionally-Based School Avoidance* Available at: https://www.ocr.org.uk/blog/a-whole-school-ap proach-to-emotionally-based-school-avoidance/#:~:text=Taking%20 a%20whole%2Dschool%20approach&text=Taking%20time%20to%20 think%20about,the%20needs%20of%20the%20child [Accessed 6.9.23]

Carpenter, L. (2022) *Trauma Informed Behaviour Policy – Where to Start* Available at: https://www.educater.co.uk/latest-news/trauma-informed-behaviour-policy-where-to-start [accessed 11.5.23]

Children's Commissioner for England (2023) *Attendance is Everyone's Business – Children's Commissioner's Submission to the Persistent Absence Inquiry* Available at: https://www.childrenscommissioner.gov.uk/resource/atten dance-is-everyones-business [Accessed 8.9.23]

Conkbayir, M. (2023) *The Neuroscience of the Developing Child – Self-Regulation for Wellbeing and a Sustainable Future* Routledge

Dix, P. (2017) *When the Adults Change, Everything Changes: Seismic Shifts in School Behaviour* Independent Thinking Press

Dix, P. (2021) *After the Adults Change: Achievable Behaviour Nirvana* Independent Thinking Press

Dowd, A. & Thomsen, B. (2021) *Learning Through Play: Increasing Impact, Reducing Inequality* The LEGO® Foundation Available at: https://cms. learningthroughplay.com/media/jxgbzw0s/learning-through-play-in creasing-impact_reducing-inequality_white-paper.pdf [Accessed 17.4.23]

Elley, D. with Morewood, G. (2022) *Championing Your Autistic Teen at Secondary School – Getting the Best from Mainstream Schools* Jessica Kingsley

European Education Area (undated) *Wellbeing at School* Available at: https:// education.ec.europa.eu/education-levels/school-education/wellbe ing-at-school#:~:text=Well%2Dbeing%20is%20a%20state,and%20a%20 sense%20of%20autonomy [Accessed 22.2.24]

Faber Taylor, A., Frances E. & (Ming) Kuo (2011) Could Exposure to Everyday Green Spaces Help Treat ADHD? Evidence from Children's Play Settings *Applied Psychology Health and Wellbeing* 3(3): 281–303 Available at: https://iaap-journals.onlinelibrary.wiley.com/doi/abs/10.1111/j.1758-0854.2011.01052.x [Accessed 29.3.23]

Fricker, E. (2023) *Can't Not Won't: A Story About a Child Who Couldn't Go to School* Jessica Kinglsey

Golding, K. (2017) *Foundations for Attachment Training Resource – The Six Session Programme for Parents of Traumatized Children* Jessica Kingsley

Greene, R. (2014) *The Explosive Child: A New Approach for Understanding and Parenting Easily Frustrated, Chronically Inflexible Children* HarperCollins

Hughes, D. & Baylin, J. (2012) *Brain-Based Parenting. The Neuroscience of Caregiving for Healthy Attachment* Norton

MacDonald, I. (2019) *Teen Substance Use, Mental Health and Body Image: Practical Strategies for Support* Jessica Kingsley

McMillan, A. (2023) *Ange McMillan's Profile Page* (LinkedIn) [Accessed 29.6.23]

Mental Health First Aid (MHFA) England (undated) *Would You Know How to Help?* Available at: https://mhfaengland.org/individuals/adult [Accessed 29.11.23]

Minahan, J. (2013) *The Flexible Classroom: Helping Students with Mental Health Challenges to Thrive* https://kappanonline.org/the-flexible-classroom-helping-students-with-mental-health-challenges-to-thrive [Accessed 14.6.23]

Minahan, J. (2018) *The Behavior Code Companion: Strategies, Tools and Interventions for Supporting Students with Anxiety-Related or Oppositional Behaviours* Harvard Education Press

Minahan, J. (2019) *Tackling Negative Thinking in the Classroom* Available at: https://kappanonline.org/tackling-students-negative-thinking-classroom-anxiety-stress-minahan [Accessed 9.9.23]

Morgan, F. with Costello, E. (2023) *Square Pegs – Inclusivity, Compassion and Fitting In: A Guide for Schools* Independent Thinking Press

Pathways to Restorative Communities (2021) *The Role of Restorative Practices in Trauma-Informed Schools* Available at: https://www.pathways2rc.com/news/2021/4/15/the-role-of-restorative-practices-in-trauma-informed-schools [Accessed 13.7.23]

Rainer, C., Le, H. & Abdinasir K. (2023) *Behaviour and Mental Health in Schools* Children and Young People's Mental Health Coalition

Rae, T. (2023) *Therapeutic Tools to Support Wellbeing in Schools* Available at: https://worldofeducation.tts-group.co.uk/dr-tina-rae-therapeutic-tools-to-support-wellbeing-in-schools [Accessed 12.7.23]

Siegel, D. & Payne Bryson, T. (2020) *The Power of Showing Up: How Parental Presence Shapes Who Our Kids Become and How Their Brains Get Wired* Scribe

The Children's Society (2022) *The Good Childhood Report* Available at: https://www.childrenssociety.org.uk/information/professionals/resources/good-childhood-report-2022#:~:text=This%20year's%20report%20shows%20that,olds%2C%20are%20unhappy%20with%20school [Accessed 29.3.23]

Thynne, R. (2022) *Behaviour Barriers and Beyond: Practical Strategies to Help All Pupils Thrive* Routledge

Treisman, K. (2017) *Working with Relational and Developmental Trauma in Children and Adolescents* Routledge

Treisman, K. (2021) *A Treasure Box for Creating Trauma-Informed Organizations* Jessica Kingsley

Young Minds (undated) *Where and Who Are Trusted Adults* Available at: https://www.youngminds.org.uk/professional/community-support/someone-to-turn-to/someone-to-turn-to-report [Accessed 7.9.23]

Whole school approaches checklist

STRATEGY	COMMENTS
Please also refer to Chapter 10	
Belonging and connectedness	
Foster a sense of belonging and connectedness, embracing difference and genuine inclusivity	
Positive welcome for all. Address any issues once pupils are settled.	
Activities with shared interests increase sense of belonging	
Whole school ethos, culture and policy	
Create a flexible, inclusive and nurturing environment for all	
Review policies to ensure that mental health and wellbeing are at the core	
Implement a robust, inclusive attendance and welfare policy which reflects understanding of school-based anxiety	
Ensure a flexible, nurturing approach, offering support and taking account of individual needs and circumstances	
Ensure everyone feels safe and knows bullying is responded to seriously and effectively	
Implement a Relational Policy instead of, or alongside, the Behaviour Policy	
Ensure regular, up-to-date whole school training	

(Continued)

Continued

STRATEGY	COMMENTS
Relational approaches	
Value and promote the importance of relationships using the PACE approach	
Regular wellbeing check-ins for vulnerable pupils	
Collaborate with pupils and caregivers	
Teach skills, regulation and restoration rather than implementing blanket sanctions	
Focus on mental health and wellbeing	
Provide training on positive mental health and wellbeing and engage with professional services	
Actively listen	
Staff wellbeing needs to be a priority	
Teach about anxiety and intervene early	
Leaders need to be aware of symptoms of staff burnout and intervene early	
Use collaborative approaches	
Strength-based approaches	
Use positive language and share successes	
Ensure policies reflect positive language reframes	

(Continued)

Continued

STRATEGY	COMMENTS
Teaching and learning	
Truly inclusive curriculum that celebrates and values diversity and difference	
Ensure curriculum incorporates trauma-informed practices, teaching of emotions, wellbeing and regulation strategies	
Celebrate non-academic success	
Value play	
Recognition and consequences	
Review policies to eliminate shame-inducing approaches	
Quiet reflection and collaborative problem-solving with a trusted adult rather than isolation and rejection	
Implement 'differentiated discipline'	
Build skills, develop executive function and teach regulating strategies	
Understand the communicative function of the behaviour and alleviate anxiety	
Clear, consistent structure alongside powerful nurture	
Be self-reflective and aware of adult impact on pupil stress	
Ensure all staff are aware of needs and implement reasonable adjustments consistently	
Avoid removing break times, where possible	

(Continued)

Continued

STRATEGY	COMMENTS
Aim for immediate praise and recognition	
Avoid public displays of attendance and aim for personalised attendance goals	
Restorative approaches	
Use restorative approaches to collaboratively problem solve and increase sense of control	
Apologise and model relational repair	
Aim to resolve issues the same day	
Environmental adaptations and unstructured times	
Use pupil surveys to obtain feedback about anxieties	
Consider how environment may impact anxiety and behaviour	
Ensure environment is inclusive and make adjustments as necessary	
Provide access to safe places and faces	
Carefully manage unstructured times	

Index

Page numbers in **bold** refer to tables

acceptance 28–9; case study 29
adaptive teaching 50, 207
alerting strategies 94
American Psychiatric Association *see DSM-5*
Anna Freud 239
anti-bullying policy 197, 240
Anti-Bullying Alliance 197, 212, 240
anxiety 3–4; alleviating anxiety checklist **71–5**; case study 15; disorders 6–9; and learning 15–16; presentations and symptoms of 9–12, **11–12**
AnxietyCanada 56, 88–9, 126
anxiety cycle 120, 202, 224–5
attachment 9, 59, 23, 245–6; figures 9; play 9
attendance 34, 63, 175–7, 188, 238–9, 249; barriers and protective factors 177, **178–84**, 200; policy 239; 'push' and 'pull' factors 184, 200
attention and focus 10, 15–16, 50–1, 56, 60, increasing 92–3
attunement 31, 78, 82
Attention Deficit Hyperactivity Disorder (ADHD) 16, 113–14, 246, 248
autism 16–17, 60, 113, 146
autonomous nervous system *see* threat response
avoidance 10, 50, 111–13, 115–16, 133, 202; as a coping strategy 25; *see also* anxiety cycle, school-based anxiety *and* Pathological Demand Avoidance (PDA)

Beacon House 24–5, 83
beginnings and endings 64, 34, 58–9, 63, 65; case study 184–5, 194–5, 228; planning for 227–8

belonging and connectedness 33–4, 206–7, 237–8; case study 34, 196; during absence 24, 195–7; reflection opportunity 33
behaviour 9–10; alternatives 97–8, 246; as communication 10–13, **11–12**, 56, 116–17, **145–6**, 247; policy 240–1, 244; reframing 24–5
Behaviour and Mental Health in Schools Report 188
blocked care 243–4
blocked trust 27
body language 14, 22, 153, 205, 225
body mapping 82
Bombèr, L. 58–9, 81, 98, 248
Bowlby, J. 221
brain 5–6, 16, 45, 78,
breathing techniques 83–4
break times *see* unstructured times
Brown, B. 157
Brukner, L. 60
bullying 225, 240, 245, *see also* anti-bullying policy
burnout 14, 243

calm bag 79, 85
calming strategies 94–5
Carpenter, L. 247
catastrophising *see* negative thinking
Cat, S. 142
check-ins 23, 46, 51, 61
Child and Adolescent Mental Health Services (CAMHS) 143, 201
Children's Commissioner for England 187–8, 212, 242
chunking tasks 51–2, 208

For Product Safety Concerns and Information please contact our EU
representative GPSR@taylorandfrancis.com Taylor & Francis Verlag GmbH,
Kaufingerstraße 24, 80331 München, Germany

Printed and bound by CPI Group (UK) Ltd, Croydon, CR0 4YY
08/06/2025
01897000-0013